ORGANIZATIONAL LEARNING AND KNOWLEDGE TECHNOLOGIES IN A DYNAMIC ENVIRONMENT

by

WALTER R. J. BAETS

Nijenrode University,
The Netherlands Business School

KLUWER ACADEMIC PUBLISHERS

BOSTON / DORDRECHT / LONDON

658.4
B14o

A C.I.P. Catalogue record for this book is available from the Library of Congress.

ISBN 0-7923-8170-X

Published by Kluwer Academic Publishers,
P.O. Box 17, 3300 AA Dordrecht, The Netherlands.

Sold and distributed in North, Central and South America
by Kluwer Academic Publishers,
101 Philip Drive, Norwell, MA 02061, U.S.A.

In all other countries, sold and distributed
by Kluwer Academic Publishers,
P.O. Box 322, 3300 AH Dordrecht, The Netherlands.

Printed on acid-free paper

1H

Printed in the Netherlands

While time is the fourth dimension...
you are my fifth.

For Erna, beyond time.

Chant XXIX Proverbios y cantares,
Campos de Castilla, 1917
Antonio Machado

Caminante, son tus huellas
el camino, y nada mas;
caminante, no hay camino,
se hace camino al andar.
Al andar se hace camino,
y al volver la vista atras
se ve la senda que nunca
se ha de volver a pisar.
Caminante, no hay camino,
sino estelas en la mar.

Wanderer, your footprints are
the path, and nothing more;
Wanderer, there is no path,
it is created as you walk.
By walking,
you make the path before you,
and when you look behind
you see the path which after you
will not be trod again.
Wanderer, there is no path,
but the ripples on the waters.

Translated by Walter Baets

CONTENTS

FOREWORD

I am not a born academic. I deliberately joined the ranks of academia at a fairly late stage as a natural progression from my professional career as an executive in what in those days was known as "decision support". My career had begun in the telecom industry before the days of deregulation in what one would call strategic planning and then I moved on to decision support in the field of banking, developing trading room software and risk management systems. As I developed decision support systems for real applications, the more I realized how very dependent these systems are on decision design. I began to question a number of basic business assumptions. I felt increasingly the need to review the way decision support systems were conceived at the time since they not only limited what one could do with computers, but also limited the decision-making capacity of executives. I thus decided to take time out from my professional obligations in order to be able to investigate the 'whys and wherefores' behind decision-making.

I experienced yet another disappointment at the beginning of my academic career as I noted the academic research style prevailing in most Business Schools. The academic community was adhering to a type of research methodology based on a single view of the way humans think. There seemed to be a lack of critical investigation into research methodology resulting in much research being mere 're-search' into prior research. I have therefore felt it necessary to annex a discussion on research methodology explaining from a scientific point of view what I aim to achieve and how I am to go about it.

But most of all, I was surprised. I was interested in exploring new ways of thinking, ingenuously expecting surprises around each corner. I wanted to search, rather than to re-search. The book invites you to share in my exploration. The main question, which I hesitate to call a research hypothesis, centers on how companies can best deal with a dynamic and transforming environment and how, given such turbulence, managers can improve decision-making processes. With this proposal in mind, one inevitably ends up investigating the properties of knowledge and the functioning of the brain as well as considering information technologies which can support new insights in these areas.

At the end of the day, not unlike fellow managers and academics, I am a child of my generation. And many of us educated in the 70s have had, and may still have, a kind of a love-hate relationship with a book which, at least in my view, sums up the 70s generation rather well: *Zen and the Art of Motor Cycle Maintenance* by Robert Pirsig (first published in 1974). If you were to ask me which management book should be given as compulsory reading to students finishing Business School, or to executives following management education courses, I would opt for Pirsig's book

The book you have in front of you is the result of a number of years touring around as a part of an environment, to use Pirsig's terminology. Let me paraphrase a few of his ideas:

> *Touring around on a motorbike, one observes the environment in a way that is quite different from most other forms of twentieth century travel. Boxed off in a car, you are removed from the landscape that runs by endlessly pictured in a frame which resembles the TV screen. You passively observe the environment passing by, distant, in a frame.*

> *On the back of a motor bike, that frame is gone: you are in contact with everything. You are no mere observer of the landscape, but an integral part of it. The feeling that you are present in it is tremendous.*

One of the most important management skills which I would wish today's managers to acquire, is this capacity to manage as part of the 'landscape'. The reader will feel through the book how I have willingly been part of that 'landscape'. Rather than being a scientific observer in a laboratory, I have chosen to be an explorer engaged in surveying the surrounding landscape.

I was astonished when a major bank asked me a few years ago to give a lecture, during their annual Quality Award ceremony, on 'Zen and the art of motor cycle maintenance' as the ultimate quality handbook. With much joy and delight, I prepared the session and the main message which I gave is the same as the one I would like to give managers today when speaking about important management skills. The message was the following.

> *The motorbike broke down and I knew I had not checked it over carefully enough; I had presumed that it was the rain which had caused the engine to fail. Perhaps what I should have done was just take a step away from the bike, take a good, long look at it and attempt to listen to it. There is nothing wrong with that. Allow it to work on you a while, just the way you would go fishing. You stare at the float and after a while you catch a fish. If you give it the time and the space, and allow it to happen, you will detect some almost imperceptible movement or detail which will attract your attention. And that is what makes the world go round: attention.*

> *Implicit in most rules is the following idea: here is a machine, isolated in time and space from its surroundings; it has no relationship with you and you have no relationship with it other than via the switches you handle and the controls you execute. This makes people who look at the same things, talk about the same things, think about the same things, able to do so from completely different dimensions.*

Compare the difference between the manager as conductor, who forms a part of the orchestra, and the manager as technician who works on the "motor bike".

The creation of the book would not have been possible without the help of a number of people. I thank them all and mention a few. Bob Galliers trained me in applying scientific research rigor to my work without, however, limiting the freedom of exploration. Other friends and colleagues, who over the last decade have greatly helped me shape ideas, also contributed directly by commenting on early drafts of the book. Gert Van der Linden co-authored the annex and we spent many hours discussing 'errors of logic'. Venu Venugopal, Leon Brunenberg, Bie De Graeve and Filip Caeldries all made very helpful comments on early drafts. They have also been involved in joint research projects which have given rise to some ideas which are reproduced in this book. I am very grateful to Jean-Louis Lemoigne and Jacques Bartoli of the Complexity Research Center of the University of Aix-Marseille (France) for the time I spent with them as visiting

xiv

faculty. The participation of certain companies in research projects mentioned in the book, has been paramount. In particular, Gerhard Schwarz has greatly inspired me and forced me to be clearer in my ideas. As a corporate sponsor, he not only struggled with the concepts, but he also had the courage to discuss them repeatedly. In 1995, I taught a mandatory course (probably the first ever in a Business School) on 'Complexity and Change' in the Masters in Management program at Nijenrode University (The Netherlands Business School). The discussions I had with students and the work they did during the course greatly encouraged me in writing the book. I used the first draft of the book as course material and student feedback contributed considerably to its improvement as did subsequent classes. The book would be unreadable without the help of Vicky Fainley and Corinne Stewart who helped me out with my English. Emilia Limia Castilla, Paola Prats Ortuño, Ana María Arias Díaz and Antonio Molina Jiménez contributed considerably to the lay-out of this book. Last but not least, I would like to thank my wife Erna, to whom this book is dedicated, for her support, encouragement and expertise which proved to be of paramount importance in the final stages of drafting.

I hope you will enjoy reading this book as much as I enjoyed writing it. My wish is to share with you a number of experiences and thoughts with a view to helping today's managers improve their management skills. If you were to feel unable to apply any aspect of the book to your business environment, I would be sorely disappointed. If, however, you were to feel you could, but were afraid of the difficulties implementing them might cause, I would wish you the courage and the drive to jump in headfirst and see how you can swim.

It is more important to travel than to arrive. Sometimes it is better to continue traveling, rather than to arrive at your final destination.

Walter Baets
Granada, January 1998

1. THE CHAOS WE CAN OBSERVE IN MANAGEMENT

1.1. Economic phenomena

We have seen over the last few decades, how Western economies have changed rather dramatically in their production pattern, both in terms of what they produce and how they produce it. While many of us were taught about the three main categories of economic activity: agriculture, industry and services, today′s reality is different. We have seen how agriculture has changed. Many small farms and farmers have disappeared in order to make way for a larger agro-industry. In doing so, and supported by the EU policy concerning agriculture, it became an industry. But probably the most dramatic changes which have taken place are in industry itself, at least in the Western world. If we compare the GNP's of different "industrialized" countries we see that a major part of that GNP is produced via services; in average around 75 %. Service economies are fundamentally different from industrial societies.

Within what we call today industrial production, an increasingly large proportion of the production cost is allocated to service type activities (e.g. research, marketing). If we take the pharmaceutical industry as an example, how much of the value added is made on the production side and how much on the research (services) side ? If we take car manufacturing as another example, how much of the price of a car is due to specific research or design, not to speak of the high marketing costs, and how much is really attributed to the production process itself ? When Lancia launches its new Y10 model which is available in around 2.5 million versions, it accepts that the client is interested in co-designing (to a certain extent) the final product. This trend which we have observed for some time in the business-to-business market is today increasingly affecting consumer markets.

This should not create major problems, albeit that a service has different properties from an industrial product. If we consider some specific examples of services, the differences will become clear. A famous story is the one of the uptake of DOS. DOS (the PC operating system of Microsoft) is far from being a good operating system. This was one of the many trials in the early age of PCs to create an operating system which combines good performance with some ease of use... (in probably both aspects) it failed comparison with other products. However, at a certain point in time, "quite by accident", IBM needed an operating system and for some strange reason DOS was chosen, and had a meteoric rise to fame. While a major PC manufacturer chose DOS as its operating system, a number of software companies started to develop software using DOS. Since more applications software became available using IBM and DOS, DOS emerged as a sort of "de facto" standard in the industry which in turn attracted more applications in DOS. Despite the fact that DOS was certainly not the best operating system available, and maybe even not a good one, it became the standard.

A number of other examples can be given, demonstrating the same phenomenon. Windows (also Microsoft product) is yet another example. Other operating systems were available (e.g. the Macintosh line of Apple) but again due to a snowball effect, Windows is today the standard in PC operating systems. A comparable evolution has been observed in the video business. VHS out-ranged Betamax which was technically superior to VHS. In the video business also it was this leverage of the VHS standard with more VHS machines (hardware) but foremost with more VHS cassettes (applications) which was responsible for this evolution. A last remarkable example is no doubt the American pre-elections. Why do candidates give so much of importance to some early and limited pre-elections which hardly give any votes in the overall total ? Since it has been observed that these pre-elections make or brake the campaign of the candidates. Either a positive snowball gets started, which will attract more support, hence more money, hence more visibility, etc. Or a negative spiral will soon kill the campaign of the candidate. In general, all mass psychoses phenomena have characteristics of this behavior. Why choose fashion brands instead of non branded clothing ? Why does Perrier need to take a full production of bottles out of the shops, based on the bad quality of one bottle and there are many more examples of what happens in markets today.

In economic theory, we don´t know how to deal with this. It fundamentally disturbs our market theories. Market behavior no longer seems to guarantee that an equilibrium will be reached, in which supply and demand get satisfied. Brian Arthur (1990) labeled these phenomena as increasing returns based on positive feed-back in the economy. If a company makes the right move at the right moment, a positive snowball effect gets started which gives this company an exponentially growing lead. Let us look into this phenomena in some more detail.

Much of the economics which we teach today in business schools is based on economic laws which date back to the previous century. Marshall's theory on economic behavior became famous. However, this theory is based on some assumptions which are undoubtedly not valid anymore today. Marshall presumes that there is a set of physical resources available and economic activity exists in combining these resources in order to create value added. The fact that one can use these resources alternatively, gives them a price, based on the competitive use of them. There is hardly any R&D cost involved in that kind of production. Producing a second copy of the same product would show some advantages of scale, but largely, the costs will be the same. There is not a lot of knowledge involved in the production process. The consequence of all this is that markets tend to go easily towards equilibrium situations. Companies' behavior settles down, based on the market mechanism. A company which has a new or remarkable product can produce that for quit a while before the competitors can copy it. In some circumstances, it is even not worth trying to copy it: developing something new is faster and maybe even cheaper.

If we now consider industrial production, we see that what we produce and how we do it has changed, but also that services have completely different characteristics. Even if we consider industrial production, the research factor has never become important. If a pharmaceutical company today finds a new drug, then they have to protect their copyright immediately. Otherwise, they would not be able to produce the drug long enough to cover the research costs before it was copied That is the difference between now and earlier industrial production. Many products today are heavily based on knowledge and hence on research. The (re-)production cost of a drug is often very low while the research cost is very high. The uncomfortable situation for a company now is that a second copy costs much less than the original one. Since all the knowledge is in the first copy anyway and since knowledge is the highest production cost involved in many industrial products today and almost all services, any second copy is very cheap to produce. Hence, products can be cheaply produced if they are based on simply a copy. The only thing which has real value is the knowledge which created the product. The first version of Windows costs a fortune; any second copy costs some dollars for some diskettes and a little bit of time to copy them. In such a market, the original assumptions of Marshall do not hold anymore. The production cost is no longer the equivalent of physical resources which can be used accordingly. The cost of production is the knowledge which is embedded in the product. Therefore we can see that markets no longer tend towards an equilibrium anymore. Instead we see phenomena of positive feed-back as described earlier. The market launch itself also becomes a knowledge based product. Even if a new product is ready, we may still want to wait a little to launch it, in order to avail ourselves of better market conditions, which in turn could produce the desired snowball effect.

Hence we can observe a number of changes in management today. Knowledge becomes a central asset in the production process. Most of the value added of production is embedded knowledge. Therefore, companies should be more aware of the knowledge they possess and manage this asset accordingly. Economic laws of market behavior do not seem to hold anymore or indeed classical theory seems to be a specific condition of a more general market behavior mechanism. Rather we see "chaotic" market behavior which seems to produce positive feed-back mechanisms. We also see that market behaves differently at different times, which only confuses us more. But one of the more frustrating observations is that economic theory does not really seem to be able to be of much help anymore. Despite some recent attempts to create a new kind of theory (which we will discuss in section 1.2), economic theory appears to be of limited use to the manager. We need to identify why markets behave as they do and how managers can get a better understanding of this market behavior in order to support their decisions.

In many respects, that is the aim of this book. This book wants to explore why managerial problems become rather "chaotic" and "complex" and how to deal with them. It will explain how important the role of knowledge has become and what knowledge means exactly. Finally it will suggest some ways to manage knowledge in-company.

This chapter will introduce the managerial changes. Later, the book attempts to explore where we can find experience which will help us to better understand the consequences of this kind of behavior. Chapter 2 describes some of the theories in other sciences which can be of use to managers in order to understand the situation and enable them to cope better. This chapter will give insight into the important role of knowledge and learning in order to understand the behavior of a system of any kind. Chapter 3 describes the basis of what we know about knowledge and learning in order to apply it in a managerial context. Some tools to deal with knowledge will be discussed in some detail in chapter 4. Chapters 5 and 6 describe examples of larger and smaller projects which have been carried out, based on the concepts developed. Chapter 7 attempts to give an overall framework for a company to deal with knowledge management and learning. Finally, chapter 8 attempts to give the reader a road-map; not to be confused with a recipe book. The map can only indicate the "nice places" which one can visit. The reader still has to decide to visit them and also whether or not he or she likes them.

Management books often give the impression that they can give the correct solution. This book will advocate, amongst others, that no theory can ever give the correct solution. The manager can only decide and may still not be sure of the quality of his/her * decision. Books can only help to provide ideas and inspiration. They can show frameworks which could make it easier for us to make sense out of nonsense. If however managers do not apply them and attempt to purely copy them, they will not guarantee success. Any solution is only a solution within the framework of reference of the person who needs the solution. Furthermore, only that person is able to judge whether the solution applied really solves his problem. Hence if the reader expects this book to give cook book solutions, he will probably be somewhat disappointed. If the reader expects this book to give new insights into how to better deal with complexity and chaos in a managerial environment and accepts it as a "work"-book, it will prove to be of assistance.

---

* Whenever the pronoun "he" or "his" is used in this book referring to a manager this is intended to be inclusive of both the female and the male manager. In no way does the author wish to discriminate against female managers. This form is only used for brevity's sake.

1.2. Information society

Recently (e.g. Boisot, 1995) an attempt has been made to describe a new approach to economic theory. It is worth spending some time on this, because of the proven limitations of classical theory. What we did not discuss at all in the previous section is the economic theory on information itself; simply because it did not exist a few years ago. One will recall from economic theory that in a market, information is assumed to be freely available. All market parties have all the available information and are able to use it. Therefore, theory persists, prices reflect all possible information available at a certain point in time and space. It is exactly the latter which currently causes a lot of problems. The economy of today makes this assumption impossible. Both "space" and "time" have a different reality. In this section we will deal with some further insights into economic theory itself. In the following section we will see how Information Technology makes both space and time different concepts.

If we consider the reality of a company, we can define information as data within a specific context: data which makes sense for the person using it. In economic theory we always reduced the reality of markets so far, that data became context free. When we speak in economic theory about information which is reflected in the price, we talk about data which is context free. In reality data is widely available, and Therefore it can not be reduced to one unique understanding or use of a particular bit of data. On the contrary. The widespread availability of networks has provided everybody with access to all different kinds of data. We also see that different people make different use of the same data. Even if two people have the same data within a certain context (hence we presume it qualifies as information) they can still use it differently in a different context or even use it differently in the same context. It is commonly known that politicians will always use economic data like inflation, economic growth, etc. to justify their policy if they are governing. The opposition parties will use the same data to prove that the government policy is a bad one. Given the growing importance of knowledge in the creation of products and services, the possibility of using data to match our needs makes a real difference. As long as knowledge was of little importance to productivity, the difference between data, information and knowledge did not matter too much.

The overflow of data today (we only need to see what is available on the Internet)
is another evolution which makes the concept of "all information available to
everyone" variable. It becomes extremely difficult for any manager to be aware of
all the data and potential information which is available and which can make a
crucial difference to him. It seems a contradiction, but the information age has
produced less equal access to data and hence information increasingly becomes a
distinctive factor. No market can be aware of all the possible relevant data (not to
speak of information) which exists. "Space" disappeared fast due to the existence
of computer networks. "Time" became a different concept since networks make
information available 24 hours a day. A manager can no longer have that
information available and under control any more. Hence no market can assume
that all information is freely available and reflected in the price anymore. It is of
no use to try and find ways to improve this. The growth of available information
cannot be stopped. It is more important to be aware of the changes which this
situation causes for the manager.

What are the changes of which managers should be aware ? First of all, it could be
that the market mechanism as we thought existed is not really operating anymore
as theory describes. This may be an additional reason why we see this kind of
strange phenomena as described in the previous section. Markets no longer tend
towards equilibrium but produce a rather complex behavior which differs if a
market is close to or far from equilibrium. Product launches seem to undergo
snowball-effects (positive feed-back) and it becomes almost impossible to foresee
or forecast anything. Remember here that we advocated in the previous section
that it was the extreme necessity for knowledge in production processes which
caused this behavior in the first place. Since the market price and the market
mechanism do not contain all the information, the manager has to manage the
acquisition of the information necessary for his company. With the growing
importance of knowledge in the production itself this stresses the importance of
knowledge management in companies. "Failure" (in this respect) of market forces
and their operation as "designed", forces the manager to pay attention to
knowledge management.

The majority of economists have not yet shown a lot of interest in this new reality.
Probably, since a consequence of a possible wider economic theory in these
circumstances would create some uncertainty in the economic community. The
academic economic community still feels perfectly happy with market theory and

pricing: presuming free and equal availability of information. They even claim that prices now reflect rational expectations of the future. From a theoretical point of view, one could attempt and develop a new economic theory, based on new assumptions of the information age. Boisot (1995) aims to do that. His developments concentrate on how a company deals with different levels of information and encoding. For the purpose of this book, however, we do not need to go into detail on the development of a broader economic theory, of which the classical approaches seem to be a particular subset.

Managers do not need a perfect theory. Managers need frameworks which describe the reality in the markets. Therefore, we only have to understand that our classical economic theory is only a subset or a specific case of a wider theory which we are to develop. The classical theory is no longer sufficient in order to understand market behavior in an information and knowledge era. Secondly, information and knowledge play such an important role both in understanding market behavior and in particular product development, that companies really have to organize themselves around their knowledge base. This should reflect the core competence of the company and this will allow them to be competitive in the market place. The knowledge base of a company and the use which is made of it will make the difference between two competitors. How else could Andersen Consulting differentiate itself from Coopers & Lybrand ?

But how have things come that far ? What has happened in order to observe the situation which we have today and is this situation reversible ? Next section will deal with the evolution which we have seen in the world of Information Technology (IT) and how this has made of "space" and "time" completely different concepts.

1.3. Information Technology (IT) evolution: from individual to group IT

It is obvious that computer technology, software development and telecommunications have developed rapidly. Since the introduction of remote terminals and more specifically of (local area) networks, telecommunications have become an integral aspect of Information Technology. Today, the borderline between Information Technology and Telecommunications has become distinctly vague. Therefore we often use the term telematics.

Given this fast and important technological evolution, infrastructural aspects of Information Systems have become increasingly important, and this has always been a highly complicated and technical matter. This technology push is responsible for the fact that within companies, IS is still considered to be mostly a technical issue. Today however, we can make technological choices. With open platforms which allow us to connect different machines and different operating systems, the manager is freer to make managerial choices concerning his information management. Too often information management questions remain limited to a small group of technologists belying the crucial importance of this matter for the competitive edge of the company.

In a short period of time we have seen promising technologies which are mainly related to networking: narrow and broad band ISDN, cable TV, cellular radio phones (PA Consulting Group, 1990). The radio spectrum can be used more economically. Cordless telephones (at home) and cordless Private Automatic Branch Exchanges (PABX in the office) eliminate reliance on the fixed telephone. Today GSM phones exist from which one can connect for applications of data communication, like reading and sending e-mail, sending files to companies, etc. from anywhere within Europe. Working from the home or from any remote place (teleworking) becomes a reality. If it were not that people are social animals and some business processes involve human contact, we would probably see more teleworking already.

A clear combination of both technologies (computer and telecommunications) is the introduction of Value Added Data Services (VADS) in Europe. VADS is a generic term and covers a range of services dealing with the exchange of structured business information. Standardization is very important in the future development of VADS in Europe. Nation-wide reservation systems are one example of such an application. The SWIFT inter-banking network is another. GSM phone networks is a third one.

However, we already know that successful in-company IS planning and implementation is more than just technology. We can learn some lessons from the past. Somogyi and Galliers (1987b) summarize the transition in the role of computerized information systems and its importance in companies since the 1950s. They suggest that the application of information technology is at the threshold of a new era, opening up new opportunities by using the technology strategically for the benefit of organizations and businesses. Ten years on, we are still struggling with the problem of exploiting new business opportunities using technology.

We still recognize today what Earl (1989, p 21, table 1.2) pictured as a number of distinguishing factors in order to describe how we have moved from what might be called the "DP era" to the "IT era". Technology for business applications are too often still situated in what Earl called the DP era. Almost ten years later, we find we have advanced little.

	DP era	IT era
Financial attitude to IT	A cost	An investment
Business role of IT	Mostly support	Often critical
Application orientation of IT	Tactical	Strategic
Economic context of IT	Neutral	Welcoming
Social impact of IT	Limited	Pervasive
MIS thinking on IT	Traditional	New
Stakeholders concerned with IT	Few	Many
Technologies involved in IT	Computing	Multiple
Management posture of IT	Delegate abrogate	Leadership involvement

More than any technical difference or evolution which appeared over recent years, the distinguishing factors have to do with the business use of IT. The changing environment from DP to IT does not depend primarily on evolving technology, but much more on evolving the business use of this technology. This latter aspect is of crucial importance.

The actual situation of Information Systems Management in companies is well summarized by Angell and Smithson (1991). Coping with IT use for business applications will be characterized by major impacts in :

linking IT to a more efficient industrial and commercial base (which relates to a better understanding of the business processes, which further relates to the knowledge inherent in a business process).

enhanced human to human communication (importance of the process of IS strategy and of organizational learning)

application and sale of expertise and of information itself (or the creation of knowledge).

However, it is the human factors and not the technology that makes the difference between commercial success or failure, and between acceptance or rejection of a system (Angell and Smithson, 1991). Thus, as a computer-based information system becomes more central to the life of the organization, the role of the information systems manager becomes more oriented towards organizational and business aspects and away from narrow technical concerns.

A first "transformation" in IS strategic thinking has been pushed by the Design School of strategic thought (e.g. Porter, 1985). These theories have been adapted to the world of IS and IT by a number of different authors (Cash et al., 1988; Porter and Millar, 1985; Cash and Konsynski, 1985; Clemens and McFarlan, 1986; Bruns and McFarlan, 1987; Vitale, 1986). In this terminology of strategic analysis, different aspects of the business in which IT plays a part are considered with respect to their role in shaping or destroying competitors. IS/IT can as such be considered as a weapon to gain competitive advantage in any sector.

One of the outcomes of a more strategic approach of IS strategy is an increasing interest in decision support and IS management. This results in a number of practical conclusions for IS design and use, but is based on a sound view of incorporating IS into the global corporate strategy (Ahituv and Neumann, 1982; Baets, 1992). Based on the definition of decision stages exceptions, discrepancies and alternatives are to be considered in each stage. In a final stage, IS policy design incorporates a better understanding of the business itself. Ten years ago one would typically think of (quantitative) models and forecasting techniques. Today new evolutions in Artificial Intelligence allow a broader understanding of business processes without too much reduction. We will discuss these new developments in chapter 4.

Among others, the banking industry gave and still gives considerable importance to technological developments and their possible (technological) implementation into particular banks (Baets, 1989). Examples of these developments are: Back-office automation at the Stock Exchanges; Automated trading for equities; From dumb terminal to intelligent workstations; Knowledge-based techniques. Therefore, banks are interesting organizations to study. In banks we observe that IT related problems have mostly to do with limits induced by regulation and attitudes, much more than with technology.

In summary, we have seen a technological push during the 1960s, 1970s and early 1980s, based on the fast growing possibilities of IT and telecommunications. Many applications have been developed, including many more functions than in other previously known applications. In the late 1980s, the organizational, human and business aspects were found to be very important for successful IS development in general.

But how do we deal with the integration of IT in day-to-day business, other than by replacing manual processes by automated processes ? Again we will take the banking sector as an example.

In the banking sector research has been done and some observations are of general interest. Morris (1986), for instance, considered innovations in banking strategies and employee relations. A clear change in the banking industry has to do with the way technology de-skills the workforce (Morris, 1986). Both tasks and skills change. The latter apparently is due to technology, and Morris' research confirms this. Whether tasks change due to technology is less evident. Only in the more "advanced" sectors of banking (international markets in complex financial instruments), does there clearly exist the link between task description and technology (Essinger and Rosen, 1989). Where most of the debate today around IS implementations is still focused on the topic of Morris' research, Essinger and Rosen seem to introduce the notion of the "knowledge worker".

A bank manager will become a consultant to his clients (Essinger and Rosen, 1989). The role of adviser will become important, since each bank will have the necessary information at it's fingertips. Competitive edge will be created with human and analytical qualities. Analysis of computer information, translation into the framework of the client, adaptation of information to specific (industrial) clients, etc. will become the core of the banking "service". Less importance will be given by the clients to the "service" on daily operations. The value added (and hence the profitability) will be created in an advice service to clients. In business-to-business markets, this could include e.g. co-design between client and producer. If this trend continues, then banks operating in different geographical and business markets (banks, insurance, trade finance, etc.) need to gather and manage the knowledge which exists inside the bank in order to use it as the basis for an improved service.

In this context, job design, or continuous job re-design during and after introduction of technology, becomes of paramount importance. The focus shifts from the combination technology and jobdesign to a combination of knowledge base and human (managerial) skills. In certain case studies (Kemp and Clegg, 1987), these trends are confirmed. One observes in real life cases important interactions between: organizational aspects of IS (job design); motivation; training; group building; industrial relations; communications; organizational aspects (co-ordination).

Considering the relation between technology and the nature of the business itself signifies the need to consider all these kinds of issues in a global systemic picture. It probably means rethinking the company around a new nucleus: the knowledge base. Information and research is still rare concerning these implications. Daniels (1991) reflects on directions of research:

> Improved communication, created by the adequate use of technology, will influence the decision making process and the way in which a consensus is reached. People will have to adapt to a "new" use of "new" information. The effect of, e.g., videoconferencing on strategic decision making, or even on negotiations, is not known. The same question can be raised on the effect of cutting down meeting times, through the use of IS/IT, and its effect on the quality of decision making.

> Knowledge workers will become crucial in any organization and hence will need to be supported adequately (motivation, information, training, etc.). Expertise is not automatically translated into expert systems. Experts remain human beings.

The tendency towards multimedia communications is apparent. The shift from paper work to more electronic work (word processors, electronic mail, etc.) is not yet fully mastered, and certainly not yet integrated in the strategic decision making process. What can be expected of the evolution of multimedia communication is unknown today.

As Daniels suggests we have seen in the beginning of the 90s the introduction of group decision support systems, a kind of affordable video conferencing, networks for exchange and electronic discussion (e.g. e-mail) on a larger scale than for experiments only. We have not investigated these evolutions enough. We also approach them as new developments in IT, which they probably are, to some extent. But more importantly, they will adapt the way IT can be used within a company. We have seen how the individual use of IT started moving gradually to more of a group-use. If each individual works on his own with data, a common knowledge base is interesting but probably less of a necessity. When we see today the emergence of electronic conferencing over the Internet and the development of the Internet itself, we are probably moving into another age. The use of IT for management is changing rapidly. Automation of processes is less of an issue today. Management itself, quality of decision, speed of decision and global coverage require a new approach to IT in companies.

Until now, decision support systems have not really been able to bridge the gap between the expectations they raised and their real use. They are still very much part of an individual type of IT use. A possible reason for that is that the computer has forced managers to think about the way a computer is able to operate. Managers have adapted their way of thinking to what is possible with computers. Maybe we should now try and create applications where the application thinks like humans; or at least in a way humans better recognize their way of thinking. As we will see, this is probably possible today.

For all these reasons, IT is still changing daily and fundamentally the "here" and "now" assumptions of economic theory. Time and space take on another meaning in the IT era. Electronic markets are operating 24 hours per day and nobody can really see where a deal is physically made. In the aerospace industry we have engineers who are co-designing an aeroplane, all remaining in their own offices. This joint design work takes place between different countries in the European

Union. Teleworking is another example of the dilution of time and space. One can work from anywhere, at any time it suits one. But independent of this dilution of time and space, there are still gaps of a different nature.

Where are the remaining gaps between the available technology and the applications we develop ? If we can identify these gaps, we can explore approaches in order to overcome them.

1.4. Gap between technology and application

It can be observed that IS management is still, to a large extent, technology-driven (Baets, 1994). Furthermore, IS development and planning does not comprise important elements of strategic policy. Evidence shows that the integration of human, organizational and business aspects in IS strategy and planning is poorly dealt with. These concerns are identified as the true nature of the problem. Not the technology development in itself, nor the kind of applications companies are striving for, but rather the gap between the two cause the problems. The strategic process of change is the problem which causes companies headaches. Applications need a more advanced knowledge component, given the evolution we see in the market and which we described earlier. There is a lot of technology available, which could support this development but it is not very clear how this fits with the Information Systems we know today. But above all, what do we need to know in order to start progressing in that direction. What insights are necessary on a corporate level in order to be able to launch this process of change. With the aim of clarifying the situation, we will describe in this section some of the elements which can play a role in launching this change process.

Research in identifying some of the reasons why companies have difficulties in balancing new information technologies (e.g. artificial intelligence) with the need for clearer knowledge management, has given some insights (Baets, 1994). Managers disagree to a considerable extent amongst themselves on the potential of the company, the economics of the market in which they operate, the specific knowledge which makes their company unique compared to others. They do agree about specific processes which are going on inside companies and between the company and buyers or suppliers. This could suggest that companies are over-stressed on business processes, rather than on the overall evolution of the company. Corporate management still seems to concentrate on a mechanistic Taylorian approach of a company, rather than considering a company as a network of people who all contribute to a common goal. In the latter approach, people management becomes more central and the management of business processes becomes of secondary importance.

A second group of important problems for improved use of Information Systems (IS) is the lack of an integrated view on the core corporate activities, the Information Technology strategy and the corporate strategy. Research suggests that this issue of integration seems to be far removed from managers' major concerns. If some consideration is given to this issue, the entire problem is seen as rather static and not at all, as a dynamic process. Integration is for most managers something which you decide on (say once a year) and then other people will execute it. Decision and execution are considered still separate from one another, which is very much based on Porter's concepts of strategy (Porter, 1985a). More modern views on strategy (Whittington, 1993) seem to contradict this. In view of a more advanced approach of knowledge management, as we advocate later, this division between decision and execution makes little sense and is at the very least, artificial. Furthermore, this classical view on strategy is very static and does not seem to correspond with the dynamic behavior in markets.

The organizational issues related to IT are well known and recognized as important by managers. However, they are perceived to be static, not dynamic in the sense that they are not perceived as being a part of a process. While different organizational models are understood, there is considerable disapproval of the existing organizational models within a specific company. Managers seem to know where the problem is, but they are not able to tackle it. They consider an organizational problem as a static problem which is imposed on a company and its employees. Too little importance is given to concepts of continuous learning, empowerment of workers, initiative of workers, etc. In view of knowledge management, this will become one of the major challenges which we will need to work at. A bureaucratic structure is identified as the most likely to improve awareness for IS planning within a company. Yet, an entrepreneurial structure is considered as more optimal for motivating people and hence for the creation of learning and knowledge. This paradox will prove to be difficult to tackle.

All this relates to an important factor which will appear a number of times throughout the book: perceptions and managerial mind sets. In our own research, managerial mind sets were defined as an attitude towards the use of "feeling" and "formal analysis" in managerial tasks. Chapter 3 will go into more detail on what managerial mind sets are. Managers recognize the importance of different mind sets, for different managerial tasks. There is a clear perception of the necessary qualities of the decision maker as an individual, but the decision making process is not well understood and not seen as important. There is still more focus on the aim, the "good" decision, than on the process of reaching that decision: the process of learning and knowledge building. This process component will prove to become very important if a company chooses a knowledge management approach. Much of the research we did and which will be reported on in later chapters, stresses the problems of dealing with perceptions in managerial research. Much of what we do in decision support these days depends on the measurement of perceptions, and there is almost no other way to generate information on these less quantifiable issues than by questioning managers.

In general we can see that managers are very skilled in performing their day-to-day work processes. Given the changes which occur on the markets, companies try to re-engineer their work processes in order to cope with some of the market shifts which they see. However, they still base their management on the design and/or improvement of work-processes. This approach supposes that work processes do exist and that they can be described "objectively". This presumes that two people (buyer and supplier, or even two people from different departments of the same company) have the same understanding of the same business process. The following chapters (and in more detail, the annex) will advocate that this approach is at least a questionable one.

Managers react on their "process" within their own framework of reference (their mindset) and so does any other person involved in the process. It is the specific expertise or knowledge of the person which allows him to deal better with a specific problem than somebody else. Does this not suggest that different people see the same process differently ? If two people can see the same process "identically" and they were both knowledgeable, why wouldn't they then both do the same ? Doesn't this suggest also that a person does not use his knowledge on a specific problem, but rather that problem and knowledge get involved in an interactive process whereby the person creates knowledge which allows the problem to be solved ? If this seems logic to us, then a new approach to combine IT and corporate applications, based on the knowledge paradigm, is emerging.

This evolution makes our society and the markets an exciting challenge for companies today. Of course, it also causes new problems. As advocated before, in Western Europe we have quickly evolved into a knowledge society, but we do not really see clearly in how a company should organize itself in order to respond to this challenge. Complex decisions need input from different people. Individual decision making, based on an individual approach of information and information support technology seems to be over. Shifting towards a more group approach to IT, in connection with group decision making needs a different managerial approach. It will be based much more on human skills and it will invite individuals to contribute to the knowledge network of the company. New types of decision support will evolve and new techniques of artificial intelligence will emerge.

Chapter 4 of this book will give some insight into intelligent decision making and the techniques which we should know as yet. Only little has been done in this area. Experiments are going on in some companies with isolated applications (Goonatilake and Treleaven, 1995; Zahedi, 1993). Finally machines are beginning to think a little like humans. For the first time we are using techniques which imitate the human brain and language. But there is still a long way to go if we want to change our companies from an individualistic information processing organization, to a networked knowledge-building company. However, the economic reality surrounding us seems to suggest that we should not wait too long.

1.5. Speed of change

We have argued that Information Technology has heavily influenced the assumption of economic theory that prices include all the required information in any specific time-space combination. This assumption made it possible to develop the market theories that we did. The most characteristic quality of such a market is that it tends towards equilibrium and that the market mechanism optimizes supply and demand. Needless to say, most of our Western thinking on management is inspired by this theory.

But today we see that Information Technology changes both time and space. Through networks, the entire world is connected and the financial markets are no doubt the most advanced example of this. It becomes extremely difficult to limit "space". The only way of doing so is regulation in many cases. But even that will not continue, in the long run. Deregulation will eventually break down the "space" limits which we were able to impose before. Globalisation is slowly becoming a fact and Information Technology is actively supporting this.

A second element of IT to which we have given less attention is that the speed of a transaction increases tremendously. The process of buying and selling has already speeded up in many industries . A lot of the processing is done automatically, but also the buyers' decision is in some circumstances, already automated. EDI (Electronic Data Interchange) is only one technology supporting this acceleration. The increasing use of IT in buying processes, speeds up the whole market behavior. What we saw ten years ago taking place over a one week time period, we may see today within the time limits of one day. If we compare with say twenty years ago, we can see time-spans of one month 20 years ago reduced to only one or a few days. Does this mean that market behavior has changed ? Maybe it is only moving faster. If we see a movie speeded up, we see things differently. The market "chaos" or complexity that we see today, has perhaps always been present. However, as the film was moving so slowly, we saw separate pictures, not the movie itself. Today, we may see the movie. And we are surprised. We see that markets do not behave in a simple and linear way "anymore". We see a lot of dynamic effects on markets, e.g. like the positive feed-back phenomena described earlier. But maybe all this is not new. Maybe this has always been the case but we have approximated it by simple linear approximations within time periods we could handle. As long as the film moved frame by frame we could do that. Now that the movie is turning at its "correct" speed, we observe the relative failure of our approaches.

There is no reason to think that markets behave fundamentally differently now than say 20 years ago. Among others, Information Technology has made the artificial limitation of markets in space and time, which we needed for our simplified approximating theories, become obsolete. We should not blame the problems we have with this on changing market behavior, but rather on our simplified approximations. We have ignored for years that markets are non-linear dynamic systems and we have approached them as linear static ones. Much of our economic theory is based on that simplification. What can a company do about this ?

In theory the solution is straight forward. Approach the markets considering them as a non-linear dynamic system and use your resources (your people) in an effective way to build on their qualities, capacities and experience. In its most simple setting, this is the heart of a knowledge-based approach of management in which learning becomes the main competitive advantage of a company. But before we can do something with this, we need more insight into a number of other things.

First we will look into the experience which other sciences have with non-linear dynamic systems. Instead of reinventing the wheel, we can learn from our colleagues. Chapter 2 will take a guided tour through what we know already about non-linear dynamic behavior and knowledge. It will allow us to see what is relevant for economics and management. In chapter 3 we will develop some ideas about dynamic non-linear behavior in economics and management. Chapter 4 will then go in some detail into useful techniques, before describing some of the applications which one can realize. After some examples and real life cases in chapters 5 and 6 chapter 7 will give a framework of use of the approaches developed. By the end of this book, the reader will not only better understand what happens around him, but he will have some indication of interesting developments one might like to explore for one's company.

REFERENCES

Ahituv N and Neumann S, 1982. *Decision Making and the Value of Information, from Principles of Information Systems for Management.* Iowa: Wm Brown Publishers.

Angell I and Smithson S, 1991. *Information Systems Management.* London: Macmillan Information Systems Series.

Arthur B, 1990. Positive Feedbacks in the Economy. Scientific American. Febr., pp. 92-99.

Baets W, 1989. The risk of implementing risk management systems. Proceedings of Computers in the City. Blenheim Online, London.

Baets W, 1992. Aligning information systems with business strategy. Journal of Strategic Information Systems. Nr. 4, September.

Baets W, 1994. The strategic use of Information Technology in banking: IS strategy alignment. PhD thesis. Warwick Business School, University of Warwick.

Boisot M, 1995. *Information Space: A framework for learning in organizations, institutions and culture*. Routledge.

Bruns W and McFarlan W, 1987. Information Technology puts power in control systems. Harvard Business Review. September-October.

Cash J, Applegate L and Mills Q, 1988. Information Technology and Tomorrow's Manager. Harvard Business Review. November-December.

Cash J and Konsynski B, 1985. IS Redraws Competitive Boundaries. Harvard Business Review. Vol. 63, Nr. 2, March/April.

Clemens E and McFarlan W, 1986. Telecom: Hook Up or Lose Out. Harvard Business Review. July-August.

Daniels C, 1991. *The Management Challenge of Information Technology*. London: The Economist Intelligence Unit.

Earl M, 1989. *Management Strategies for Information Technology*. Prentice Hall.

Essinger J and Rosen J, 1989. *Advanced Computer Applications for Investment Managers*. Canterbury: Financial Technology Publications.

Goonatilake S and Treleaven P (eds.), 1995. *Intelligent Systems for Finance and Business*. Wiley.

Kemp N and Clegg C, 1987. "Information Technology and Job Design." In *Towards Strategic Information Systems,* Somogyi E and Galliers R (eds.). Abacus Press.

Morris T, 1986. *Innovation in banking business strategies and employee relations*. Croon Helm.

PA Consulting Group (PACTEL), 1990. Information Technology: The Catalyst for Change. London: Mercury Books, W Allen & Co.

Porter M, 1985a. *Competitive advantage: creating and sustaining superior performance*. The Free Press.

Porter M, 1985b. Technology and Competitive Advantage. Journal of Business Strategy. Vol. 5, Nr. 3.

Porter M and Millar V, 1985. How Information Gives You Competitive Advantage. Harvard Business Review. July-August.

Somogyi E and Galliers R, 1987b. From Data Processing to Strategic Information Systems: a Historical Perspective. Journal of Information Technology. March.

Vitale M, 1986. The Growing Risk of Information Systems Success. MIS Quarterly. December.

Whittington R, 1993. *What is strategy - and does it matter ?* London: Routledge.

Zahedi F, 1993. *Intelligent Systems for Business: Expert Systems with Neural Networks.* Wadsworth Publishing.

2. WHAT CAN WE LEARN FROM DYNAMIC BEHAVIOR OF SYSTEMS

Increasingly, management scientists have paid attention to developments in other sciences, which could be of interest for improved understanding of the complex behavior of systems in a managerial context. The sciences which are working with non-linear and dynamic systems are multiple and therefore we want to limit this overview. Those sciences which we have a look into are: physics, neurobiology, cognitive psychology and computer sciences. For a better understanding of systems behavior (e.g. market behavior) we need to attack some theoretical concepts. We will limit them as much as possible. For each concept a brief theoretical introduction is given but we also try to make it more accessible for the manager via examples. Each of the concepts refers to a limited bibliography in itself. Some reference works will be given which allows the interested reader to go a little further, without becoming too involved in the details. The suggested books, in turn, all have an extended bibliography for the very interested or very advanced reader.

The concepts introduced in this chapter do not only have an intellectual value. They all contribute to the further development of the concepts developed in this book and the approach advocated. Hence it is crucial for the understanding of how to develop knowledge management in your own company. Keep in mind that the scientific approach is not so important in itself, though it can be intellectually very challenging; rather the managerial implications deserve all your attention. This tour of scientific concepts should be an exciting one in its own right and gives a background to enable the reader to cope easily with the managerial framework which is proposed further on in the book.

2.1. Dynamic non-linear systems behavior

Science dealing with non-linear dynamic systems is sometimes called "chaos" theory or "complexity" theory. Dynamic non-linear systems are called complex, which includes at the same time two different types of behavior. The same complex system can at one point in time behave chaotic as described later, but on other occasions it can show a perfectly deterministic and obviously simple behavior. One does not really know when a complex system becomes chaotic and when it (re)becomes simple. In any case, chaotic systems are still supposed to be deterministic, which means that there is no random behavior behind such a system. A set of non-linear and dynamic equations should still be able to describe this system. However, as an observer we may observe behavior which we cannot immediately and easily write down in such equations. The reason to stress the deterministic character of chaotic systems is that it is important to understand the consequences of its deterministic nature. If they were not deterministic at all, it would be extremely difficult to make any sense out of them. Furthermore, if they were not deterministic, that would imply that behavior cannot really be managed, which would further imply that everything would happen "by accident". Complexity theory shows us that even chaotic systems have some determinism. The consequence for management is that there is more than just good luck in management even if a system appears to be chaotic. The other side of the coin is that we cannot hope for good luck either. If something happens, there has to be a good reason. Therefore, we have to investigate a little further into complexity theory and gradually we will discover more detailed consequences for management. As we need to give some definitions, we will begin by referring to some mathematicians and their theories. They were the first to study the behavior of dynamic systems.

Stewart (1989) defines chaos as an inherent feature of mathematical equations in dynamics. It is the ability of even simple equations to generate motion so complex, so sensitive to measurement, that it appears random. An introduction to the phenomenon of chaos is given in Gleick (1988) and Holden (1986). Basic mathematics are discussed in Stewart (1987) and more advanced pieces of theory (mathematics) are found in Abraham and Shaw (1983), Crutchfield et al. (1986), Devenay (1986), Schuster (1984), Thompson and Stewart (1986) and Mandelbrot (1982).

The phenomenon of chaos is best known from Lorenz's studies of the stability of weather, the equations of fluid motion and his "Butterfly effect", proving the sensitive dependence on initial conditions (Gleick, 1988). Lorenz advocated that since weather is a non-linear dynamic system, a butterfly which flaps its wings in the Amazons could (via the dynamics of the weather system), cause a hurricane in the Sahara. Though it is a metaphor, it shows the impressive consequences which dynamic systems can cause. Angell and Smithson (1991) illustrate this Butterfly effect in a managerial context by highlighting the point that physicists no longer accept the universality that "similar systems in similar environments will undergo similar changes". They interpret the Butterfly effect as an understanding that the behavior of certain computerized deterministic models (e.g. many decision support systems) can only be explained with hindsight. In managerial terms this means that decision support models using non-complex equations are only able to predict or explain in the very short term conditional to a rather static behavior of the environment.

Gleick (1988) describes how sometimes classic models are kept from becoming dynamic. He reports the manipulation made on a number of "a priori" deterministic models, when these models did something obviously bizarre (like flooding the Sahara, or tripling interest rates). Programmers would revise the equations to bring the output back in line with expectations. In practice, econometric models proved dismally blind. In fluid systems terminology, the non-linear terms tend to be left out.

In the few references made to chaos theory in managerial literature (Angell and Smithson, 1991; Merry, 1995), it is said that based on this theory, one can conclude that too often management deals with mechanisms and functions, and not with the systemic nature of business. "It does not take into account the magnifying effect of positive feed-back in ill-structured and turbulent environments such as the business world, and so ignores the 'Butterfly effect' where the marginal and insignificant trends of today become the major business opportunities/risks of tomorrow" (Angell and Smithson, 1991). More recently, Merry (1995) describes chaos theory in an accessible way for managers, also giving many examples of the consequences of a simplified approach of management. Peters (1991) attempts to use chaos theory on stock exchange behavior which is probably the market whose behavior we least understand.

In summary, Gleick (1988) describes the actual status of knowledge on chaos theory as follows :

- Chaos appears, and within the chaos we find astonishing geometric regularity. This relates to problems of non-linear, dynamic (feed-back) functions. These kinds of functions can be observed in many managerial problems.

- Behavior produces information, it amplifies small uncertainties, but it is not utterly unpredictable. This is the promising and good news about it. We need a different approach, but we can still do something about it.

- There exists a development in mathematics, based on "strange attractors" and "fractals", which proves promising to describe chaos (Peters, 1991).

Stewart (1989) has identified properties of chaotic systems and he highlights the solutions on which physicists work in order to get a better understanding of the complexity of systems. Can we also recognize some of this in a managerial environment ? In Stewart's terminology, the concept of multi-dimensional space plays a crucial but behind-the-scenes role in the development of topological dynamics and the discovery of chaos. In managerial terms this can be interpreted as the fading away of our market assumptions that price includes all the information in any given time and space ? In scientific terminology again, the existence of strange attractors is observed in chaotic systems which sometimes give them a sense of stability. A complex system seems to turn around such a strange attractor, before going off in another direction suddenly and without any warning. A complex system can have a number of these strange attractors which does not make it easier to recognize them. Don't we see sometimes that chaotic markets seemingly suddenly become calm and fluctuate within certain narrow boundaries ? But then equally sudden they go off in a direction, either never to come back to any stability, or to achieve a local stability for a certain time on another level.

Genuine chaos has four curious properties:

- sensitivity to initial conditions
- existence of random itineraries
- common occurrences of random itineraries
- cake-mix periodicity/a-periodicity.

This implies that chaotic systems are not based on the past. They need the past to get to their initial condition. But from their initial position they start a whole new life independent of the past. Any slight difference in initial conditions (say a starting position which is different only in the 7th decimal digit) can create a completely different behavior. From a scientific point of view, Prigogine (Nicolis and Prigogine, 1989) identifies this as the "irreversibility" of time and has proven this phenomena to be a valid one in dynamic systems. If we were be able to forecast the future out of the past, then we would be able to reverse time, which of course we cannot. In managerial terms that means that if markets are dynamic systems, then we have in markets the phenomenon of irreversibility of time, hence the future cannot be forecast out of the past.

In the field of physics research, physicists work in the direction of the identification of chaotic attractors in a non-periodic regime added to a randomness caused by small changes in the "environment". This is known as Feigenbaum's Mapping (Stewart, 1989). Furthermore, a new type of mathematics evolved, capable of describing and analyzing the structured irregularity of the natural world. The new geometric forms involved were named "fractals" (Mandelbrot, 1982). However interesting this development may be for science, it is of less importance for managerial applications.

Stewart (1989, p 286) remains realistic as to the scope of what we can expect as a result of chaos theory in the short run :

> "Don't jump to conclusions. Irregular phenomena do not require complicated equations, or equations with explicit random terms. This message cuts both ways. On the "loss" side, even if you are fortunate enough and clever enough to have devised good equations, you still may have trouble understanding the system that they model. Even if equations are simple, the behavior of the system may not be. On the "profit" side, a phenomenon that looks complicated may not really be. It may be governed by a simple - but chaotic - model. Now we are getting into Designer Chaos, using know-how about typical types of dynamics to build plausible models."

According to Stewart, the brightest ray of light that chaos sheds focuses on the nature of complexity. We know now that simple equations can have simple solutions - or complex ones. Complex equations can have complex solutions - or simple ones. What controls the relationship of equation to solution, of model to behavior, is not form, but meaning. Therefore we need to become critical about some of our decision support approaches and/or knowledge approaches. Instead of using approaches which focus on the form (on equations) we need to shift for approaches which focus on behavior and meaning. These approaches will be described in more detail in chapter 5. This coincides with a number of other research findings on which we report further on in this chapter. However, a warning. It would be wrong to conclude that the simplicity of a theory is the easiness with which we can express it (de Callatay, 1992). Sometimes, we cannot find a cause for all actions.

A person who contributes a lot to research in behavior of complex systems is Nobel Prize winner Ilya Prigogine (Nicolis and Prigogine, 1989). He did a lot of research specifically in fluid systems. In many respects, fluid systems can be compared to managerial environments. One of the things which Prigogine observed and which we mentioned already is the "irreversibility" of time, an idea which deserves some further explanation. Prigogine observed that the same dynamic system behaved differently, starting from a different set of initial conditions. Together with many management scientists one would probably expect that the same system, which was correctly based on past behavior, would predict the future in the same way. This would imply that such a model is based on the past and that once the past has been captured in a model, it can predict the future. Hence, the past and the future become part of the same truth and we could reverse time. A model can describe what happened say 5 periods ago equally good as it could predict what will happen 4 periods into the future. Despite the fact that we all know that this is not true in reality, we have built models based on that principle and we use them again and again in management.

What Prigogine shows us is that the initial state is important together with the behavior of the system from there. This initial state is reached via a past path, a path of experience and learning, but this past path in itself does not give an indication of future behavior. Dynamic behavior also causes a system which we see at different places in its development path to show a completely different development path, depending on its initial state. The same complex market

behavior, based on the same complex model may look very different at a different
point in time if it started from an even very slightly different starting situation. If
we compare this to the market penetration models which we know today, then we
can see that dynamic behavior causes disruption in these classical models. Static
market penetration models may prove to be rather useless, if the market which it
attempts to describe shows complex behavior.

This has important consequences for management science. These observations
suggest that we do not waste time in extrapolating models out of past behavior, but
rather spend more time on describing the initial state clearly, as well as the
dynamic non-linear properties of the system. Such systems create during their
"life" stepwise an exponentially growing set of alternative development paths that
could be followed (bifurcation). These observations would suggest that
forecasting the way we do now is of little use, other than in the very short term.
Rather it is necessary for companies to gain understanding and insight into the
complexity of the problem.

Human beings have the quality to cope with complexity very easily since we are
able to reduce variety quickly and easily for complex tasks. If one wants to cross a
street, one faces a large number of different observations, like: cars coming at
different speeds, from different directions; other vehicles which are around; the
weather conditions have an influence; sound and light; etc. We do not even think
about this while crossing a street but we do it with ease. In the next chapter we
will discuss in more detail how humans deal with these kinds of problems since
what we wants is to imitate this behavior in management applications.

Prigogine made further interesting discoveries in his research. He observed that
knowledge is not something which is present and resident in any system, but rather
it is built up each time over and again, bottom-up. This is a remarkable
observation and we will see that other scientists in other disciplines have observed
very much the same. This goes against the common idea which many of us still
have that knowledge is something one acquires via a teaching process. Once the
knowledge is acquired we store it in our memory and we retrieve it any time we
need to use it. A teacher who has more knowledge than a student passes on
knowledge, which the student needs to store for future use. Our pedagogical
system is (unfortunately) still very much based on this idea. But this pedagogical
concept which is equally a concept on the nature of knowledge, continues to be

applied in companies too. This implies that the manager of a business unit needs to know everything. He will pass on parts of his knowledge to some co-workers when necessary. In this process of "knowledge transfer" the co-workers will gain more knowledge and eventually they will be able to do the job of the manager. That is what we often call "on the job training". If Prigogine's observations apply to the managerial world, and there is no reason why they would not, this could be an illusion.

Knowledge is built bottom-up, each time over and again. People create and use a reference framework and they use this framework dynamically to create knowledge. This reference framework is built up over their lifetime of learning and experimenting. Knowledge is not structured and not stored in units of any kind. Other scientists have made additional observations which we discuss further on in this chapter. Once we have seen what scientists have observed and identified with respect to knowledge, we can go into more detail in the next chapter about how knowledge creation takes place and how the individual's reference framework gets created. This will then prove to be an analogy for the creation of corporate knowledge networks which we will describe in chapter 7.

This vision on knowledge has important consequences for knowledge networks, defined as a co-operation of individuals who produce, share or use a common resource or repository of knowledge. Often we try to organize a group of human beings and very often we install a kind of a hierarchy. In this vision of knowledge, a hierarchical organization of a knowledge network of any kind, other than for ease of communication, becomes obsolete. There does not appear to be anything like a hierarchy of knowledge (or experience). Rather, there is a system in which human beings interactively for each given problem confront each others reference frames and come up dynamically with the knowledge necessary to tackle the problem. Equality of humans in their input in the knowledge process, dynamic knowledge creation and interacting reference frameworks become the rules for knowledge-based decisions and the creation and management of knowledge networks. In chapter 7 we consider in more detail the consequences of this for knowledge-based management. Linear approaches which we still use very often to approximate management situations could catastrophically fail in such knowledge networks. We do not need to go further into the specifics of knowledge networks now. For the time being it is enough to have an understanding of the underlying observations which are made in the sciences about these systems.

The changing economic behavior which we described in chapter 1 seems to have properties of this complex behavior. These views on systems and knowledge building in complex systems coincide with what we have identified as positive feed-back loops in economics. Prigogine also mentions them in his research in fluid systems. First movers seem to perturbate systems beyond reasonable expectations. At least, what we observe as market behavior seems to match with what we have learned about complex systems up to now.

2.2. Far from equilibrium behavior

Another interesting observation which Prigogine made is that systems behave differently when they are close to an equilibrium or when they are far away from an equilibrium. Typically, closer to an equilibrium a complex system becomes more stable and farther from an equilibrium, a system behaves more chaotically. However, complex systems never really seem to get into an equilibrium. This is a consequence of the nature of dynamic systems as described in the previous section. This observation reinforces the idea that when markets are close to an equilibrium (and slow moving) they look rather stable. However, this only hides the complex nature of the system and gives the false idea that specific market behavior could be described easily via a linear approximation.

Some authors have seen these sudden changes and have developed some rules of thumb for managers to cope with them (Genelot, 1992; Stacey, 1992). Independent of how useful these rules are for managers, they do not give a better understanding of the behavior of the system itself. If managers want to be more equipped to deal with complex systems, some deeper understanding is necessary.

Different behavior far from equilibrium compared to close to equilibrium could be yet another reason why a few decades ago we thought we were in stable markets. It remains true that time and space have other dimensions, but it could equally be true that economic systems like markets, happened to be closer to an equilibrium than they are today. Most probably, both phenomena reinforced each other.

One main advantage which sciences have over management is that sciences have laboratories where they can test systems under a higher speed of development.

Unfortunately in management we need to live through the experience in order to observe. The only possible way out is to design simulators which simulate complex systems describing managerial problems. This allows us to experiment with dynamic behavior, much like the science does. As of today, business schools are not yet into this kind of research. It would probably imply such an important paradigm shift, that it would need another few years before forming a part of academic research. Companies, however, cannot wait for academic research to cope with this. Therefore, the few textbooks dealing with complex systems in management should be carefully studied (Merry, 1995).

2.3. Computer sciences and knowledge creation: experiments with artificial life

The concept of knowledge creation bottom-up and the fact that knowledge is not stored but dynamically created is also observed in a particular field of computer sciences, i.e. artificial life. The godfather of artificial life is Chris Langton who did lots of research on this particular field in the computer sciences (Langton, 1989), amongst others at the Santa Fe Institute. Artificial life became a particular development in artificial intelligence which builds further on the genetic approach of systems which we explore in this section.

Artificial life simulates the behavior of simple elements which eventually in their conjunction show complex behavior. This approach is opposed to attempts to build models of complex systems (like the human brain) via simple approximations. Artificial life research chose this way of exploration since it is interested in finding out how "life" starts and functions. This research provides fascinating results on which reports can be found from different sources. A very readable book is the one by Franklin (1995) which is anyway a good tour guide of the world of Artificial Intelligence and therefore also of artificial life.

Important for management is what Langton derives from his study of artificial life. He observes, in line with Prigogine, that knowledge is built up again each time, also in these artificial systems. The building blocks of these artificial systems are very simple elements and they show hardly any intelligence if one considers them separately. However, whenever a system of simple individual elements becomes confronted by a specific problem it develops intelligence which allows it to tackle the specific complex problem. An example of this behavior is a simulation of an insect (hence an artificial insect) which is built up from of a number of very simple elements, none of them having any intelligence. The artificial insect is programmed to walk around in a closed zone, say a closed room. It is programmed to avoid walls and if it finds a wall, it changes direction. When an additional wall is put in the middle of the room, the artificial insect develops the knowledge, based on its previous knowledge of avoiding walls, to also avoid this wall. Once the insect is able to avoid this additional wall in the center, the researcher moves the wall. Again we observe the insect developing the knowledge to avoid this new position of the wall.

Of interest to us is the observation that a system of individual elements which show hardly any individual intelligence can develop, completely autonomous, knowledge which goes far beyond the individual's capacity. This knowledge is not stored, but created each time again in an interaction of the different elements. Here we can make an interesting parallel to a company ? Doesn't it happen often that managers think that some people (e.g. with lower education or less experience) are unable to contribute to the corporate knowledge ? We often presume that an individual should have the necessary knowledge to tackle a specific problem. We forget that a number of individuals who do not have specific knowledge could develop it in co-operation. Based on which criteria do we hire people in a company ? Do we consider the capability they have to work in teams in order to create dynamically knowledge and get tasks done, or do we rather attempt to judge on individual capacity for producing intelligent behavior (if indeed we can judge that) ? In many companies and circumstances we are interested in finding the bright individual, who, if possible fits the corporate culture. We often accept that managers do not have the necessary people skills to manage teams. We think that an intelligent manager is more important than a manager who can activate the knowledge creating process with his co-workers. Research in artificial life suggests us that this is, at the very least, a dangerous illusion.

What we can observe in artificial life theory invites us to rethink these approaches dramatically. An efficient knowledge management and elicitation approach may well be more rewarding for a company than a set of bright intellectuals. Provided that a company can support teams of "knowledge workers" (which is not necessarily the same as bright intellectuals) with the adequate infrastructure (as we will discuss in chapter 7), the knowledge creation process could be improved consistently which would allow companies to deal with complex and changing environments more easily.

A final lesson we can draw from the research into artificial life is that despite the need to support knowledge workers with an IT infrastructure, this support is not the crucial element for success. Human behavior and attitude, dealing with adequate resources, will be the key to success. For that reason, a learning attitude is equally as important for success as a correct infrastructure. This will be discussed in more detail in chapter 7.

2.4. Self-organizing systems

As argued before, the distinctive feature of any knowledge network will be the human beings who use it. Therefore it should not surprise us that neuro-biologists have done some interesting research which is relevant to the managerial context. In the first place they also confirm the findings of e.g. Langton and Prigogine. Amongst others, Maturana and Varela (1984) have done a lot of research into the behavior of biological species and into the knowledge creating process of these species. What Varela observed and identified as a striking quality is the capacity of self-creation of systems ("autopoèsis"). Whenever we bring a number of biological elements together, they organize themselves in a way that they can deal with their survival in an intelligent way.

One of the most simple examples is the bee colony. Each individual bee does not have a high intelligence. As a colony, however, they are able to do tremendous things. In the beginning we were convinced that somebody had to be the leader (the queen) and that she would "organize" all that. Research, however, does not confirm this. Rather, the colony organizes itself, with no specific pre-defined rules.

The principle of "autopoèsis" is a principle according to which groups of biological species organize themselves for survival. This development does not always deliver and guarantee success if defined as survival. According to the same principles, colonies and animal sorts disappear since they cannot be adapted any further. From an "autopoetic" point of view this is optimal behavior of the group.

Needless to say that this refers in managerial terms to bankruptcy. The self-organizing principle guarantees the best structure and organization for a company to survive, given that survival is the best possible state for that specific structure, in this example, for a particular company.

Varela has observed this kind of behavior in many other groups or systems. Any system creates its own structure which is optimal for its task. In such a structure, knowledge is built dynamically in order to be able to tackle each new situation which is encountered. If you break down a network or a self-organized organization, the new organization has to start all over again in order to get self-organized again. Any specific organizational structure is not transferable to another organization or company.

Some parallels can be drawn with companies. This research suggests that frequent job changes (job rotation) necessitates each time again a new team to be re-created. Any structure which is forced onto a group top-down, could cause a group to function sub-optimally. Provided that the structure is really forced against the will of the group members, they will dysfunction. Alternative group organizations may emerge, doing very useful work, but not according to the structure which the company desires. In organizational behavior terms we call this the informal power structure. Furthermore, this research confirms the observation already made in earlier sections that any member of the group (independent of its individual capacity) can provide interesting input for the group. If the aim is to create knowledge networks, then group members (and after all a company is a group of people) should be selected on their capacity for dynamic knowledge creation in a network of co-workers.

Varela also observed that within an auto-organized group, knowledge creation never stops. Given the dynamic nature of knowledge creation, it is not at all certain that a group of people will come up with the same solution for the same problem on a second occasion. Given that each individual continuously adapts his reference framework based on his experience working in the group and since any group meets at a different time with different dynamics, further knowledge can be created any second time. A second brainstorming on the same subject with the same group can result in another outcome. Knowledge produced during a first meeting is not necessarily retractable. The relevant bits of the first knowledge building exercise will be partly integrated in the individual's framework, but in itself it will cease to exist. Hence knowledge creation continues on and on. Any interruption which a company would like to bring to this process can only cause under-performance. This does not mean that the constitution of any particular group needs to be fixed for the rest of its life. Only, the creation and operation of the knowledge capacity of a group needs to be managed by the group itself. Any external action should be carefully considered before it damages the knowledge creating process. On the other hand, well conceived training which stimulates precisely this knowledge creating capacity of a group can be of good use to support knowledge workers.

In a corporate environment, these theories could have consequences for e.g. product design and launch; the organization and management of project teams; marketing of products.

2.5. Organizations as neural networks

Varela compared what he observed in his biological colonies with what we know about human intelligence. It needs to be said that we do not know a lot yet about human intelligence. Different people have different, but all very interesting ideas about it. Khalfa (1994) edited an interesting book about the different dimensions of intelligence: a sometimes rather philosophical but always interesting exploration of different forms of intelligence. On a more episthemologic level some work is done about what human perception is, but this does not give conclusive evidence either (Caverni et al., 1991; Ehrlich et al., 1993). We will have to do with the experimental research in which Varela is one of the front-runners.

The human brain is composed of millions of small very simple cells which are called neurons. They are highly interconnected via a dense network of synapses. Each of the individual cells is only able to perform very low level tasks and shows hardly any intelligence. The network, however, is able to solve any complex problem which is presented. This happens via a very simple process of parallel activation of a huge number of individual cells. We will explore this phenomenon in more detail in chapter 4, since this will become one of the main concepts of the use of knowledge-based management. For the purpose of understanding what is going on in other sciences we will leave it at that, for the time being.

Interestingly Varela has observed in biological colonies that the colony reacts as a group very much like a neural network (our brain) reacts. When a group is confronted with a problem, in parallel, different members of the group will be consulted who in term then consult other members. Needless to say, there is a lot of cross-consulting, where one member is consulted by different other members via different routes. That member will probably do the same with other members in the group. This process continues until a solution to the problem is reached. It is important to observe that all members of the group contribute to the creation of the knowledge and the answer and that this knowledge is created dynamically. None of the individual members has the ultimate answer, even if they have been confronted beforehand with the same problem. This is the kind of behavior one can observe in colonies of animals hunting, or colonies trying to survive. Though they have already encountered a particular problem a number of times, each time they will construct the most reasonable solution. Animals do not have the answer somewhere stored in their memory, but they have developed a reference framework which allows them to tackle any problem of the same type (e.g. survival, food, hunting). It is worth mentioning here that it is the ever changing environment which makes this kind of action necessary. No decision can be the same on any other occasion, since a lot of parameters will have changed, and not least, the (tacit) knowledge which the group has already acquired via the earlier experiences.

Just as our brain has a learning capacity, biological colonies also show learning behavior. They do not copy their behavior from the first time, but rather they learn from the first time and create a second reaction which builds partly on the first. Learning behavior of a company and the individuals within the company prove to be essential when a company wants to get organized around a knowledge base. Each individual in a group learns from the experiences of the group and puts this experience into his individual framework. As we will see in more detail later, experiences and perceptions are very individual and therefore if we want to work with knowledge based management, we need to give due importance to the individuals' perceptions of the problems. Perceptions and experiences co-create individual mental models and individual mental models is what people bring with them in the group. Therefore we need to understand in more detail what perceptions are and what role they play in knowledge management. Chapter 3 will deal with this problem.

So far, the observations made in neuro-biology seem to confirm the earlier observations in physics and computers sciences. The same kind of managerial consequences could be drawn from these observations. If we could assume that a company operates like a human brain does, we will see that knowledge-management and learning become crucial for modern management. Comparable to how millions of simple neurons constitute the brain and that this network of simple neurons is able to deal with very complex matters, so will a network of employees duly organized, trained via experience and supported, be able to cope with complexity.

We gave a lot of attention to what sciences have observed about knowledge. We have mentioned that knowledge creation does not exist without a learning attitude. Therefore we should pay attention to what the sciences know about learning. We should get some more insight in what other sciences have identified about learning. Before that, we will describe some research going on in Artificial Intelligence. It has been researched and confirmed that using very basic rules of genetic manipulation on decision processes produces results which outperform other more classical approaches. The obvious parallel with human reproduction and the importance which the human neural nets seem to play in knowledge networks makes it an interesting side-step to at least position genetic programming within the broader area of Artificial Intelligence.

2.6. Artificial Intelligence and genetic programming

Knowledge management is probably the main "raison d'être" of Artificial Intelligence as a research field. Therefore it is interesting to get a short overview of the developments which are going on in what we call the field of Artificial Intelligence (AI). Much of what we have already discussed in this chapter is part of what is researched in AI. For the interested reader, Franklin (1995) designed a very interesting tour through the world of AI with lots of emphasis on the underlying concepts, rather than on the techniques themselves. What is interesting for us is to see how AI evolved over time and gradually brought more insight in what knowledge is and how it operates.

AI started very much with expert systems: rule based systems which seem to follow some human thinking. The system is based on a number of rules which are deducted from a human expert (or a panel of human experts). A combination of rules, using a set of if-then-else constructions allows us to navigate through a kind of a knowledge base. In case the application domain considered is very narrow and the knowledge dealt with very specific, expert systems have shown some success. From a knowledge point of view, experiments with expert systems gave more insight in the fact that rules are a bad representation of knowledge. Expert systems can be considered as the first generation of AI techniques.

Connectionist systems (like neural networks are) are based on the assumption that knowledge is built dynamically, based on a framework of reference. Connectionist models learn from past experience and the real basis for the knowledge they generate is the network they have trained. One could consider this network as a framework which implicitly holds the knowledge. This network allows the reproduction of knowledge when necessary; the knowledge itself is not stored in any form. These kinds of applications are considered as second generation AI.

These days experiments continue with yet another generation. Based on what has been observed in the neuro-biology and the research on artificial life scientists think that even a context is not necessary in order to be able to (re-)produce knowledge. Rather, knowledge is built up bottom-up. If we can bring enough simple elements together and combine them in a very natural way (e.g. via the eternal law of the fittest) strong and healthy systems will occur which are able to tackle a lot of complex systems. Artificial life experiments are part of this third generation, as well as genetic algorithms. The latter combines strings of very simple elements, based on a survival law, in order to create the best solutions. Though most of these third generation developments are still highly experimental, they are interesting to follow.

For our purpose, the second generation of AI tools will prove to be very helpful and stable enough to be of use in a business environment. Managers are not interested to experiment with new techniques. They want solid solutions for their problems. Only, in a few more years we may have to start learning all over again.

The reader should now have enough detail to understand what knowledge is and how we can deal with it. Furthermore, it should have given some insight in what has been observed and researched in other sciences which can have effect in management. Much of what we have seen indicates the importance of knowledge as the basis of behavior of any living system. It has also been advocated that second generation AI tools have the capacity to develop knowledge or even to produce knowledge since they are trained with examples, not with rules or equations. Neural networks, e.g., learn from cases with which they are confronted. Hence, we should know a little more about learning and therefore we also have to consult different scientific disciplines.

2.7. Implicit learning

Research in Artificial Intelligence did not concentrate only on the characteristics of knowledge. It also needed to investigate the properties of learning: acquiring knowledge. Interesting research which has implications for management is on the theme of "implicit learning". In many cases people are not aware of what they are really learning. Teachers claim to know what students should learn but in reality this often is not the case. People learn a lot of things in an implicit way, via a certain context. This unintentional learning process is important for information-processing. Often with AI, language is used as a research object. Cleeremans (1993) has made an attempt to study whether one can model human performance in sequence-learning and in this particular case he took grammar as the example. His research confirms how complex knowledge, which grammar is, may emerge through the operation of elementary mechanisms. His findings seem to confirm that sequence learning is very much an exercise of building up building blocks until enough complexity can be dealt with.

This experience and these experiments confirm further the importance of a knowledge structure, build up of simple building blocks. It is interesting also to refer to these experiments, since they deal in many instances with language learning; an act which all human beings are confronted with and is considered as a typical case of learning.

2.8. Organizational learning

Applied to management, theories about learning got increasing attention, specifically those on organizational learning. Organizational learning is not a new concept. Argyris, in 1976, devoted lots of his time on the subject. However, it took another 10 to 15 years before the management community took up some of his original ideas. Extensive literature (Argyris and Schon, 1978; Daft and Huber; Dixon, 1992; Garvin, 1993; Swieringa and Wierdsma, 1993) indicates that there is no clear unique definition for organizational learning. Argyris and Schon have defined organizational learning as " ... a process in which members of an organization detect error or anomaly and correct it by restructuring organizational theory of action, embedding the results of their inquiry in organizational maps and images". Lee et al (1992) have defined organizational learning as a process in which "individuals' action leads to organizational interaction with the environment; the environment responds; and environmental responses are interpreted by individuals who learn by updating their beliefs about cause and effect relationships". Most of the definitions proposed by the researchers consider organizational learning as a dynamic process of creating, acquiring and transferring knowledge (Garvin, 1993) and converting a company into a "knowledge-based" organization (Drucker, 1988; Applegate et al., 1988; Quinn, 1992; Shukla, 1994). Hence learning is seen as a way of feeding the knowledge based nucleus of the company.

A knowledge based approach seems to be a pre-requisite for learning. Without the adequate knowledge base and the capability to update and put it into practice, it is difficult to live up to the expectations of the changing environment (Applegate et al., 1988). Lessem (1991) has defined organizational learning-constructs, viz., knowledge origination, knowledge development, knowledge refinement , knowledge promotion, knowledge adaptation, knowledge implementation (dissemination), and knowledge application and has suggested that organizations build up these constructs to become a learning organization. In most of the literature, a learning organization is not really defined either. However, we agree that these kind of definitions are difficult to give and by giving them, we are already influencing the idea itself. In the next chapter we will deal in more detail with how learning takes place within companies.

According to Lessem, knowledge origination is the process which opens up entirely new fields of knowledge. Knowledge development is the process which uncovers potential for the application of newly discovered knowledge across a wide diversity of fields in organizations. In the context of organizations, both knowledge origination and development take often place in Research and Development activities. These two processes are becoming increasingly important if organizations are to keep apace with technological innovation. Gradually, knowledge origination and development also take place outside the R&D context, the more a company becomes a "learning organization".

Knowledge refinement is the process which refines the originated and developed knowledge into systems, policies, routines and procedures. For instance, marketing analysts would refine and specify the system required for the introduction of a new product.

Knowledge promotion is the process of promoting the knowledge so that it can be used by others. Promotion does not involve any original or developmental activity other than customization of knowledge. Knowledge adaptation is the process of adapting the knowledge which is specific to a situation / field to solve an *analogous* problem. Such a process is conventionally used in management services.

Knowledge implementation (dissemination), is the process of ensuring that the knowledge physically reaches the right place at the right time. Information technology plays a major role at this stage. Knowledge application is the process of putting the acquired knowledge into action.

To summarize, learning from a knowledge-based perspective is the combination of building up these processes. All these processes can be classified into two categories, viz., knowledge acquisition and knowledge management. When the knowledge is generated within the organization or from outside the organization, learning is said to occur.

To be specific, learning in the context of organizations occurs when

> a) Individual members of the organization *form* their views/ knowledge ("mental models") on the action-response of organization and environment (Lee et al., 1992).

> b) Individual members *share* their knowledge and form pooled knowledge.

c) Individual members *update* their knowledge in a changing environment.

Organizational learning is inherently a collective and shared individual learning. Organizations learn from their own past experiences and also from the experiences of other organizations. But no learning can take place on an organizational level, other than via individual learning.

The next level is then inter-organizational learning which involves learning from other companies and competitors. Inter-company learning takes place as the members of the organization go on meeting the business partners, suppliers, customers and competitors. Especially, learning occurs when a company watches and uses the experience of another firm in resolving a problem. Sometimes learning occurs between organizations due to joint-ventures with other companies. An example of inter-company learning is benchmarking with the best practice in other industries (Pedler et al., 1991).

Learning may take place within the organization due to *internal information exchange, participative policy making* and *a learning approach to strategy formulation. Internal information exchange* and *participative policy making* leads to learning as they enable members of the organizations to share their knowledge and values. In a *learning approach to strategy*, formation of strategy, its implementation, evaluation and improvement are consciously treated as a learning process as it enables the companies to interrelate their performance and anticipated environmental changes. In practice, certain organizations do consider planning as a learning process. For instance, at Shell "Planning means changing minds, not making plans " (de Geus, 1988).   Needless to say, a part of inter-company and intra-company learning takes place during the planning process.

Organizational learning literature describes all these different processes and how to improve them. Less attention is given to the link between learning and the "body of knowledge" which a company will need to develop in order to maintain its competitiveness. While we are interested here in knowledge-based management, we need to investigate a little more the link between learning and knowledge as will be done in the next chapter.

However, before taking that step, some recent developments need to be mentioned in the knowledge management field.

2.9. Tacit knowledge

Nonaka (1988, 1991) has given a lot of attention to what he calls tacit knowledge. He means by that the kind of knowledge which is used by individuals but which is almost impossible to transfer. If somebody tries to transfer tacit knowledge, it becomes explicit and hence it loses its distinctive character. Nonaka´s research made it clear that it is probably this tacit knowledge which is the real value adding knowledge in a company. A knowledge base for a company should therefore by preference target the tacit knowledge, rather than the explicit, if it wants to constitute the distinctive competence of the company.

Enlarging the body of tacit knowledge is only possible if we empower people to do as much as they can by themselves. The experiences they live through will enrich their tacit knowledge and in doing so a company will enlarge the overall "volume" of tacit knowledge. Empowering people to do more and new things, however, has some risks. A company has to be willing to accept mistakes and not to immediately punish somebody who took initiative. This confirms the importance of the corporate culture in that respect. Knowledge building goes via learning and learning can only be effective if the person himself undergoes the experience. This trade-off, is in many companies, difficult to make.

Transferring tacit knowledge can only go via a process of joint learning. If people live together through the same experiences, they can learn from each other without making their mutual knowledge explicit. This mutual experimenting also reinforces the trade-off risk already mentioned in the previous paragraph.

A useful deduction of Nonaka's theory is that knowledge cannot be transferred in an explicit way, if it wants to keep its value. Attempts to lock knowledge into rules (which are in a sense relaxed equations) are bound to fail, as the knowledge which rules can describe is only a simplification of the real knowledge. These observations coincide very much with what we have been able to observe in the sciences with respect to knowledge.

They further coincide with some criticism on earlier AI results (Dreyfus, 1993; Winograd and Flores, 1986). They all stress the importance of context for knowledge, up to the point that a specific kind of knowledge makes different sense for different people in the same circumstances, just as it makes different sense for the same person in different circumstances. Students in the same classroom learn different things from the same teacher who is teaching or from the group exercise they are doing together. A person will learn how to ski much faster in the snow with the skis on his feet than from a movie which he is watching at in some exotic warm place. Knowledge is not something which exists in its own right. Knowledge is part of a context and a process and the identifiable structure of knowledge may well account for only a limited part of the knowledge base of individuals or groups.

We could go into much more interesting developments, but we have covered those concepts which are of immediate use for the further development of the book. Management science has been reluctant to take up some of the consequences of the phenomena discussed. In the next chapter we investigate what the consequences are of these new developments in a managerial context. How does knowledge creation and learning coincide and how do these processes take place within a company ? If we consider a company as the learning arena, how do we understand corporate knowledge, how can we build it and how can we manage it ? What are the kind of developments we have to look into in order to support knowledge-based management?

REFERENCES

Abraham R and Shaw C, 1983. *Dynamics: the Geometry of Behavior (4 vols.)*. Santa Cruz : Aerial Press.

Angell I and Smithson S, 1991. *Information Systems Management*. London: Macmillan Information Systems Series.

Applegate L, Cash J and Mills D, 1988. Information Technology and Tomorrow's Manager. Harvard Business Review. Vol. 66, November-December, pp. 128-136.

Argyris C and Schon D, 1978. *Organizational Learning: a theory of action perspective*. Reading Mass: Addison-Wesley.

Caverni J P, Bastien C, Mendelsohn P, Tigerghien G, (eds.), 1991. *Psychologie cognitive: Modèles et Méthodes*. Presses Universitaires de Grenoble.

Cleeremans A, 1993. *Mechanisms of Implicit Learning: connectionist models of sequence processing*. Cambridge: MIT Press.

Crutchfield J, Farmer J, Packard N and Shaw R, 1986. Chaos. Scientific American. December, pp. 38-49.

Daft R L and Huber G. *How organizations learn: a communication framework in Research in sociology of organizations* (Edited by Bucharach S and Tomasso N), Vol. 5. Greenwich, CT: JAI press.

de Callatay A, 1992. *Natural and Artificial Intelligence: Misconceptions about Brains and Neural Networks*. Amsterdam: North-Holland.

de Geus A, 1988. Planning as learning. Harvard Business Review. March/April, pp. 70-74.

Devenay R, 1986. *An Introduction to Chaotic Dynamical Systems*. Menlo Park: Benjamin-Cummings.

Dixon N M, 1992. Organizational Learning: A Review of the literature with implications for HRD Professionals. Human Resource Development Quarterly. Nr. 3 (Spring), pp. 29-49.

Dreyfus H, 1993. *What computers still cannot do*. MIT Press.

Drucker PF, 1988. The coming of the new organization. Harvard Business Review. Jan-Feb, pp. 45-53.

Ehrlich M F, Tardieu H and Cavazza M (eds.), 1993. *Les Modèles Mentaux: Approche cognitive des représentations*. Paris: Masson.

Franklin S, 1995. *Artificial Minds*. MIT Press.

Garvin DA, 1993. Building a Learning Organization. Harvard Business review. July-August, pp. 78-91.

Genelot D, 1992. *Manager dans la complexité*. Insep Editions.

Gleick J, 1988. *Chaos: Making a new science*. London: Heinemann.

Holden A (ed.), 1986. *Chaos*. Manchester: Manchester University Press.

Khalfa J (ed.), 1994. *What is Intelligence*. Cambridge University Press.

Langton C (ed.), 1989. Artificial life. Santa Fe Institute Studies in the Sciences of Complexity. Proceedings. Vol. 6. Redwood City. Addison-Wesley.

Lee S, Courtney J F, and O'Keefe R M, 1992. A System for organizational Learning Using Cognitive Maps. OMEGA. Vol. 20, Nr. 1, pp. 23-36.

Lessem R, 1991. *Total Quality Learning - Building a Learning organization*. Oxford, UK: Bassil Blackwell Ltd.

Mandelbrot B, 1982. *The Fractal Geometry of Nature*. San Francisco: Freeman.

Maturana H and Varela F, 1984. *The tree of knowledge, The Biological Roots of Human Understanding*. Scherz Verlag.

Merry U, 1995. *Coping with uncertainty: Insights from the new sciences of chaos, self organization and complexity*. Praeger.

Nicolis G and Prigogine I, 1989. *Exploring Complexity*. Freeman.

Nonaka I, 1988. Towards middle-up-down management: accelerating information creation. Sloan Management Review. Vol. 29, Nr. 3.

Nonaka I, 1991. The knowledge creating company. Harvard Business Review. Year 69, Nr. 6.

Pedler M, Burgoyne J and Boydell T, 1991. *The Learning Company - A Strategy for Sustainable Development*. London: McGraw Hill Book Company.

Peters E, 1991. *Chaos and order in the capital markets*. NY: John Wiley & Sons.

Quinn J B, 1992. *Intelligent Enterprise*. New York: The Free Press.

Schuster H, 1984. *Deterministic Chaos: an Introduction*. Weinheim: Physik-Verlag.

Shukla M, 1994. Knowledge-based Organizations : How companies use knowledge as a Strategic Leverage (Unpublished manuscript). XLRI Jamshedpur (India) / ESADE (Barcelona).

Stacey R, 1992. *Managing Chaos*. Kogan Page.

Stewart I, 1987. *The Problem of mathematics*. Oxford: Oxford University Press.

Stewart I, 1989. *Does God Play Dice: The Mathematics of Chaos*. Oxford: Basil Blackwell Inc.

Swieringa J and Wierdsma A, 1993. *The learning organization*. Addison-Wesley.

Thompson J and Stewart H, 1986. *Non-linear Dynamics and Chaos*. NY: John Wiley.

Winograd T and Flores F, 1986. *Understanding computers and cognition*. Addison-Wesley.

3. ABOUT KNOWLEDGE, PERCEPTIONS AND LEARNING: MANAGING THE MENTAL MAP OF A COMPANY

In the first chapter we saw how the managerial context has changed and an attempt has been made to identify some structure in the chaos. We have seen some of the paradoxes of modern management theory. We have identified knowledge as a prime resource of the modern company and a learning attitude as a prime attitude. In the second chapter we have investigated what we can learn from the sciences. Different disciplines have made important progress both about knowledge and learning. We need some understanding of the basic concepts which are handled in the sciences. Though we have given some examples in chapter 2 about some of the possible consequences of some of the concepts for management, we have not really applied those concepts to management. This chapter will apply the concepts of chapter 2 in a managerial context.

Considering the first chapter on the changing managerial context and drawing the lessons of what other sciences have experienced, we should now focus on what the combination of both the observations and lessons could mean for management. This chapter attempts to get a better understanding of how concepts of complexity can be used by companies. Complexity and chaos are theories which, when applied in management, need tools like knowledge and learning in order to deal with these theories. We will see in this chapter how companies can work successfully with knowledge and perceptions and how this links to change processes.

This chapter describes and explores a way for managers to work with their perceptions and to derive tacit knowledge from these. We accept the difficulty of measuring observations, and we specifically question if management phenomena are really objective. The annex discusses this topic in much detail. We accept that managers are human beings showing intelligence, rather than robots executing rules which others invented for them. Despite what we sometimes think, it is not the use of computers which makes robots out of managers.

Management education suggests that procedures exist to manage better and it further suggests that these techniques can be taught and easily applied. If managers believe this, then computers can support them in doing so. In that case, the manager accepts he should not think and decide according to pre-programmed rules. It is not the computer which forces management. Too often we are very glad to have a computer to blame for our own lack of creative thinking and for our own lack of courage in decision making. We blame the way we use a machine, as if it was the machine which was conscious of what it was doing. This is turning the world upside down. Rather, it is a simple linear and static thinking, which we then try to label as rules, which reduces management to the pure execution of rules. If anybody is to blame for that, it is probably ourselves. It is our freedom to use IT for a deeper understanding of complexity; for a dynamic and non-linear approach of management problems in order to obtain richer information. Only, this necessitates a "richer" and often more courageous decision making process from the manager.

However, it would put the accent of management where it should be: how can we generate, manage and distribute more knowledge across more people within the company ? How can we multiply the body of knowledge existing in our company ? How can we transform ourselves from the industrial organization, which we still are to a large extent even in service companies, to the company which can survive in a turbulent world. How can we reorientate the production and data driven approach into a people and knowledge driven organization ?

Management of knowledge in all its aspects increasingly becomes the value adding resource of a modern company. Knowledge management as the basis of corporate strategy could make up the competitive difference between two companies. However, we cannot consider knowledge without learning. If knowledge is the resource, then learning is the way to create and use it. As we will advocate, they are inseparably linked. In this chapter, we will discuss this link in detail. The critical role of perceptions will be highlighted since knowledge management and learning are processes which do not exist independent of a context. The widespread move of companies into a quality culture may make this subject a little more open for discussion. In an adequate quality culture we do not exclusively see quality rules and norms, but rather we see companies, groups and people working on motivation and individual's input. Real empowerment seems to go via routes of knowledge.

The specific paradigm which we will explore in this chapter is the following route to the creation of corporate knowledge:

individual experiences - individual tacit knowledge - individual mental model - shared mental model - repository of corporate knowledge - repository of core competencies - proactive management - positive feed-back loops

as the basic logic of the knowledge creating company. Learning is then a process based on the manager's ability to take part in such a knowledge creating company. We do not yet discuss specific tools to be used for knowledge creation. Chapter 4 will do that. In this chapter we discuss in detail knowledge management in companies. This chapter argues that the most difficult step in the cycle of the paradigm is to get hold of the (shared) mental model. If we can make mental models, both individual and shared, more explicit, then we also have a first version of a knowledge base. Once we have identified a knowledge base, we can start to get interested in proactive management, using the positive feed-back mechanism which appear on the market and which we have discussed in chapter 1.

In summary, this chapter deals specifically with knowledge and learning in a corporate environment. It discusses theories and practice in this respect. It does not yet discuss any tools to create or manage knowledge: that is done in chapter 4. It does not specify any particular approach to organize knowledge management inside a company: that is done in chapter 7.

3.1. What do we know of managerial processes ?

Based on experience and research both in industry and banking (Johansson et al., 1993; Baets, 1992, 1993a), indications are found that management processes are poorly understood amongst managers. Most managers are mainly interested in their day-to-day job to the degree that they miss the overall picture. Most views on managerial processes are reduced to a reality which is very close to the individual's view on his job. This confirms a new management paradigm which makes the distinction between management of the "whole" versus management of "operations". The latter is often called "immediate management" (Borucki and Byosiere, 1994). It appears that both in industry and banking managers do not have a holistic and/or multidisciplinary view of their business. In spite of that observation, theory also suggests that the integration of social, managerial and technical issues in respect to management processes seems key for a better understanding of the process itself. These findings challenge in the first place what is going on in the area of business process re-engineering. Business process re-engineering (BPR) often presumes that management processes can be reduced to a unique reality which is recognized and shared by all managers and which is context free. Hence, we can identify this process and re-engineer it. Maybe therefore a large number of BPRs have limited success. The more important the scope of changes is, the more a reduced and context free view of that process can cause disruption. Let us discuss BPR in a little more detail as an example of a type of a change process.

It goes without saying that within the broad area of Information Technology and Organizational Change (Scott Morton, 1991; Galliers and Baets, 1997), Business Process Re-engineering (BPR) and organizational change get manager's attention (e.g. Ramaswami et al., 1992; Benjamin and Blunt, 1992; Rockart and Hofman, 1992; Niederman et al., 1991). Gradually, BPR was considered key for gaining competitive advantage within a specific industry (Knorr, 1991; Johansson et al., 1993; Peppard and Rowland, 1995). The company which is able to reorganize its business processes (with minimum slack), integrating customers and suppliers in a chain, does create important barriers for competitors. In that respect, BPR is also sometimes considered as key for organizational success.

In practice, it appears that one of the more interesting by-products of BPR proves to be the identification of some of the core competencies which a company may have. These core competencies receive increased attention with respect to (re-)focusing a business (Kaplan and Murdock, 1990; Hamel and Prahalad, 1989; Prahalad and Hamel, 1990). But at the same time it becomes apparent that BPR in itself does not do enough with these competencies. While BPR aims at reducing management processes to its core path, it can be considered as a reductionist approach to a change process. In the ideal event that BPR was not reductionist and if BPR produced a clear view on the core competencies, one could consider BPR as a dynamic way of reshaping the company around its core competencies. The synergy and/or balance between BPR (if it were defined in a non-reductionist way) and core competencies create the potential for an organizational change process. The dynamics of this process of organizational change is what some authors call a learning process (de Geus, 1988; Senge, 1990; Leonard-Barton, 1992). Organizational learning - in a way a corporate mind set regarding change - is an enabling attitude during change processes.

A number of reasons can be identified for the difficulties which organizations seem to have with organizational change. An important one is that managers have difficulty in formulating the desired direction of change. It could be questioned whether or not they are able to define this direction at all. This could be caused, either by a fragmented view of their own situation as a manager, or because the environment is changing rapidly (changing strategy, increased competition on the market, chaotic behavior of markets, etc.) (Stacey, 1993). Hence, any change process should be a dynamic one. This not only allows flexibility for the continuously changing environment, but it also allows to be hostile for the different perceptions which top executives and line managers have on their involvement in the process. It allows them the necessary time to change.

If we want to understand a management process within its context and in its dynamic properties, it is not sufficient to reduce management processes the way BPR does. Knowledge should be at the basis of a better understanding of the dynamics of the process, as well as of the context. Can we make "knowledge" a little bit more concrete for managers in such a way that we can do something with it at a later stage ?

3.2. Knowledge and experience

In the cognitive sciences and even more so in the epistemology a lot of work has been undertaken in order to identify and define knowledge. Unfortunately, in managerial sciences, we do not know a lot about what managerial knowledge really is and though we all have a vague feeling for what this kind of knowledge is, there are not a lot of definitions within a managerial context.

Kim (1993) suggests that knowledge is a combination of "know-how" and "know-why". Other authors identify (two) types of knowledge (Firebaugh, 1989; Nonaka et al., 1994). On the one hand we have explicit knowledge. This kind of knowledge is transmittable in formal, systematic language. This kind of knowledge is dealt with in knowledge based systems. On the other hand we have implicit knowledge or tacit knowledge. This latter kind of knowledge deserves most of our attention. Originally, implicit knowledge was defined as that knowledge which is logically entailed in the system (Firebaugh, 1989). Tacit knowledge has more of a personalized quality. It is deeply rooted in action, commitment and involvement in a specific context (Nonaka et al., 1994). Tacit knowledge involves cognitive and technical elements, but it also involves context.

Tacit knowledge gets used in managerial tasks and tacit knowledge is the knowledge which makes the difference. Key to acquiring tacit knowledge is experience. A well identified example of tacit knowledge in management is the decision making behavior of dealers on financial markets. Based on what they learned from their past experience, the things they read and hear, probably the "climate on the market", they make decisions on buying and selling in a few seconds. We like to call this "instinct" or "fingerspitzengefuhl" but the behavior of different dealers is different. Each individual dealer seems to have his own way of dealing based on his experience and his reference framework. It proves extremely difficult to extract this kind of "knowledge" from dealers and not because they do not want to share that. It seems extremely difficult for dealers to express the knowledge which they use, or in technical term to make tacit knowledge explicit. However, since some dealers are persistently better than others, it would be of interest for a company to understand why they score better, in order e.g. to reproduce the "winning" behavior. Furthermore, if a dealer acquires his experience/knowledge during his stay in a particular bank, how can this bank keep this acquired knowledge (this asset), in case the particular dealer leaves the company ?

Many different types of cognitive elements are involved. Those of interest for managerial problems seem to center on "mental models" (Johnson-Laird, 1983) in which human beings form working models of the world by creating and manipulating analogies in their mind. Senge (1990) describes mental models as deeply held internal images of how the world works which have a powerful influence on what we do because they also affect what we see. Mental models represent a person's view of the world, including explicit and implicit understanding. Mental models provide the context in which to view and interpret new material and they determine how stored information is relevant to a given situation (Kim, 1993). Based on these definitions and analogies to individual learning, organizational learning is defined as increasing an organization's capacity to take effective action (Kim, 1993). What seems to matter is not reality but rather perceptions of reality. It is clear from this description how crucially important context is for learning and knowledge.

This capacity of an organization to take effective action is based on tacit corporate knowledge (Baets, 1993b). The more this corporate knowledge is accessible (which does not necessarily mean explicit) and shared, the easier it becomes to take advantage of it. Perceptions of reality become more important than reality for management. Hence the role of corporate mental models becomes extremely important since the ultimate aim of corporate mental models is to visualize the shared mental model on any chosen subject. In that case fundamental to corporate learning, and hence to proactive management, is a shared mental model (Kim, 1993) more than anything else. Further in this chapter we will detail more how mental models get created and how they appear. If we want to take this reasoning one step further, one could even consider that it is the manager's role to identify the shared elements within the diversity (complexity) (Van der Linden, 1993): this idea introduces management of corporate (tacit) knowledge as a strategic mission.

If we want to understand more about mental models, we need to have some idea how the human brain works. The PDP Research Group (Rummelhart and McClelland, Vol 1 and 2, 1986) demonstrates, based on extensive research, that the human brain is characterized by a high degree of parallelism. This means that a large number of elements (in this case neurons) are used at the same time alongside each other. A second important characteristic of the human brain is the Micro Structure of Cognition (distributed knowledge) of which it is built. The human brain has no clear equation for what happens in a given situation, but is able to reconstruct solutions, actions, etc. fast and easily, based on this micro structure of knowledge. Consequently, we can assume that knowledge is not sequential (but parallel) and deals with variety (and not with averages).

Despite the many problems with definitions, the organizational capability for knowledge creation is gaining momentum in managerial sciences and some consider it as a potential source of competitive advantage for companies (Toffler, 1990; Badaracco, 1991; Quinn, 1992). Whereas companies have long been dominated by a paradigm that conceptualizes the organization as a system that "processes" information and/or "solves" problems, we now consider an organization as a knowledge creating system (Nonaka et al., 1994; Borucki and Byosiere, 1994).

This body of knowledge, this repository of core competencies, this capacity to manage knowledge and to learn from it has recently attracted some attention in management research. A number of concepts point to the body of differentiating ideas, skills, capacities, etc. of a company. Eden (1988) introduced the idea of a "cognitive map" as a sort of pool of knowledge in the company. A cognitive map is a map in which a person expresses via blocks and connecting arrows how he reasons about a particular subject or how he sees that things fit together. Haeckel and Nolan (1993) introduce the "corporate IQ" for a comparable "repository" of corporate knowledge. Keen (1993) argues for a more quantitative representation of this "repository" and calls it a "fusion map". They all aim to identify and make explicit the differentiating core competencies of a company. All of them seem to agree that there exists a "repository of knowledge", which is the resource for the differentiating capacity of a company.

3.3. Learning and mental models

Learning, then, can be considered as the way to fill the "repository of knowledge". Kolb defines learning as the process whereby knowledge is created through the transformation of experience (Kolb, 1984). This definition of learning relates to the "know-how" and "know-why" of Kim (1993). According to this definition, learning takes place in a cycle of four steps: first an experience is made; in a second stage observations and reflections on that experience are created; thirdly, abstract concepts and generalizations are formed based on these reflections; fourthly these ideas on the new situation get tested which in turn gives new experiences. These latter new experiences can become a first step in a new loop. This cyclical learning loop is called the OADI-cycle (Observe; Assess; Design; Implement) and pictures it as demonstrated in figure 3.1.

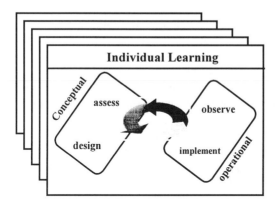

**Figure 3.1: Simple model of Individual Learning: the OADI-cycle
(after Kolb, 1984 and Kim, 1993)**

An easy example of this learning process is to observe how a child "learns" not to put its hand on a warm plate. In many cases, a child cannot be taught not to touch a warm plate. The first time (even if told different) a child tries and put its hand on a warm plate. The child observes something which it assesses as heat. It designs, and of course this design does not necessarily need to be very deliberate, an action: probably to take away its hand. Eventually, the child implements that design and does take away its hand. A new observation follows which is assessed as "better". Probably no further design takes place. In the case of the hand having been burned already, the child again observes something different which does not feel very nice. It would (or in the beginning somebody else would) assess it as "burned". A possible design would be to put its hand under cold running water, which it eventually does. This cycle can continue for a number of rounds. Via this process of "learning the hard way", a child learns a number of things. Individual learning, independent of how adult we are, still goes via experience. Instruction can shorten the learning cycle, but only if the person can make sense out of it. The latter means that the instruction given should fit into the existing framework of the person.

Based on this OADI-cycle, Kim proposes a second stage of individual learning, where he links up individual learning with individual mental models (figure 3.2).

Figure 3.2 shows in a way a double loop learning process: double in the sense that it includes both learning based on external impulses (OADI-cycle) but it also includes learning from connecting what is learned from external impulses with the individual mental model. The reason to put so much emphasis on mental models is that mental models in individual's heads are where a vast majority of an organization's knowledge (both know-how and know-why) is imprinted (Kim, 1993).

When a child goes through the above mentioned "experience" a number of times, it will not do it again. The child does not necessarily know what happens and it does not necessarily understand why it should not touch a hot plate anymore. It has implicitly developed a framework of knowledge which allows it to deal with a new comparable case. It can deal with a new case, without knowing the correct "equations". In some respects it can be argued that this is not a true example of learning, but rather of human reflex. Probably this is true, however, it indicates clearly how the learning cycle operates in interaction with the environment (single loop learning) and how it leads to the individual mental model (via individual double loop learning). According to the same principle, the trader "learns" and creates by doing, his own mental model about trading. Any learning experience (courses, or books read) could speed up the process, if and only if the experiences fit into the existing framework (mental model) of the person. If the gap between the existing mental model and the taught material is too large, hardly any learning can take place. Teaching is no guarantee at all for learning. Teaching is only one kind of experience which an individual can choose to use for learning purposes and ultimately to learn from. Field experience can be another experience leading to learning. Hence, different people react completely different to the same learning experience. No unique best way of teaching exists, no unique best way of learning can be identified. Learning remains very much a free act of people.

On an organizational level, a comparable double loop learning model can be designed (figure 3.2). The individual single-loop learning translates the implementation phase of the OADI-cycle into an individual action, which in turn creates an environmental response. This response is a new input to the OADI cycle as described earlier.

The organizational level is introduced in figure 3.2 in two different ways. Comparable to the single-loop learning in the individual model, each individual action can be part of an organizational action (right under in 3. 2) which in turn causes an additional environmental response. This is called organizational single-loop learning. Organizational double-loop learning takes place when the individual mental models are brought into relation in order to form shared mental models (shared on a corporate or group level), which in turn have an influence on the individual mental models. In figure 3.2, shared mental models are also defined as organizational routines. Improved learning via knowledge creation and management, takes place, for a major part, in the organizational double-loop learning in the left under corner of figure 3.2. Explicit shared models (the explicit organizational routines) will improve the learning ability of an organization.

Organizational double loop learning can only take place via bringing together individual mental models in a learning space. Individual mental models only get created via individual learning experiences. One cannot have direct impact, neither on the individual mental models, nor on the corporate mental model. Any change in the shared mental model goes via individual experiences, which in the first instance need to change the individual mental models and only then a new shared learning activity would be able to change a shared mental model. This does not mean to say that shared mental models are an addition to individual mental models nor that they are only the addition of a number of individual mental models. It is only said that one cannot have a direct influence on shared mental models. Any attempt to change a shared mental model, has to go via new experiences at the individual level (even if these experiences can take place in groups). If an individual learns, which means that he fits the new experience into his mental model and produces a different mental model, some change could occur on the shared level. However, it remains almost impossible to foresee the impact on the shared model of any action on the individual's level, before it comes via the individual mental model into the shared mental model. Therefore, a shared mental model is not a static entity. It should be monitored continuously and that is what we understand as picturing and comparing mental models. Knowledge management also attempts to visualize mental models with the aim of learning from them and sharing them.

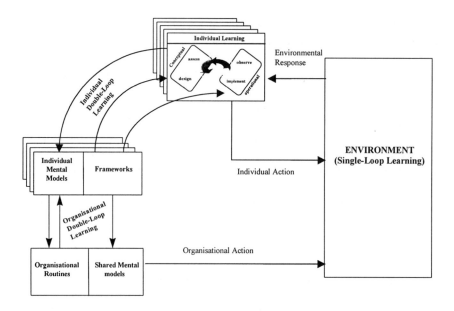

**Figure 3.2: An Integrated Model of Organizational Learning
(after Kim, 1993)**

The most famous example of how a shared mental model differs from the addition
of a number of individual mental models is no doubt the one of the cage of
monkeys and the bananas. If one puts 20 monkeys into a cage with a step in the
middle and a bunch of bananas on the ceiling, the smartest monkey runs up the
steps and takes a banana. This monkey follows its "individual mental model". For
sake of correctness, it is not argued here that monkeys have a mental model. This
story is mainly used as a metaphor. When the monkey takes the banana it starts
pouring with rain. Monkeys do not like that at all. One monkey is taken out of the
cage and a new one is brought in. The second smartest monkey runs up the step,
and following its mental model takes the banana. It starts pouring rain again.
Allow us to draw your attention to the fact that each monkey individually feels the
pouring rain, which gradually will influence its mental model in that respect.
Again a monkey is replaced. This story continues until the smart monkeys have
understood the mechanism. Individually they still like the bananas but they

understand the consequences. The most stupid monkey then tries to take a banana.
That one has not understood it yet. Again it pours with rain and we change again a
monkey. The new monkey will try and run up the step. All the others, having
understood, will not try anymore. But all the monkeys in the cage will also try to
stop the new monkey taking a banana. The new monkey does not understand, but
he cannot get to the banana.   He follows the shared behavior without
understanding.   Another 20 replacements will be delivered to a cage full of
monkeys which all individually would like to take the banana. As a group they do
not do that and none of them knows why. The shared mental model is clearly
different from the individual mental models. The change has taken place via
continuous new observations and experiences which all the monkeys had
individually. None of them has the same number of experiences since they were
replaced at different times.

This story illustrates the learning process and also shows that a shared mental
model can be completely different from the sum of the individual mental models.
Change in a shared mental model only occurs via experiences on an individual
level, influencing the individual mental model first. The latter, in turn, will
influence the shared mental model. How many times do we recognize this in a
corporate environment ? "Why do we do that here the way we do ?" Answer:
"Since we always did so". Nobody necessarily knows why and the individual
models could well differ from the shared one. Is this what we call "corporate
culture" ?

If we would like to change that, say if we would like to change corporate culture,
we cannot dictate cultural change. Actions have to be undertaken in order that all
individuals get new experiences. If the atmosphere is positive enough around these
new experiences, individuals may (but cannot be forced to) integrate these new
positive experiences into their individual mental models, which in turn, eventually,
could change the shared model (the culture). It is a long process, which goes via
individual learning and no guarantee can be given about the success. Again,
monitoring seems the best thing one can do.

When we concentrate on the "shared mental model" of figure 3.2 only and we
zoom in, we can represent this "map" as we do in figure 3.3. We can re-arrange
the "ins" and "outs", in order to be able to get a picture of the repository itself. In a

way, figure 3.3 is another way of representing the ins and outs of the shared mental model; the repository of knowledge.

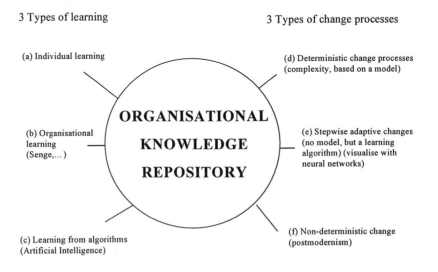

Figure 3.3: Learning, Knowledge and Change
(Baets, 1995, figure 1)

Figure 3.3 pictures three different levels of learning: individual learning, organizational learning and learning of algorithms (systemic learning). Each of them has an input in the corporate knowledge repository. In turn, this repository is used in order to feed three different types of change processes: deterministic change; stepwise-learning change and non-deterministic change processes. These two lists of types of learning and change are not exhaustive. It only defines some of the most common ways of creating knowledge (via different types of learning) and applying knowledge in corporate change processes. Let us have a closer look into the different ways of learning and the different types of change.

Probably best know is individual learning {a}. School systems are based on theories about individual learning and even a lot of in-company courses are based on it. Pedagogy became a science in its own right. Piaget (1966), amongst others, contributed a lot to this science.

A few decades old, but recently revamped, are the ideas of organizational learning {b} (Argyris and Schön, 1978). It was probably Senge (1990) who gave these ideas a second life. Groups and organizations show characteristics which allow individuals to learn more within the group than what they would be able to learn on their own. The question remains unanswered in these theories whether learning is an individual or a group process (Nonaka, 1994). In our opinion, as argued before, group learning can only take place via individual experiences.

Recently, some successes have been reached in the theory and applications of learning algorithms {c}. Within the broader area of artificial intelligence there is a lot of attention for systems which appear to have learning behavior. Artificial neural networks are only one example of these systems (Dayhoff, 1990). Experiments with such learning algorithms or self-regulating systems (Morin, 1990a and b) give insight in how systems behave while they learn without guidelines. Artificial life applications and implicit learning are other approaches in systemic learning.

These three forms of learning contribute to the creation of the corporate knowledge repository on which a number of corporate actions can be based. This repository is sometimes called "corporate intelligence": the real distinctive quality between company A and company B. For that reason some have written that probably the only durable competitive advantage for a company is the capacity to learn continuously (de Geus, 1988). Even further, Nonaka (1994) suggests that the capacity to create and manage knowledge would be the only durable competitive advantage.

This "corporate intelligence" is the basis for successful activities in a company, of which change processes are only a subset. Comparable to the different ways in which this "intelligence" is created, it can be used in a number of different ways too. Figure 3.3 pictures some of these ways.

Our classical economic thinking about managerial problems has known successes in what is seen as "scientific management". Deterministic and by preference quantitative thinking became the common way of considering management processes. Economic phenomena are reduced in order to fit linear, deterministic and non-dynamic models. Reality, however, proves to be different. As argued before in chapter 2, chaos theory (Cohen and Stewart, 1994), complexity theory (Nicolis and Prygogine, 1989) and research into artificial life (Langton, 1989) have changed our understanding in that respect. The Santa Fe Institute (Bulletin of the Santa Fe Institute) has produced remarkable output on these topics. We now have a better understanding of the underlying constructions of managerial problems. We still need to translate that understanding into improved management practice, but we are underway on an exploration of what is possible. We do not consider linear, non-dynamic change approaches. We have argued that they have limited scope. Transforming deeper understanding into adapted practice needs different approaches.

Foremost, complex but deterministic processes {d} get a lot of attention. These differ from more classical approaches in the form of the equations of the models used. These equations can be non-linear and dynamic, in which the dynamic character appears via the positive feed-back phenomena, as described in the previous chapter. Complexity theory is one example, as well as systems dynamics (originated in the 1970s but again popular) and knowledge based systems. The base idea of this approach for change processes is that a deterministic (change) model exists which can be represented by a set of complex equations or rules.

A second approach to change processes is stepwise or "learning" processes {e}. This approach still accepts the existence of a (deterministic) model, but it also accepts that it is impossible to describe this model with equations or rules. In this approach a "workable" change process is more important than the "best" one. Stepwise change is considered as a normal procedure and during the change process adaptation and learning takes place. The choice between deterministic change and stepwise processes is one between, on the one hand, the need for a simplified but detailed model and, on the other hand, a less detailed but richer picture of the reality. Added to that dilemma, the second type of model is accepted to change throughout the entire process itself, which only makes it even less accessible for detailed representation. Artificial neural networks is an application of this approach and is therefore discussed in more detail in next chapter.

A last possible approach is the one of non-deterministic change {f}. This approach does not assume any model behind change processes and it is claimed that one should not waste time in order to find such a model. Some theories on the learning organization are based on this theorem (e.g. Swieringa and Wierdsma, 1993). Though it seems a "contradictio in terminis", a manager can try and guide change processes which pairs up with approaches on managerial leadership and empowerment. This approach is called postmodernist (Hassard and Parker, 1993; Hassard, 1993) and in this book we will not deal with it further.

In summary: learning is not the accumulation of useful knowledge. Rather, it is the operationalisation of perceptions and experiences in a framework. We don't really know what knowledge looks like, we only know that different types exist (e.g. explicit and tacit) and that most probably knowledge is kept in a distributed form. Corporate intelligence is a "repository" of knowledge which drives corporate change processes. Any visualization of the repository can improve management based on corporate knowledge. The richer the picture, the more complex problems management can tackle. Reductionist deterministic models seem to contribute less than what we anticipated over the last decades to improve management in complex situations.

If we wanted to model or map this "repository", we would need to investigate into new systemic techniques and/or new ways of thinking which constitute an improvement compared to Operations Research and/or Decision Support Systems' efforts of the 70s and 80s. Most of these classic techniques are rather prescriptive. They fail to deal with variety, since they focus on central tendencies. Along the lines of Soft Systems Methodology (Checkland, 1981; Checkland and Scholes, 1990), it is arguable whether it is possible even to try to be prescriptive in managerial processes. These analytical techniques assume that management processes are something which exist "objectively" "outside" the manager. It is argued that the manager perceives any management process through his own filter, his own mind set. For that reason there is no one single way to manage but a choice needs to be made between different possible approaches to a managerial situation and different aspects of each particular managerial situation to be dealt with (Van der Linden, 1993). The best combination of "approach" and "aspects dealt with" will constitute the managerial act. The "repository" will be the "in-put" for the manager who tries to handle any particular situation.

In order to improve this process of knowledge creation, management and learning an approach is proposed in this chapter which is new in a number of respects. It is based on the very operation of the human brain (our neural network). The approach aims to attack management processes via the mind sets (and not the claimed knowledge of the processes) of the concerned stakeholders (and not only the concerned managers). This approach keeps the diversity of mind sets accessible for all involved people. They can be translated into an IT based tool, which allows individual learning and sharing.

Without going in detail yet on the tools and techniques which we need (they are dealt with in the next chapter), we introduce here the idea of a connectionist approach to knowledge and managerial analysis. Connectionism has proved successful in the transfer of issues to relationships, of individual to corporate mind sets and of perceptions to knowledge (de Callatay, 1992; Firebaugh, 1989). Connectionism came up with the increased computing power available today, but connectionism, as already discussed in an earlier chapter, is not a novel idea: its application in management is.

3.4. Measurement and mapping of mind sets: a connectionist approach

As argued before, learning takes place via individual experiences. Shared mental models are created via confronting individual mental models. The latter can be done in different ways. What we are most familiar with is management meetings: a number of managers meet in order to get a consensus or a decision. Each manager has his own individual mental model. In the process of the meeting a shared mental model gets created. Needless to say that in this kind of meetings, the knowledge creating potential is rather low and limited to the small number of people around the table. The exchange of ideas has not always proved to be ideal and therefore a number of brainstorming techniques have been developed over time. However, all these techniques are based on the presumed parallel nature of the knowledge creating process. When one person brings in a idea, another person may get yet another idea. Ideas build on each other and while one person is speaking, others are thinking. The knowledge creation process works in parallel. We have observed that for years in management meetings all around the world.

Before, however, we concentrated more on the rationalization of the outcome which was in line with reductionist views on management which prevailed. We have ignored the parallel character of the process for a while, since we did not see the role of parallelism in the knowledge creating act. We have concentrated on rationalization. Based on the concepts developed until now, we feel it would be an important contribution if managers would pay more attention to the parallel character of the knowledge building process: both to the process and to the parallel character of it. Connectionism is advocated here as a fundamentally different approach to the management of corporate knowledge. For the correct understanding of connectionism, let us first describe some process oriented techniques with which managers may be familiar.

A number of techniques exist which try to improve that process and which attempt to generate common shared perception. Most of them are known as tools for organizational learning (Senge, 1990). Best known are probably scenario analysis, brainstorming (hexagon method), systems dynamics models and simulations, etc. A disadvantage of most methods dealing with group processes (and attempting to create corporate mind sets) is that they are based on a specific consensus, reached in a specific (limited) group at a specific time. There is limited guarantee that this consensus is general. These consensus groups are in general rather limited in number, whereas the eventual concerned group (people involved in the business process) is much larger.

If we want to improve these techniques and broaden them throughout large companies, we need to target different aims. First, more people should be involved in the process of the creation of shared beliefs. Secondly, we should find a way (a tool) to communicate these shared beliefs throughout the company (hence, to a larger number of people). Thirdly, diversity should prevail over centralism, variety should prevail over sharing in order to be used as a distinctive power. Post modernism (Hassard and Parkers, 1993) even advocates that unity or centrality can never be reached. For them, management is dealing with limited order in chaos. Finally, individuals should be targeted by preference since it seems broadly accepted that most learning takes place on the individual's level (Kim, 1993).

It is commonly accepted that (relationships are made explicit) and that the measurement of maps or models is mostly done by quantitative (statistical) methods. Research in the banking industry (Ramaswami et al., 1992; Baets, 1993a) dealing with the indirect and direct impact of organizational context factors (such as strategy and environment) on the emphasis placed by firms on strategic information support, allows for the identification of some limitations of classic measurement. In the annex we discuss in detail about the measurability of managerial concepts and the difference between quantitative approaches and connectionist approaches. We cannot avoid it completely here, since it is an important element in the reasoning into why connectionism is an alternative.

Quantitative techniques are of limited use in complex managerial problems since they presume that managerial acts can be isolated and measured. The weaknesses of quantitative methods are detailed in the annex. What we need is an alternative for the creation of relationships, as close as possible to equations (Norden, 1993), avoiding most of the problems, suggested by e.g. Ramaswami et al (1992) and Baets (1993a). These alternatives should be based on what we know today about knowledge and human behavior. These alternatives should be able to deal with complex (non-linear dynamic) entities like markets.

Connectionist approaches are approaches which are based on the theory that a lot of simple basic elements, all interconnected to a high degree, are able to solve complex problems. These many basic elements are all used in parallel. In a first stage they are trained in order to recognize a number of cases and to be able to deal with them adequately. In a second stage, a trained connectionist system is then able to tackle new problems which it has never seen before, but which generally fit into the overall category of comparable problems. The best known connectionist system is our brain. We train a child to cross the street while doing it a number of times with the child. If the child crossed the street 100 times it would be able to deal with a situation which is close to another situation which it has already seen. A dramatically different situation (like a car which is driven too fast) will cause serious problems for the child. After further training (say crossing streets another 1000 times) the child would be able to cross a street in more difficult situations. Accidents occur when the child's brain (the connectionist system) is not able to deal with a specific new situation. Either the new situation is too different from what the connectionist system recognizes, or the connectionist system fails. Our brain is the best know connectionist system and is called our neural network. Other connectionist systems are the bee colony discussed earlier or a project group of people. A company can be considered as a connectionist system and so can a management team.

Connectionist systems, through parallel distribution processing, imitate our brain-like thinking, which has everything to do with perceptions, filtering assimilations, etc. The classic sequential equation approach needs a valid theory to underpin estimation and needs the definition of these complex equations. Today, nobody seems to be able to define these kind of complex (dynamic and non-linear) equations in enough detail. The knowledge does not yet exist to write these equations (Venugopal and Baets, 1994).

For introduction only, since the next chapter discusses neural networks in detail, it is useful to briefly describe the parallel between our brain (our neural network) and Artificial Neural Networks (ANNs). For the time being ANNs are only to be considered as another example of connectionist systems. In the next chapter we will describe them as appropriate tools to manage knowledge.

Artificial Neural Networks (ANN) attempt to model the architecture of biological neural systems. Biological neural networks are made of millions of simple, tightly interconnected processing elements called neurons. The interconnections are made by the outgoing branches, the "axons", which again form several connections ("synapses") with the other neurons. When a neuron receives a number of stimuli and when the sum of the received stimuli exceeds a certain threshold value, it will fire and transmit the stimulus to adjacent neurons. Knowledge is not stored somewhere in the network. Rather, the network is activated each time a question is asked or an action needs to be processed. In parallel, a vast number of neurons are activated which produces the correct answer. Knowledge is created over again each time using possibly different neurons. Each neuron is a very simple processor. Only in the densely connected network do they deliver the human performance which we all know. In no way, our brain is to be compared to the architecture of an electronic storage device. In real life cases, these ANNs have proved success in "assimilated thinking" (Lodewijk and Deng, 1993; Fletcher and Goss, 1993; Baets, 1993b; Venugopal and Baets, 1994).

When we choose connectionist approaches as an alternative to measure or visualize management processes via human perceptions, we are interested in getting a map of those individual and shared mental models, which are indicated on figure 3.2 and explained earlier. If we can construct such a map, we can get a little closer to the "tacit knowledge" existing in a company. But connectionist approaches do not only allow us to visualize mental models. If connectionist approaches were only able to measure, they would be less interesting. Managerial change is dealing with complex processes of change and durable change can only take place if it fits into the appropriate mental models of the individuals involved or if these mental models are themselves part of the change process. That is probably where learning and change meet each other.

During the phase of the creation and development of a connectionist network, we are working with concepts and operational issues on the individual's level. We try to identify and list all relevant issues, without linking them with individual mental models and certainly not with corporate mental models. In the child's example we can draw its attention to the speed of cars, rain, light, etc. without, however, trying to explain how they all influence the process of crossing the street. This stage, learning and change moments take place during the elicitation of these issues.

During the training phase, connectionist approaches try to develop the mental models, based on the issues and concepts raised. During the training phase, the child crossing the street a number of times will create its mental model, its connectionist structure, which allows it to deal with comparable cases. Each new case it experiences adapts the mental model. In as far as the first phase included elements of organizational frameworks and organizational routines, we will be able to get insight into some shared mental models: shared not in the sense that all people involved tend to share a specific vision but in the sense that the variety in the shared mental model remains operational but is accessible to everyone. This variety in the shared mental model is where the know-how and know-why of a company is "stored".

A connectionist network as described here is, in a way, comparable to a moving picture of a corporate mental model. As such, an ANN e.g. makes (mostly tacit) knowledge explicit, manages it, but also assists the creation of knowledge. If a manager is interested in pro-active management, he needs to learn from experiences. He needs to be able to adapt his mental models He needs to be able to fit new experiences into his individual mental models and in a second stage also into the corporate mental model. The reflection of experience into a mental model (whether individual or corporate) would be much easier if an explicit form of such a mental model existed. Learning can take place more easily and, hence, change can take place more easily.

individual experiences - individual tacit knowledge - individual mental model - shared mental model - repository of corporate knowledge - repository of core competencies - proactive management - positive feedback loops

is the basic logic of the knowledge creating company. Learning is then a process based on the manager's ability to take part in such a knowledge creating company (as described by the above mentioned paradigm) and this in a number of aspects. A connectionist network can be used to make a moving picture of the shared mental model. A learning organization is an organization able to manage this cycle of knowledge creation and apply it in its daily operational and tactical management.

If we want to re-orient our company to a knowledge creating company in order to manage the overall managerial complexity we should put more emphasis on mind sets, learning and knowledge. This has consequences, both for approaches and for structures (architectures). There is still a long way to be gone in this respect. Knowledge management in business situations could benefit from joint efforts and developments between artificial intelligence, cognitive sciences and modern human resources management (Nonaka, 1994). Ideas on organizational learning could be boosted by such a cooperation.

3.5. Knowledge is not rule based, but parallel, or how connectionism is positioned against rule based systems

Successes with expert systems have suggested that knowledge is rule based: if we cannot express knowledge in equations, maybe we can express it in rules. How are connectionist approaches placed in comparison to expert systems or more generally rule based systems. Let us consider some examples of every day decisions.

Let us first continue with the example of crossing the street. If one asked us how we crossed a street we would probably be unable to describe it. Only if we were forced would we probably say something like: look first left, then right and probably left again and then cross. As humans, we do much more while crossing a street, but we are not aware of it. We have learned that behavior via experience.

probably left again and then cross. As humans, we do much more while crossing a street, but we are not aware of it. We have learned that behavior via experience. By crossing (a number of times) a street, as described earlier as a child, and probably with some help in the beginning, we learned how to do it. Maybe our parents gave us the simple rules described above, but we very quickly found that they were not sufficient. However, we never updated the rules. We only updated the framework which allows us dynamically to cross any street at any time. This updated framework is the "body of knowledge" which allows us to behave intelligently. Could we have updated the rules too ? This is less probable. We cannot even trace the rules from an act that we do that many times a day (and clearly successfully).

If we give a presentation before an audience, many people do not really prepare a written text. Words come out fluently, based on a rough framework of ideas. Could we actively influence the words we use ? Let us try and do that for once. If we gave a presentation and we tried to think over which word to use next, the first thing we would immediately observe is that we would slow down. The second thing we would observe is that we were searching for words, whereas before they came out more fluently. Eventually, we would stop as it would probably begin to embarrass us. Certainly, there are rules of grammar behind a language and in school we learn those. The living language, however, does not always obey them. The most lively speakers do not always use correct constructions, do they ? Automated language research failed to a large extent while it was using rule based approaches. Much of what we see today as speech recognition or voice recognition is based on a network based approach. A system is trained with a number of cases which develops the system's framework. This framework will allow us to speak or to recognize speech any time a word is "fired" onto the system.

Some other examples of the way humans make decisions maybe helpful. Let us take the example of driving a car. In the very beginning , a teacher gave us some simple rules. We tried them out, made the necessary mistakes and with a lot of experience, we eventually became safe drivers. Did we ever update the rules ? Probably not and we find that out when we try to teach somebody else to drive. It is extremely difficult, even for the best driver, to give driving lessons. We do not exactly know the order in which we take the different steps of changing gears, turning into a street, not even braking quickly. We are able to work out some parts of some rules, but we are unable at any point in time to trace down the complete set of rules. If we would operate rule-based, why wouldn't we be able to trace down the rules. Since again, via a learning process we developed a framework which allows us to very quickly reproduce the correct action, given any new circumstances. Rules would allow us to deal with situations we already saw before. A framework allows us to deal with new situations, via derived knowledge.

Another example is getting up in the morning. Without elaborating too much on it, we clearly have no rules to get out of our bed. We can get out of bed during the night sometimes without wakening. Do we have rules for that ? Can we do it without mishap?

Even more fundamental decisions in a human's life are not really based on rules. Let us take the choice of studies we made. Many people do have a checklist of criteria they will check while choosing a subject. However, eventually, they will decide based on a combination of factors, and in many cases criteria which have not been taken into consideration before force the decision. It sounds strange but a small test amongst peers will give some limited evidence of that. Human beings like to think that they are very rational in their decision making. In many cases they are not.

The last example refers to the choice of having children. We all think that this is a very rational decision and in the age of contraception, even a positive act is necessary in many cases. However, don't we often decide to stop contraception, rather than to decide to have children ? We of course know the possible consequence, but we rather see it as "let us see what is going to happen". Do we think about all the consequences of having children ? Or rather, do we think about what the consequences are of stopping contraception ? Though this is of course arguable, how do we reason about marriage ? How do we reason about divorce ? Do we have good reasons for doing any of these ? Probably we have. But it is extremely difficult to make them explicit. We can indicate some of the framework we have used to make a decision. We cannot give the rules we have followed while taking the decision.

Why, if we take decisions like that in real life, do we suddenly want to change when taking management decisions ? Why would management decisions be any different from decisions in every day life, if management decisions are also based on human behavior. When we take management decisions, we suddenly accept that humans should think like machines do: based on rules and equations. But as humans we do not do that ourselves. Why shouldn't we try to think humanly about management problems, just like we think about any other human problem ? Can't we support our (human-like) decisions? It is our mindset which makes it difficult for us to do so. Management is declared to be a "science" and hence it should follow scientific rules. The Western European culture has educated its managers with the idea that scientific rules automatically mean equations (or rules like in expert systems). As we will see in the next chapter, other approaches exist, which are much closer to the human way of thinking.

If we want to improve managerial decision making, or only managerial understanding of problems, we all have an interest in approaching managerial problems in an appropriate way, which is the way humans deal with knowledge. In summary this way consists of building individual mental maps or models via experience. These maps are very much a framework which allows us at any time to respond to any question (and of course not always correctly, but almost always). If an individual works together in a group, a group mental model gets created. This group's mental model will direct the activities of the group, as much as an individual mental model drives an individual. A group's mental model can differ considerably from the sum of the individual mental models.

These examples show that knowledge is not rule based (or equation based). We can say that knowledge is parallel: it is based on a network structure in which different knots are activated in parallel. Developing corporate knowledge in this sense means, therefore, developing the correct framework which is based on the corporate experience and which will allow one to tackle new problems. We need to get the context correct. Then the rules will be produced dynamically each time it is necessary. Knowledge gets created dynamically (as argued in chapter 2) if we have the framework correctly trained, which then supports this process. A company needs to focus on the framework and not on the rules. It needs to focus on understanding (holistic) and learning, rather than on reducing (analytical) and teaching.

Rather than putting too much effort into forecasting, we can build a framework (the initial state as scientists call it) which would allow us to evaluate and learn dynamically, starting from different initial situations. In each new circumstance, the system will be able to re-create itself, giving the manager a new initial state. As Prigogine says, if we could forecast the future based on the past, this would imply that time is reversible. Since time is non-reversible, forecasting based on the past is, except in a very short time period, of rather limited use. Management comes close to directing an orchestra where each moment the director decides on corrective measures to be taken. The same is true in sailing a yacht. Each moment the skipper has to decide what to do. The past has brought the ship to the situation it is in but the past is not going to be of any help to design a future action. Basing future actions on past behavior seems at the very least to be dangerous. Managerial behavior is emerging, starting from an initial state. The quality of managerial behavior is based on the quality of the knowledge framework which the manager can use.

3.6. The corporate mental map: what is important ?

This chapter has dealt in some detail with knowledge and management. Before introducing some of the tools which can be used, it is worth trying to summarize what we have observed until now.

We have discussed the idea that knowledge is not identified and stored in a specific location of the human brain, but that knowledge is built up dynamically, using a network of closely connected cells. This approach of how humans deal with knowledge should be transferred on to the activity of corporate knowledge building. This would suggest that we can approach knowledge building and management in companies via building closely connected networks of people. These networks of individuals will generate more knowledge of a higher quality than any individual can. Remember the neurobiology argument that these composing elements (in this case people) could each be very simple and individually not show lots of intelligence. This has no direct consequence on the overall performance potential of the network. As already stated earlier, this could have consequences for the recruitment policy of a company if this company would like to build a knowledge based management approach. Hence, connectionism seems a logical approach if we are interested in understanding better how groups operate, how companies behave or how markets behave. Building knowledge, in order to support decision making and management, therefore, should best be based on this connectionist approach.

In line with this connectionist approach, sciences show that knowledge is re-built each time and again, from very simple elements. Knowledge cannot be transferred as such; the knowledge framework has to be created by each individual and that framework will create the knowledge necessary to deal with an action. Knowledge cannot be imposed; may be, knowledge cannot even be passed on via formal education. Knowledge gets created when a number of people bring their experiences together, in order to organize themselves with the aim of performing a task. Self-organization (advocated both by the neuro-biologists and the researchers in artificial life) goes against the prevailing idea of Taylorian organizations. Self-organization implies that changes can only take place stepwise This stepwise approach is very typical for self-organized systems. Radical change processes have little chance of success. "Tabula rasa" approaches have not proven successful and are not likely to do so (Probst, 1987). Be aware of the hype around radical change processes !

Our concern remains with the manager, who has to lead his team, who is hired or put in charge of a major change process and who does not really like to experiment with self-organizing change processes. After all, if our own survival depends on it, the human being produces a survival instinct. This instinct is not necessarily helpful, but if we do not have alternative tools to support self-organized, knowledge based change processes, nobody should blame a manager for taking his responsibilities seriously. Therefore, the next chapter gives more detail on specific tools and techniques and some examples are described in the following chapters. We deal with these tools since we believe that self-organized learning systems perform better than others. We have already mentioned a few times that these ideas are also a little culturally bound. The French, e.g. even developed a term for these kinds of economic systems: "auto-eco-organization" (Morin), which could be translated as the "economic self-organized system" which suggests a difference with other self-organized structures. In France, more research has been done on the socio-economic consequences of these theories. However, the approach proposed in this book is different from the rather post-modernist approaches in France. We suggest the use of knowledge tools which are today commonly characterized by artificial intelligence in order to develop, show and allow adaptation of individual and corporate mental models.

Independent of the underlying theories of change processes or learning as such, we agree that managers or "change teams" need support tools giving insight into the change process considered. As Shakespeare already suggested is "perception the truth" and so we need to map change processes via perceptions of everybody involved, not via so called objective observations. Companies have launched many change processes ever since, without much attempt to get a picture of the process considered. The present idea is very much that since the quantitative or rule based approach has failed, we have to work with our feeling and experience. Yes this is a possible approach, but one could do much better and use the change process to create corporate knowledge. One could gain twice as much by obtaining a better managed change process, which also creates additional knowledge.

Furthermore this approach allows some measurement of possible change. An easy way of measuring change can be measurement of changed perceptions. This does imply that we also need initial perceptions. We need the initial knowledge framework in order to be able to compare with the obtained one.

To summarize, learning is not considered as sampling lots of useful knowledge. Rather, learning is making perceptions and experiences usable. We do not really know what knowledge looks like; we only know that there are different kinds of knowledge (e.g. explicit and tacit) and that knowledge, most probably, is stored in a distributed form. Corporate intelligence is a pool of knowledge, which probably drives corporate change processes. It would be useful to have some idea of the processes we want to change, as they are perceived by the different stakeholders, before we attempt to change them. But based on the ideas developed thus far, this is highly unlikely to be successful if we continue to use our classical deterministic (linear and non-dynamic) way of problem solving.

In corporate problems, we consider individuals within a group. This chapter has argued that learning always takes place via the individual. The individual learning process is a non-linear process. Specifically at group level, the creation of knowledge is even more dynamic than on the individual level. How could we approximate this non-linear dynamic approach to learning and change via linear and non-dynamic approaches ? Knowledge based systems which we build should be based on non-linear models, which are allowed dynamic (learning, adaptive) behavior. In order to build such a kind of knowledge networks, we have to use some techniques which are known and have proven success in other fields.

A last remark to be made is that learning and change are here presented as somewhat separate. In reality, they are not. In many corporate circumstances, learning, knowledge creation and change go hand in hand. For conceptual reasons, we needed to separate them a little, to improve the understanding of the differences and similarities. In real life, there cannot be a reductionist approach of knowledge, learning or change giving success on an overall level. If the three do not go together in one interconnected picture, we are losing the value added of the holistic picture we are attempting to create.

In order to create, maintain and allow change of corporate processes we want to consider artificial neural networks (which were already mentioned before) in conjunction with fuzzy logic in order to build knowledge based representations, able to support change management. The next chapter will give some insight into both artificial neural networks (ANN) and fuzzy logic. The subsequent chapters will give some examples based on our own research of what is possible with these systems.

REFERENCES

Argyris C and Schon D, 1978. *Organizational Learning: a theory of action perspective*. Reading Mass: Addison-Wesley.

Baets W, 1992. Aligning information systems with business strategy. Journal of Strategic Information Systems. Nr. 4, September.

Baets W, 1993a. IT for organizational change: beyond business process engineering. Business Change and Re-engineering. Vol. 1, Nr. 2, Autumn.

Baets W, 1993b. Information Systems Strategic Alignment: A case in banking. Working Paper. Nijenrode University, The Netherlands.

Baets W, 1995a. "Artificiele neurale netwerken: het in kaart brengen van veranderingsprocessen en het meten van leren." In *Handboek effektief opleiden*, 4.131.

Baets W, 1995b. Ecosip study day on Business Process Reengineering and Information Technology (Paris): Business Process Re-engineering: A corporate mind set.

Badaracco J, 1991. *The Knowledge Link: Competitive Advantage through Strategic Alliances*. Boston: Harvard Business School Press.

Benjamin R and Blunt J, 1992. Critical IT issues: The Next Ten Years. Sloan Management Review. Vol. 33, Nr. 4, Summer.

Borucki C and Byosiere P, 1992. Toward a Theory of Enlightenment of Middle Management in Globally Competitive Firms. Annual Meetings of the Academy of Management. Las Vegas, Nevada. August.

Checkland P, 1981. *Systems thinking, systems practice*. Chichester: Wiley.

Checkland P and Scholes J, 1990. *Soft Systems Methodology in action*. Wiley & Sons.

Cohen J en Stewart I, 1994. *The collapse of chaos*. Viking.

Dayhoff J, 1990. *Neural Network Architectures*. NY: Von Nostrand Reinhold Book.

de Callatay A, 1992. *Natural and Artificial Intelligence: Misconceptions about Brains and Neural Networks*. Amsterdam: North-Holland.

de Geus A, 1988. Planning as learning. Harvard Business Review. March/April, pp. 70-74.

Eden C, 1988. Cognitive mapping. European Journal of Operational Research. Nr. 36, pp. 1-13.

Firebaugh M, 1989. *Artificial Intelligence: A knowledge-Based Approach*. Boston: PWS-Kent.

Fletcher and Goss, 1993. Forecasting with neural networks. Information and Management. Vol. 24, Nr. 3, March, pp. 159-167.

Galliers R and Baets W, 1997 (eds.). *Information Technology and Organizational Transformation: Innovation for the 21st Century Organization*. Wiley.

Haeckel S and Nolan R, 1993. Managing by wire. Harvard Business Review. Vol. 71, Nr. 5, Sept.-Oct.

Hamel G and Prahalad C, 1989. Strategic Intent. Harvard Business Review. May-June.

Hassard J, 1993. *Sociology and Organization theory: Positivism, Paradigms and Postmodernity*. Cambridge University Press.

Hassard J and Parkers M (eds.), 1993. *Postmodernism and organizations*. London: Sage.

Johansson H, McHugh P, Pendleburry A and Wheeler W, 1993. *Business Process Reengineering - Breakpoint Strategies for Market Dominance*. Whiley & Sons.

Johnson-Laird, 1983. *Mental Models*. Cambridge: Cambridge University Press.

Kaplan R and Murdock L, 1990. Core Process Redesign. The McKinsey Quarterly. Nr. 2.

Keen P, 1993. Information technology and the management difference: A fusion map. IMB Systems Journal. Vol. 32, Nr. 1.

Kim D, 1993. The link between Individual and Organizational Learning. Sloan Management Review. Fall.

Kolb D, 1984. *Experiential learning: Experience as the Source of Learning and Development.* Englewood Cliffs: Prentice Hall.

Knorr R, 1991. Business Process Redesign: Key to Competitiveness. The Journal of Business Strategy. Nov./Dec.

Langton C (ed.), 1989. Artificial life. Santa Fe Institute Studies in the Sciences of Complexity. Proceedings. Vol. 6. Redwood City. Addison-Wesley.

Leonard-Barton D, 1992. The Factory as a Learning Laboratory. Sloan Management Review. Vol. 34, Nr. 11, Fall.

Lodewijk and Deng, 1993. Experimentation with back-propagation neural networks. Information and Management. Vol. 24, Nr. 1, Jan., pp. 1-8.

Morin E, 1990a. *Sciences avec conscience*. Paris: Fayard.

Morin E, 1990b. *Introduction à la pensée complexe*. Paris: Esf.

Nicolis G and Prigogine I, 1989. *Exploring Complexity*. Freeman.

Niederman F, Brancheau J C, and Wetherbe J C, 1991. Information Systems management issues in the 1990's. MIS Quarterly. Vol.16, Nr. 4, pp. 474-500.

Nonaka I, 1994. A dynamic theory of Organizational Knowledge creation. Organization Science. Vol. 5, Nr. 1, February.

Nonaka I, Byosiere P, Borucki C and Konno N, 1994. Organizational Knowledge Creation Theory: A First Comprehensive Test. Annual Academy of Management Meetings. Dallas. August.

Norden P, 1993. Quantitative techniques in strategic alignment. IBM Systems Journal. Vol. 32, Nr. 1.

Peppard J and Rowland P, 1995. *The essence of business process re-engineering*. Prentice-Hall.

Piaget J, 1966. *La naissance de l'intelligence chez l'enfant*. Neufchatel: Delachaux Niestlez.

Prahalad C and Hamel G, 1990. The core competence of the corporation. Harvard Business Review. May-June.

Probst G, 1987. Organiser par l'auto-organization. Les Editions d'organizations.

Quinn J B, 1992. *Intelligent Enterprise*. New York: The Free Press.

Ramaswami S, Nilakanta S, Flynn J, 1992. Supporting strategic information needs: An empirical assessment of some organizational factors. Journal of Strategic Information Systems. Nr. 2.

Rockart J and Hofman J, 1992. System Delivery: Evolving New Strategies. Sloan Management Review. Vol. 33, Summer.

Rummelhart D and McClelland J, 1986. *Parallel Distributed Processing: Exploration in the Microstructure of cognition. Vol. 1: Foundations*. Cambridge, MA: MIT Press.

Rummelhart D and McClelland J, 1986. *Parallel Distributed Processing: Exploration in the Microstructure of cognition. Vol. 2: Psychological and Biological Models*. Cambridge, MA: MIT Press.

Santa Fe Institute. Bulletin of the Santa Fe Institute. 1987 - present.

Scott Morton M (ed.), 1991. *The Corporation of the 1990s: Information Technology and Organizational Transformation*. Oxford University Press.

Senge P M, 1990. *The Fifth Discipline: The Art & Practice of the Learning Organization*. NY: Doubleday.

Stacey R, 1993. Strategy as Order Emerging from Chaos. Longe Range Planning. Vol. 26, Nr. 1, Feb.

Swieringa J and Wierdsma A, 1993. *The learning organization*. Addison-Wesley.

Toffler A, 1990. *Powershift: Knowledge, Wealth and Violence at the Edge of the 21st Century*. New York: Bantan Books.

Van der Linden G, 1993. Een Essay over en Empirisch Onderzoek naar Betekenissen van Loon en Beloning. Casus van een postmoderne visie op bedrijfsbeheer. PhD thesis. Rijksuniversiteit Groningen.

Venugopal V and Baets W, 1994a. Neural Networks and Statistical Techniques in Marketing Research: A conceptual comparison. Marketing Intelligence & Planning. Vol. 12, Nr. 7.

Venugopal V and Baets W, 1994b. Neural Networks and their Applications in Marketing Management. The Journal of Systems Management. September.

4. ARTIFICIAL INTELLIGENCE FOR KNOWLEDGE MANAGEMENT AND LEARNING

In the previous chapter we identified what we understand as corporate knowledge and knowledge management for companies. We have discussed why it is advantageous and how knowledge management can make the competitive difference between two companies, specifically for service companies. We have highlighted the power of connectionist thinking for knowledge management and the example of our brain was used to introduce the concept of neural networks. In this chapter we will discuss two specific techniques which can be used while building connectionist networks: artificial neural networks and fuzzy logic. They are both considered as part of what we call artificial intelligence techniques. The combination of both promises to be able to generate some intelligence in decision making. In a first stage we will describe and elaborate the techniques. The next chapter gives examples of straight applications of connectionist networks (artificial neural networks) in real life corporate situations. There after we discuss some examples of real life cases in knowledge management or connectionist approaches to complex management cases.

4.1. Artificial Neural Networks

Neural network techniques

Though the use of neural networks in management science is rather young, and the applicability of these techniques to business problems experimental, both successes in related fields and the conditions for use of these methods appear promising.

The technique of Artificial Neural Networks (ANNs) is highly interdisciplinary and
brings together, "inter alia", mathematics, computer science, psychology and
biology. We already briefly described earlier how the prototype of a neural
network (our brain) operates. Inspired by physiology and biology, artificial neural
networks (ANNs) mimic the neurons and synaptic connections of a human brain
(see figure 4.1). ANNs are "by-products" of the search for understanding (and
imitation) of the operation of the human brain.

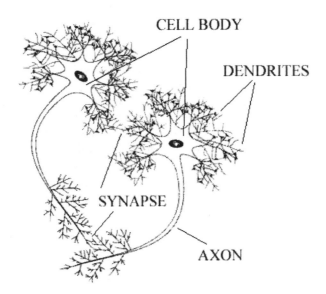

Figure 4.1: Biological Neuron

Recently, some remarkable successes have been reported in a number of different
applications. Most of these have to do with one or other form of pattern
recognition. In this area, conventional computers do poorly compared to neural
networks. This does not automatically imply that neural networks are good for
classical estimation in physics and/or economics, however.

Widrow and Stearns (1985) report on a range of applications in which neural networks have been used successfully, such as weather forecasting, speech recognition, adaptive control and adaptive noise filtering. Collins et al. (1988) report on some interesting results in using neural network techniques for financial evaluations. They tried to apply the neural network technique to credit files, in order to develop an application of credit scoring. Additional success was obtained with stock value forecasting. Applications in marketing have been reported on by Venugopal and Baets (1994) and van Wezel and Baets (1995). Duda and Hart (1973) report on successes in the field of image analysis, related to target identification (military). Yoon et al. (1989) have some good cases in the field of medical diagnosis. Dietz et al. (1989) and Marko et al. (1989) have good results in jet engine failure detection and related automotive problems. Hart (1992) reports on some experiments with classification problems. For an overview of these success stories, one can refer to Dayhoff (1990).

As we argued before, many managerial problems contain both aspects of pattern recognition (map) and dynamic non-linear behavior. Neural networks, therefore, seem promising in helping to solve this kind of problem, whereas the classic techniques of analysis seem less adequate. As such, neural networks are a promising tool with which to analyze an ill-structured and turbulent environment, bringing some system to the chaos.

The successful applications of artificial neural networks suggest an important resemblance between neural networks and characteristics of the human brain (Wasserman, 1989). They both learn from experimentation. Neural networks generalize from previous examples. They seem to be able to abstract essential characteristics from "irrelevant" data. A brief history of neural networks will clarify some remaining issues and will illustrate the scientific growth of this discipline.

History of neural networks

Without claiming to be complete (for which, e.g., Wasserman, 1989 can be consulted, providing the background for the following treatment of the topic), a brief historical overview of the early years of neural networks introduces some important issues.

Time and again, human beings have been wondering about human thought and the workings of the human brain. Research on the brain and the nervous system has shown us the existence of "neurons" as central knots in brain and thought. Neuro-anatomy and neuro-physiology are the sciences which brought us this insight. On the other hand there were psychologists who tried to develop models of human learning. Back in 1949, Hebb created what was known as the "learning law", which afterwards became the basis for neural network learning.

In the 1950s and 1960s, biologists and psychologists developed the first artificial neural networks, which gave rise to a burst of optimism. According to Marvin Minsky, Frank Rosenblatt and Bernard Widrow, the single layer artificial neurons (called perceptrons) were the key to our intelligence. A number of tests, however, caused major disillusionment of this view. In 1969, Minsky and Papert proved that this single layer network cannot solve many of the easiest logical connectors. Researchers dropped this area of development, with some exceptions (e.g. Tervo Kohonen, Stephen Grossberg and James Anderson).

In the 1970s and 1980s, scattered efforts were published in various journals, without clear direction. During these years, multi-layer networks were developed and today these are quite successful. In the late 1980s, however, the subject of neural networks became much more popular. Four major international conventions and over 500 technical papers indicate the level of activity. Sejnowski and Rosenberg (1987) made progress in speech recognition. Burr (1987) worked in recognition of hand-written characters. Cottrell et al. (1987) were active in image compression, and Werbos (1974), Parker (1982) and Rummelhart et al. (1986), contributed extensively to the concept of Backpropagation Learning, which is the central heuristic today in neural network applications.

Some remarks on the architecture of neural networks

Based on extensive research, the PDP Research Group (Rummelhart and McClelland, Vol. 1 and 2, 1986) demonstrated that the human brain is characterized by a high degree of parallelism. A second important characteristic of the human brain is the Micro Structure of Cognition (distributed knowledge) on which it is built. The human brain has no clear equation for what happens in a given situation, but it is able to reconstruct solutions, actions, etc., quickly and easily, based on this micro structure of knowledge. Classic analytical techniques require a complete and correct equation before being able to handle such situations. This is no doubt one of their most severe limitations in dealing with perceptions, as opposed to quantitative data.

In summary, this "Parallel Distributed Processing" of our brains is in contrast to the classical sequential equation approach with which we try to solve complex real world problems. This is above all others, the reason for using neural networks in order to create knowledge maps.

Computer architecture should reflect this "parallel distributed processing" way of solving problems. We are most familiar with the "Von Neumann" machines, in which operations are executed sequentially on the basis of a time clock. Such processors are capable of executing hundreds of basic commands (add, load,....).

Neural Network Processors (Dayhoff, 1990) are only able to process a few calculations. Summations are performed on the inputs and incremental changes are made to parameters associated with interconnections. In themselves, neural network processors are much less impressive than the classical "Von Neumann" processor. However, in a neural network architecture, these processors operate in parallel processing mode. Processors are massively interconnected and the number of interconnections far exceed the number of processors. As an imitation of our human brain, these neural network processors achieve promising results.

Why neural networks are interesting for these kind of problems

In the annex we deal in some detail with the problems of classic quantitative methods to deal with non-linear dynamic systems, showing learning behavior. Here, we will only briefly summarize them. The main focus of the argument is on the strict assumptions underlying all quantitative methods, and the important numerical problems when using them with perception-like data. The "quality" of the data (observations) and the relationships are characterized by the fact that :

Equations are non-linear, dynamic and most certainly very complex

The data deal with perceptions and are, by definition, less clear-cut than quantitative data

The observations are of a highly contingent nature

Observations (e.g. questions in research questionnaire) are highly interconnected.

Managerial problems are either deterministic or stochastic and they contain few or many variables. We deliberately exclude here the alternative of non-deterministic change, as argued earlier. For deterministic problems with few variables, calculus can bring the solution. For stochastic problems with few variables, statistics are an adequate tool. Many variables in a deterministic (linear and static) environment are addressed by mathematical programming. Finally stochastic problems with many variables are partly addressed by econometrics, but they need other tools, specifically when behavior is non-linear and dynamic. Behavioral science, fuzzy and chaos models and neural networks are the tools to be used in this context (Benjamin and Levinson, 1993). For stochastic problems with lots of variables or for deterministic problems, where the behavior is non-linear and dynamic, a combination of neural networks and fuzzy logic is proposed here. Not a lot of research has been done yet on this subject and managerial applications are hardly reported.

Neural network techniques, through their parallel distributed processing, imitate what we understand to be our brain-like thinking, which is concerned with perceptions, filtering unstructured thinking, etc. The classic sequential equation approach needs a valid theory to underpin each equation and permits the definition of these complex equations. Today, it seems difficult to define this kind of complex (dynamic and non-linear) equation in enough detail. Possibly, the knowledge of the underlying business processes does not yet exist in order to write these equations. Solving knowledge maps needs a research approach which is best able to simulate this "assimilated thinking". Neural networks seem an appropriate technique in achieving this.

What artificial neural networks do exactly

Artificial Neural Networks (ANN) attempt to model the architecture of biological neural systems.   Biological neural networks are made of simple, tightly interconnected processing elements called neurons. The interconnections are made by the outgoing branches, the "axons", which again form several connections ("synapses") with the other neurons. When a neuron receives a number of stimuli and when the sum of the received stimuli exceeds a certain threshold value, it will fire and transmit the stimulus to adjacent neurons. The aim of ANNs is to extract concepts from the biological networks, with which new powerful computational methodologies can be developed.

ANNs consist of many non-linear computational elements called nodes. The nodes are densely interconnected through directed links. Nodes take one or more input values, combine them into a single value, then transform them into output value. Figure 4.2 illustrates a node that implements the macroscopic idea of a biological neuron.

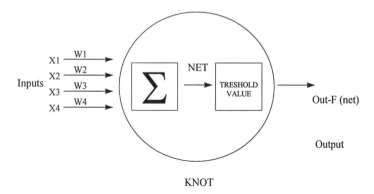

**Figure 4.2: Artificial neuron
(after Venugopal and Baets, 1994)**

In figure 4.2, a set of inputs labeled X_1, X_2, ..., X_n is sent to a node. Each input is multiplied by the weights of the interconnections W_1, W_2, ... W_n before it is applied to the summation block. Each weight corresponds to the strength of a synaptic connection.   The summation block adds all the weighted inputs algebraically, producing an output denoted as NET. The block labeled "threshold value" accepts the NET output. If the NET output exceeds the threshold level, the OUT node is said to be activated.

The power of neural computing comes from connecting artificial neurons into artificial neural networks. The simplest network is a group of neurons arranged in a layer. Multilayer networks may be formed by simply cascading a group of single layers. Figure 4.3 shows a three-layer neural network: an input layer, an output layer, and between the two a so-called hidden layer. The nodes of different layers are densely interconnected through directed links. The nodes at the input layer receive the signals (values of the input variables) and propagate concurrently through the network, layer by layer.

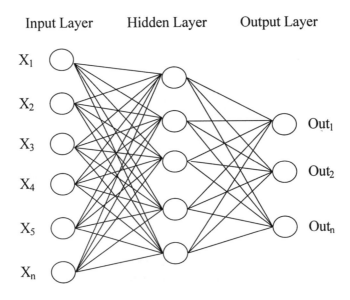

**Figure 4.3: Schematic representation of a three layer Neural Network
(after Venugopal and Baets, 1994)**

The numbers of layers and neurons and the weights to be attached to the connections from neuron to neuron can be decided in such a way that they give the best possible fit to a set of data. Different types of neural network models have been developed in the literature.

ANN models are characterized by their properties, viz., the structure of the network (topology), how and what the network computes (computational property) and how and what the network learns to compute (learning or training property). Learning means here the process in which ·a set of input values is presented sequentially to the input of the networks and the network weights are adjusted such that similar inputs give the same output. Learning strategies are categorized as supervised and unsupervised.

Supervised learning requires the pairing of each input value with a target value representing the desired output and a "teacher" who provides error information. In unsupervised learning, the training set consists of input vectors only. The output is determined by the network during the course of training. The unsupervised learning procedures construct internal models that capture regularities in their input values without receiving any additional information.

The massive number of processing elements makes neural computing faster than conventional computing. They are robust and fault tolerant due to their parallelism. They are fault tolerant in the sense that their performance does not degrade significantly even if one or few of the nodes fail. Also, based on current results, neural networks adapt themselves, i.e., adapt their structure and/or connection weights to achieve a better performance.

As we already argued earlier, we want to use ANNs in order to create "corporate intelligence", via mapping of business processes. These maps could then be used in order to support change processes. ANNs do not give the completely detailed picture, but they do show a workable and correct picture which contains the complexity of the considered business process. If this picture can be visualized with a user-friendly software interface, different people can use it in order to get a better understanding of a particular business process and its context. Stakeholders can learn from each other in a non-confrontational way and they can get hold of each others "knowledge" about a specific business process. The stakeholders can get an idea of what is important in a specific business process for all the involved stakeholders, based on their respective perceptions, and they can approach that via a system from which they can learn.

The most important value added of ANNs is that they are able, by definition, to simulate non-linear behavior and it is not necessary to know beforehand whether behavior is non-linear or not. ANNs show learning behavior. New information will allow the system to learn and gradually to internalize the new information. ANNs are non-parametric, which means that we do not need to know the exact form of the equation beforehand. When we simulate complex, chaotic and dynamic systems, this quality is no doubt of paramount importance. ANNs are fault tolerant which implies that they can easily deal with "non-available" values, without replacing them by averages. Replacing the non-available values by averages would bias the result. If a value is non-available, that should not deteriorate the result, indeed it should be a neutral operation. The big disadvantage is that the eventual result of a trained network is not easy to interpret in managerial terms. ANNs are a trade-off between quality of the result and insight into how the result is obtained.

In summary, ANNs give a more global and holistic picture of a managerial problem, which shows adaptive (learning) behavior. To a certain extent, it remains a numerical approach. The combination of ANNs and fuzzy logic (which we describe in the next section) can help here, in order to make the interpretation of the ANNs more accessible. However, now we would like to give some additional insight into ANNS via a comparison with other techniques and a summary of weaknesses and promises.

Statistical use of neural networks versus their use as a knowledge tool

Since the early 1950s, two opposing visions of what computers could be and do struggled for recognition (Dreyfus and Dreyfus, 1988). One sought to use computers to instantiate a formal representation of the world; the other to simulate the interactions of neurons. One took problem solving as its paradigm of intelligence; the other, learning. One school was the heir to the rationalist, reductionist tradition in philosophy; the other viewed itself as idealized and holistic. The first way of looking at computers also became the way of looking at brains (Dreyfus and Dreyfus, 1988). Even today, acceptance of neural networks struggles with the same reductionist tradition. Very often, neural networks are considered as part of, and equally comparable to, statistical methods.

In general, neural networks provide a means of mapping a set of inputs to a set of outputs in a way that allows the network to perform the same mapping on new data that has not been seen before. These networks are particularly useful for classification of a set of input features into various categories. During the training stage, examples of the mapping of the input domain into the output classes are presented to the network. Once successfully trained, the network can generalize the learned mapping to classify new data.

Weaknesses and strengths/possibilities of neural networks

Applications of neural networks in a managerial environment is still rather novel, as already illustrated. If applications have been developed, it was mainly an attempt to do better than via classical quantitative techniques. Therefore, many of the applications are of a kind which have already been investigated for years via quantitative techniques. Though neural networks can do a good job in these fields, the real value added is most probably elsewhere.

The value added of neural networks is specifically present in those applications where other techniques fail or perform badly. Though it is difficult to generalize those types of applications, they all have to do with processes in which *perceptions* are important. Also for situations in which we attempt to map *complex situations*, maybe not in its full detail, but certainly in its full complexity, neural networks seem appropriate. Finally, applications in which we attempt to make *tacit knowledge* explicit, changing as little as possible of its distinctive feature, seem promising applications for neural networks. If we have a closer look into each of these domains, we can immediately observe the distance which we still have to make before we can reach guaranteed success.

Perceptions are crucial in many managerial applications. In the near future we will see more research coming up in the use of neural networks for problems in which classical methods failed, due to the appearance of perception-like data. Specifically in marketing, a number of potential applications can be identified, like brand imaging or quality control. The applications are rather straightforward. The chances for success are high and the degree of difficulty of the developments is manageable.

The second group of promising applications are those where we make an attempt to map *complex situations*. Management literature today seems to suggest the management of the future will consist of coping with uncertainties, complexity and chaos, rather than the plan-and-control mechanism which has been applied in the past. Complexity and chaos theory are only new fields of development in the social sciences and since it causes some uncertainties, it will take a certain amount of time for these theories to become accepted. Managers do not feel comfortable with uncertainties and furthermore we are taught that we cannot manage what we cannot observe and/or make explicit. Only, in these terms making explicit often means describing it in linear non-dynamic systems. This could be equations (for simulation models) or knowledge rules (for expert systems) or even contracted rules (like in the case of performance evaluation of staff). We seldom ask ourselves whether or not these rules are a simplification of the reality.

Probably we will have to get acquainted with working with representations of the holistic complex reality (with the aim of simulations), but we have to accept that the price we have to pay is the lack of detail. We simply do not have enough information to be able to write equations of complex systems. By definition, neural networks can be a good and workable representation of complex systems, if we accept a lower level of detail but a higher level of aggregation. In that case, we could even use neural networks in order to simulate complexity. Research in management still has a long way to go in that respect. Hopefully, we will see in the future more research in how neural networks can be helpful in providing a better understanding of complex systems, but rather applied to managerial situations.

In the corner of the cognitive sciences and the organizational sciences there is a growing interest in knowledge management. Without going into too much detail, there is an entire field of research into how tacit knowledge can be used within a corporate context, without loosing the qualities of the "tacitness" of the knowledge. Our own research (Baets, 1993, 1995) shows that neural networks have some potential there. Hopefully, some research into organizational learning will go in that direction. Only the future will tell.

Neural networks are promising in applications where perceptions are central and where no quantitative equations can be identified. Neural networks are also promising for supporting organizational change processes (of which we give an example in chapter 6). Neural networks in order to get a better understanding of complexity is very promising, but as yet, not a lot of evidence has been collected. Finally knowledge based management, as advocated in this book is a promising field for neural networks. That is what will be illustrated in the real life case studies.

The limits of neural networks are their numerical character. Human beings do not readily understand the language of neural networks. However, this has to do a lot with the Cartesian logic in which we are all educated. This logic is one which is not really human and does not really come close to the way we think as human beings. Fuzzy logic is much closer to human thinking, only it is again one of these theories which does not really fit into our Western management culture. The Asiatics have much less problems with it. We, at least, should be interested. Therefore, let us try and get some more insight. Eventually the combination of neural networks and fuzzy logic will allow for intelligent decision making. Beforehand, we will have to go through some detail on fuzzy logic.

4.2. Fuzzy logic

The logic which forms the basis of Western mathematical and statistical thinking is based on the Cartesian 0-1 logic: something is red or it is not red; if it is for 60 % red, then it is for 40 % not red. Other variations or combinations of colors are not possible. In our day-to-day life, however, we think differently. Most apples have different colors at the same time. They are members at the same time of the group of green apples, red apples, yellow apples and some combinations of these. When does an apple become a "core" while eating ? What is large exactly ? If 1.8 meters is large, is 1.79 then small ? Of course not; humans are able to reason in gradation, in memberships of different groups at the same time. However, most of what we have attempted to do in decision support is not really based on that capacity. We have forced ourselves to think like computers do. While they think digital, we feel we should do the same. Application of fuzzy logic is the first attempt to make a machine think the way we do: in fuzzy and overlapping groups.

Fuzzy logic approaches the way people think. Combined with the learning capacities of neural networks we approach, to some extent, the way humans think.

Fuzzy logic is an integral part of the Asiatic way of considering the world. Asiatic people have learned to live with good and bad in the same person, in the same situation. They do not consider them as mutually exclusive, but rather an integral part of each and all things. Asiatic people can be at the same time happy and sad, be white and black and they do not feel the necessity to be a member of only one group at the same time. In our Western world, fuzzy logic is still very controversial. In the US more than in Europe, fuzzy logic does not find a lot of application. In Japan, on the contrary, they have a fully automatic metro operating on only 54 fuzzy rules. They have fully-automatic washing machines and microwaves and autofocus camcorders. All these fuzzy machines decide themselves, based on observations of a number of sensors, continuously what to do next. No washing program excludes another. All programs are used to a certain degree at the same time.

Within the scope of this book we can only limit ourselves to a brief description of fuzzy logic. For more detail a number of books can be consulted. Most readable are Kosko (1993) and Mc Neill and Freibergen (1994). For the more technical side of building fuzzy logic systems, Pedrycz (1995) is an interesting reference, as well as the Fuzzy logic CD-ROM library (Cox et al., 1995).

Using some very simple examples, we can get an idea of what fuzzy logic does and what it could be useful for. Let us first take the example of "tall": when is somebody tall ? In the classical 0-1 logic we have to define a cut-off level, above which somebody is tall and under which somebody is small. Say that we agree that this cut-off level is 1.8 meters. If somebody is larger than 1.8 meters, then we say he or she is tall. Somebody smaller than 1.8 meters is considered small. If somebody is 1.79, does he then suddenly become small ? If he were 1 cm taller, would he be considered tall ? Hence the difference of 1 cm on a scale from 150 to 200 cm makes the entire difference. As human beings we feel that this is a little stupid. On the other hand, when we design decision support systems, we follow these rules.

Another example is the artificial cut-off of becoming an adult. At the age of 18 one becomes an adult. As we all know, that cut-off level is rather artificial. Some people never become adults and some children are (sad but true) complete adults early on. Somebody who is 17 years and 360 days, therefore, is not an adult. We could cite many more examples of this kind.

If now we want to consider the same problems via a fuzzy logic approach, it would look different. In Figure 4.4 we show the concept "tall" as a fuzzy set (which is a fuzzy variable). If somebody is 150 cm tall, he is not a member of the group of tall people as can be seen on the diagram. If somebody is 185 cm tall, then this person is 70 % member of the group of tall people. From 200 cm upwards, one is a 100 % member. Of course, this is much closer to the normal way human beings think.

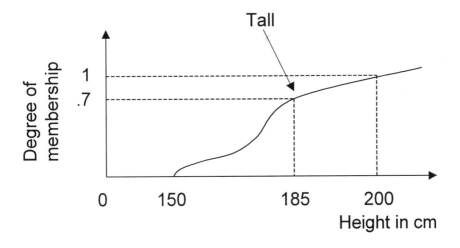

Figure 4.4: Representation of the concept *tall* using fuzzy sets
(after Dutta, 1993)

Figure 4.5 combines four fuzzy sets: "short", "medium", "tall" and "very tall". As can be seen from figure 4.5, these curves are overlapping. Hence, a person can be a member of different groups at the same time. These groups are not mutually exclusive like they are in our classical 0-1 logic. The person who is 185 cm tall is for 0.7 member of the group of "tall" people, for 0.5 he is also a member of the group of "very tall" people, for 0.3 he is a member of the group of "average" people and for 0.2 he is a member of the "short" people. For our 0-1 logic it is very strange that this sums up to more than 100 %. The reason, therefore, is that these memberships are not probabilities but really memberships. One can be a member of different clubs (a sailing club, a basketball club, etc.) at the same time. In management, we always immediately think that these "clubs" need to be mutually exclusive. That is the big difference between Cartesian logic and fuzzy logic. The particularly strong quality of fuzzy logic is the overlapping sets. Our world is not constructed of mutually exclusive variables. Many of the variables we use in management are not mutually exclusive, which does not exclude the fact that we can organize them in a way that they are defined as being mutually exclusive. However, this exclusivity is artificial.

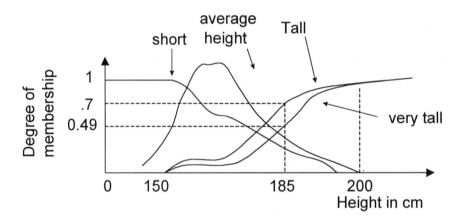

**Figure 4.5: Fuzzy sets *very tall, tall, short and average* height
(after Dutta, 1993)**

If we try to apply fuzzy logic in a real application, we combine a group of fuzzy sets via fuzzy rules. We will give here an easy example with only 5 fuzzy sets on each of the two axes. In a second stage, they are connected via fuzzy rules. As can be seen of figure 4.7, a fuzzy rule pictures exactly the way a human being would like a machine to be commanded. Figure 4.7 gives the complete application. The example dealt with is a fuzzy airconditioner. As we all know from nights in hotel rooms, most airconditioners operate on a certain speed (and noise) level, until the desired temperature is reached. Then suddenly the machine switches off. By the time you are almost asleep again, the machine turns on again, since the temperature has increased. It is this eternal switching on and off, instead of smooth changes, which keeps us awake in hotels instead of improving sleeping conditions. Where the airconditioner is meant to improve the quality of a night's sleep, in practice the contrary happens. The aim of the fuzzy airconditioner is to do this differently. Instead of switching on and off suddenly, this airconditioner changes speed gradually, which implies that the noise levels change very gradually too. Not only does this airconditioner consume less energy, it also allows people to sleep. That is, after all, the aim, isn't it?

Figure 4.6 shows the 5 fuzzy sets which were defined for the temperature of the room and those for the motor speed. If the temperature is between 7 and 10 degrees Celsius, then we call that "cool"; between 16° and 21 °C we call that "just right". As can be seen this is exactly the way human beings express temperature: too cold, just right, hot, etc. The essential thing, again, is that sets are overlapping. Of course, not all sets need to be overlapping. It could be that some sets do not overlap. The case of 0-1 logic is a special case of fuzzy logic, in which the sets do not overlap. The consequence is that such a combination of all non-overlapping sets does not show the value added of fuzzy sets either.

On the second part of figure 4.6 we have another 5 sets which identify the motor speed. A speed of between 50 and 90 rounds per minute for example, is identified as "fast". The fuzzy rule which combines both sets "warm" in temperature and "fast" in speed is "if the temperature is warm, then the speed should be fast". In any case, this type of rule is very recognizable, isn't it ? Figure 4.7 combines both variables and gives the overview of all the fuzzy rules used in this application. In this case too, we see that not only the sets, but also the rules are overlapping. It is these overlapping rules which guarantee a smooth change of speed, in which case a smooth change of temperature occurs.

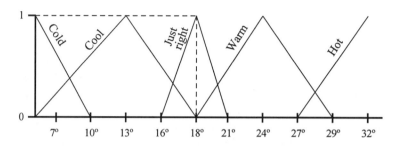

Temperature in Degrees Celsius

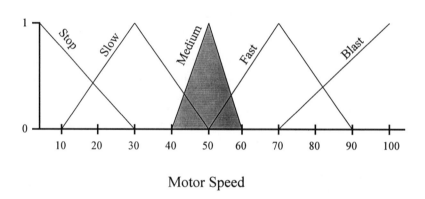

Motor Speed

**Figure 4.6: Temperature in Degrees Celsius and Motor Speed
(after Kosko, 1993)**

Fuzzy rules

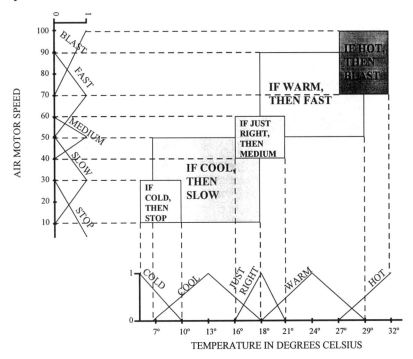

**Figure 4.7: The fuzzy airconditioner
(after Kosko, 1993)**

In practice, a sensor measures the temperature. This temperature will be a member of a number of fuzzy sets, all describing the temperature. These memberships will then activate a number of fuzzy rules each of them to a higher or lesser degree. These different rules will then activate to different degrees the sets on the speed side. Via a process of de-fuzzification (say a process of weighted averaging) a new motor speed is identified and produced. This process is a continuous process of change, which makes the motor speed change continuously but gradually.

In commercial applications, trading room systems are best known. Japanese banks operate today with fuzzy trading systems. Apart from this application there are not a lot of applications known within management. In engineering applications there are a lot of commercial fuzzy products on the market already, almost exclusively produced by Japanese companies. The Sendai subway system (already mentioned) is no doubt the most famous. It is a fully automatic subway which operates without a driver. The subway produces no shocks, neither when accelerating nor when braking. Passengers can stand up without holding on. Furthermore, the Japanese have fuzzy microwaves, fuzzy washing machines, fuzzy camcorders, etc.

The big advantage of fuzzy logic is that it allows a reasoning which is very close to human reasoning. In practice this means reasoning in vague rules, rather than in exact probabilities and chance distributions even if the latter are a bit artificial. Furthermore, due to the overlapping memberships, it is an outstanding quality of fuzzy systems that they produce very smooth behavior and change. Stepwise change, or rather changes with shocks, which are rather classical in most decision support applications, are smoothed out via fuzzy systems. This is an approximated simulation of the incremental learning process which we have described in earlier chapters. This fuzzy way of reasoning also approaches the incremental but dynamic change processes which we have identified as so important in the sciences.

An argument could be made that applications developed on the basis of control theory can perform the same tasks. In theory they can. However, it would need a tremendously large computer and a comparably complex application to do so. In practice, simulating fuzzy behavior by control mechanisms would be expensive and difficult. Other than for theoretical reasons, this comparison is not realistic in real life applications.

The really promising development, however, is the combination of neural networks (perceptions, patterns and learning behavior) with fuzzy logic (natural language construction and incremental change). In this combination we start speaking about intelligent systems. These systems are able to simulate the dynamic and non-linear reality which we have described thusfar in previous chapters. Therefore, if we want to base our management on knowledge, fuzzy neural networks are a tool or technique of importance with the aim to picture complex systems. It supports development of knowledge, it assists management of knowledge and it organizes knowledge in order to evolve gradually. The next section will give a description of the kind of applications we can expect in the coming years where we observe some human intelligence.

4.3. Intelligent systems

A kind of intelligence in systems occurs when we combine the learning and adaptive qualities of neural networks with the vagueness and natural language use of fuzzy logic. This combination has some remarkable qualities which cannot be reached by any of the techniques in isolation. This combination shows some human reasoning, in the sense of reasoning which is easily understood by humans, without any mathematical training. Hence, this kind of reasoning gives us interesting insight into problems. Therefore again, this combination is a good one for the purpose of knowledge management. Also, this is a way of reasoning in which we attempt to use the computer to reason in a way a human being does. No longer do we need to adapt our way of thinking to what computers can deal with. In practice this means that we no longer have to think in equations or rules (which is artificial for a normal human being), but rather in adaptive systems, based on natural language.

The subject of fuzzy neural networks is rather technical (for detail, see e.g. Kosko, 1992 and Lin and Lee, 1996) and is not yet applied well in managerial applications. Therefore we limit ourselves here to summarize some of the characteristics, rather than to give lots of technical detail. In chapter 6 we give an example which will probably indicate, much better than anything, the kind of problems we can deal with.

The aim of fuzzy neural networks, or better, the aim of intelligent systems, is the combination of the learning capacity and the capacity to picture complex systems via neural networks, with the "human" language interface of fuzzy systems. This adaptive behavior, the complex environment and the overlapping rules is what we recognize in many managerial applications. Vague but learning behavior is very human, hence it is very recognizable for managers. Therefore this approach is very interesting in view of knowledge management.

In summary we can describe the qualities of fuzzy neural systems as follows:

- Combination of adaptive and learning ability with vague rules.
- Overlapping and vaguely defined groups. The answer is never yes or no, but always a little yes and no together.
- The use of vague decision rules, just the way managers make decisions.
- Adaptive and learning behavior which is very human.
- This combination allows the building of knowledge via perceptions and language, rather than via pre-defined rules.

What can we expect to see as the kind of applications of intelligent systems in the future ? Without claiming to be exhaustive, we can identify a number of potential applications for the combination of neural networks and fuzzy logic (what we will call intelligent systems for the purpose of this book). Roughly, we can group these applications into five groups :

- Decision support based on perceptions, mainly in marketing applications.
- Better insight into complex systems and environment.
- Management information systems and control systems (risk management systems) with mankind reasoning.
- Support for and mapping of change processes or learning processes.
- Machine intelligence.

In the group of *decision support* based on perceptions, a typical example is brand imaging. Brand imaging is the problem that the perceptions of the clients are central to the confirmation of their interest in any particular brand. Brand perception is not always related to technical factors (like taste, weight, speed, etc.). It is in many cases very difficult for a buyer to say why he or she really wants e.g. a specific coffee brand. For the company, of course, brand loyalty is crucial. Given the availability of huge volumes of scanner data, we will see applications which combine these scanner data with broader behavioral data. An example can be to relate the results of one's own sales in respect to a publicity campaign, but also in respect to the perceived publicity of the competitor. Another example in this group could be measurement of emotions in buying behavior. Many modern advertisements actively use emotional elements but it is very difficult today to measure the impact of emotions on buyer behavior. In general we see improved decision support in any application where the data are perceptions, rather than physical variables.

The second group is the one of applications oriented to a better *insight into complex systems*. Many of us have understood by now that market behavior is rather non-linear and dynamic, but still we try to describe market behavior via static, rather non-linear descriptions. Market behavior simulations could benefit from fuzzy neural systems. Introduction strategies in new markets are an example of this group of applications. Any application in which a company wants to get a better understanding of how a particular international market behaves is an application which attempts to gain insight into a new complex system. Of a different order, but sharing the same qualities, we can use fuzzy neural systems in order to study behavior of groups of people. In many respects, that is what we do in market studies anyway. Studying group behavior (e.g. the organization of a specific company) but also the study of organizational structures seems a promising application of fuzzy neural networks. On a more macro-level, fuzzy neural systems could give us deeper insight into the dynamics of socio-economic (or should I say political) systems. These systems could contribute to a better understanding of e.g. the development of Euro-Arab economic relations. It could help to identify the underlying variables and structures. Of course, these are highly dynamic systems, which can only be simulated via adaptive systems.

The third group of applications has to do with control systems, or in a broader sense *management information systems*. Many companies are interested in improving their management (control) on e.g. their sales networks. They are interested in using dynamic data, both for better decision support, but also for better management control. Far too often we ignore non-quantitative elements in management control, which causes very limited insight. Since management is not an act of quantitative optimization (as already argued in earlier chapters), rather these qualitative differences are decisive for the difference in quality of management. A specific example of an application in this group is risk management or Assets and Liabilities Management. Ideally, they should combine quantitative and qualitative variables in a language oriented environment. What happens today far too often is that risk management is an exercise in number crunching.

The fourth group of applications could be categorized as *supporting change processes*. Chapter 6 will give an interesting example of such an application. While companies seem to pay more attention to the creation of open and learning environments, they need more and more, an adapted support for these change processes. Then we would definitely be going in the direction of knowledge creation, knowledge management and knowledge distribution within a company (or even larger, within an industry). These kind of applications come closest to knowledge management applications. Therefore we will devote a lot of importance to the development of a particular example in chapter 6. Good understanding of this example will make the potential of fuzzy neural networks much clearer for these kind of applications.

The last group of applications can be called *machine intelligence* applications and are applications where machines try to imitate mankind reasoning. This is an extension of what we have already tried for years, with expert systems. Bankruptcy forecasting, creditscoring, loan advice, etc. could be made much richer today compared with what we have seen up to now from expert systems. Inclusion of human decision factors becomes infinitely easier. Even more important, via the learning capacity of neural networks it is much easier to keep these systems up to date in their capacity to decide. This is a kind of application which is a group in itself. This is what artificial intelligence and computer sciences in a larger sense are interested in, though in this case it is applied to a corporate environment.

As already indicated, this list is far from complete. Hopefully, it gives an idea of the broad groups of applications which are possible with fuzzy neural networks and what the value added is of bringing machine intelligence closer to human intelligence. Applied to a corporate environment this means running a knowledge based company for an improved adaptive management style. The least we aim for is to make computers think the way humans think. This is now possible to a certain degree. In saying this, it should not be understood as a claim that machine intelligence could replace human intelligence. However, the richer we can make machine intelligence, the richer human thinking can become, since the machine can take over more of the rather routine activities. Humans could then concentrate more on the deliberate act of management: or are we not really interested in doing this ? The more routine and structure we can take away from human thinking, the more human thinking can be creative and the more interesting the manager's role becomes. Managers are interested in creating, not reproducing, aren't they ?

We could go much further in this chapter, but we only aim here to give the necessary background in order to be able to understand the next few chapters of real life examples. The aim is to give a better understanding of the practical value of what is advocated thusfar, as well as to give an indication on how this can be achieved. The examples cover a wide range of companies and applications. All that is described can still be improved considerably. On the other hand, all these applications are real. They have been developed and/or thought out through real life cases.

After the few chapters of concepts on complexity, perceptions, learning and knowledge, we have dealt in this chapter with formal techniques of knowledge management, i.e. neural networks and fuzzy logic. These techniques are described and arguments are given why they would do better than other techniques which have been already around for a long time. Whereas the first chapters discussed the reason why knowledge management and learning are important, this chapter illustrates which techniques can be used. However, we are very well aware that it could still be unclear. The reason for this is that we are all educated with a rather different view on management, learning and knowledge than what we know today of these subjects. Instead of merely asking to believe and apply, we would like to give some examples of realizations. The aim of the following chapters is to give a better understanding of the previous chapters. Then we can propose a global approach for knowledge management within companies.

REFERENCES

Baets W, 1993a. IT for organizational change: beyond business process engineering. Business Change and Re-engineering. Vol. 1, Nr. 2, Autumn.

Baets W, 1993b. Information Systems Strategic Alignment: A case in banking. Working Paper. Nijenrode University, The Netherlands.

Baets W, 1995a. Artificiele neurale netwerken: het in kaart brengen van veranderingsprocessen en het meten van leren. Handboek effektief opleiden. 4.131

Baets W, 1995b. Ecosip study day on Business Process Reengineering and Information Technology (Paris): Business Process Re-engineering: A corporate mind set.

Benjamin R and Levinson E, 1993. A Framework for Managing IT-enabled change. Sloan Management Review. Vol. 34, Nr. 4, Summer.

Burr D, 1987. Experiments with a connectionist text reader. Proceedings of the First International Conference on Neural Networks. M Caudill and C Butler (eds.). Vol. 4, pp. 717-724. San Diego, CA: SOS Printing.

Collins E, Ghosh S and Scofield C, 1988. An application of a multiple neural network learning system to evaluation of mortgage underwriting judgment. IEEE International Conference on Neural Networks. Vol. II: pp. 459-466.

Cottrell G, Munro P and Zipser D, 1987. Image Compression by Backpropagation: An example of extensional programming. Advances in Cognitive Science. Vol. 3. Norwood, NJ: Ablex.

Cox, McNeill and Thro, Dubois and Prade, Zadeh, 1995. *Fuzzy Logic CD-ROM Library*. AP Professional.

Dayhoff J, 1990. *Neural Network Architectures*. NY: Von Nostrand Reinhold Book.

Dietz W, Kiech E, Ali M, 1989. Jet and Rocket engine fault diagnosis in real time. Journal Neural Network Computing. Vol.1, Nr. 1, pp. 5-18.

Dreyfus H and Dreyfus S, 1988. "Making a Mind versus Modeling the Brain: Artificial Intelligence Back at a Branchpoint." In *The artificial intelligence debate: false starts and real foundations*, Gravbard S (ed.). MIT Press.

Duda R and Hart P, 1973. *Pattern classification and scene analysis*. New York: Wiley Interscience.

Dutta S, 1993. *Knowledge Processing & Applied Artificial Intelligence*. Butterworth-Heinemann.

Hart A, 1992. Using Neural Networks for Classification Tasks - Some Experiments on Datasets and Practical advice. Journal of the Operational Research Society. Vol. 43, Nr. 3, March.

Lin, C-T and Lee G, 1996. *Neural Fuzzy Systems: A Neuro-Fuzzy Synergism to Intelligent Systems*. Prentice Hall.

Marko K, James J, Dosdall J and Murphy J, 1989. Automotive control systems diagnostics using neural nets for rapid pattern classification of large data sets. Proceedings of International Joint Conference on Neural Networks. Vol. II: pp. 13-15.

Mc Neill D and Freibergen P, 1994. *Fuzzy Logic*. Touchstone. Simon & Schuster.

Parker D, 1982. Learning-logic. Intervention Report. S81-64, File 1, Office of Technology Licensing, Stanford University.

Pedrycz W, 1995. *Fuzzy Sets Engineering*. CRC Press.

Rummelhart D and McClelland J, 1986. *Parallel Distributed Processing: Exploration in the Microstructure of cognition. Vol. 1: Foundations.* Cambridge, MA: MIT Press.

Rummelhart D and McClelland J, 1986. *Parallel Distributed Processing: Exploration in the Microstructure of cognition. Vol. 2: Psychological and Biological Models.* Cambridge, MA: MIT Press.

Sejnowski T and Rosenberg C, 1987. Parallel networks that learn to pronounce English text. Complex Systems. Vol. 3, pp. 145-168.

van Wezel M and Baets W, 1995. Predicting Market Responses with a Neural Network: the Case of Fast Moving Consumer Goods. Marketing Intelligence & Planning. Autumn.

Venugopal V and Baets W, 1994a. Neural Networks and Statistical Techniques in Marketing Research: A conceptual comparison. Marketing Intelligence & Planning. Vol. 12, Nr. 7.

Venugopal V and Baets W, 1994b. Neural Networks and their Applications in Marketing Management. The Journal of Systems Management. September.

Wasserman P, 1989. *Neural Computing: Theory and practice.* NY: Von Nostrand Reinhold Book.

Werbos P, 1974. Beyond Regression: New tools for prediction and analysis in the behavioral sciences. Masters thesis. Harvard University.

Widrow B and Stearns S, 1985. *Adaptive signal processing.* Englewood Cliffs, NJ: Prentice Hall.

Yoon Y, Brobst R, Bergstresser P and Petersen, 1989. A Desktop Neural Network for dermatology diagnosis. Journal on Neural Network Computing. Vol.1, Nr. 1, pp. 43-52.

5. EXPERIMENTS WITH NEURAL NETWORKS

In order to introduce more complex examples of knowledge management and change management in the next chapter, we first concentrate in this chapter on some examples of the use of neural networks. They illustrate the concepts described in previous chapter and they also show how neural thinking can help to solve problems of decision support, where other methods have failed or perform badly. The aim of these examples is to make the advantages of a connectionist approach clear. As such, these examples are not yet real examples of knowledge management. Though they all create knowledge which did not exist before or which could not be obtained in other ways.

Though the knowledge creation focus is not of prime importance in these examples, attention is given to the way knowledge is represented in order to share it afterwards with large numbers of people. The examples given deal with market response, brand imaging, and international introduction strategies. It can be observed that many of these applications have to do with marketing or marketing related activities. We have already mentioned a few times that market behavior increasingly is considered as "chaotic". Classical approaches of market response or market forecasting give a weaker performance. Therefore, the approaches discussed here can be used as a solution to deal with "chaos marketing" (Nilson, 1995): marketing in a turbulent and changing market. The three examples discussed are based on research projects executed for specific companies. They report on real life cases addressing problems which these companies were really concerned about.

The aim here is only to give a brief introduction in order to apply the readers' thinking to his own practical work environment and to introduce connectionist thinking in real life cases. Only limited numbers of examples exist on the use of neural networks in management. As argued earlier in this book, only if experience and experiments get translated via the individual mental models into a corporate mental model, are we creating knowledge. This is equally true in the use of knowledge management and connectionist thinking itself. There exists no shortcut to being able to use connectionist models than via using them.

5.1. Market response models for fast moving consumer goods

Markets are highly dynamic non-linear systems which we have attempted to forecast for years already via static and rather linear approaches. Still widely used in market research in companies (different from academic market research) are multiple linear regression models and/or multiplicatif models. In the first type of model, an addition is made of a number of influencing factors, each multiplied with a coefficient. Econometric estimation calculates the coefficients which make the model best performing with the aim to reproduce past behavior. The second type of model differs from the first one in the fact that instead of an addition of factors like in the first model, it is composed of a multiplication of factors. The "coefficients" then appear as exponents of each variable. Estimation also calculates these coefficients, often after linearisation of the equation via logarithms. The first type of model is purely linear. A linear combination of often a limited number of variables is estimated based on the past and then used to forecast the future. This approach presumes that the market is not dynamic. As Prigogine (Nicolis and Prigogine, 1989) said: "If we could forecast the future as an extrapolation out of the past, time would be reversible which it is not". The second type of model, the multiplicatif model, contains also a limited number of variables but given its multiplicatif form, the exponents are elasticities. For the reader with less mathematical background it is only important to understand that both models are static ones and either linear or close to a linear form.

A burning question for many researchers is how good are neural networks as a the technique per se. Therefore they are interested in a comparison between the performance of neural networks under exactly the same conditions as the above mentioned techniques. In the annex, this comparison is discussed in much detail and the interested reader in these comparative matters should consult it. For general purposes, however, a comparison can be useful as an introduction. This example is one of pure comparison. Hence, the way neural networks are used here are not an example of their knowledge building capacity as described in previous chapters. This experiment only suggests its knowledge extracting capacities which in this example clearly proves to be better than what we most often, even if the data on which training has taken place, was not optimal for the use of neural networks.

Breweries are operating in a highly competitive market with often limited profit margins on their products. Therefore, market share and market response are important and require to be followed closely. They also differ in each different market and the different markets behave differently. For a particular major European beer brand we have investigated market response of a number of beer brands on a specific European market. In general, the breweries themselves use both multiple linear regression (MLR) models and multiplicatif (MUL) models for this research. In this particular case the brewery wanted to test the performance of neural networks. In practice this meant that neural networks were trained on the same data and using the same variables as was done with the classical methods.

As we argued in earlier chapters, neural networks can deal with a much larger number of variables and indeed perform better with more variables. Classical approaches intentionally limit the number of variables dramatically in order to avoid multicollinearity: mutual dependence of variables which causes bad estimates. Economic variables are always somewhat correlated and therefore it is necessary for classical approaches to keep the number of variables, used in any specific equation small. This avoids problems of collinearity but it also limits the validity of the model. We improve the statistical performance of the model and we pay for that via a reduced view of reality. If neural networks had been used in their entirety, we would have used more variables and data which were less prepared. For the sake of comparison, however, the number of variables had been kept exactly the same as those used in the classical models and the data used for training and testing were also the exact same data as those used in the other approaches. The training took place on a specific data set, of which half was used to train the neural network and the other half was then used to test its performance. Therefore, the test was a real forecast since it forecasts a series which was not used for the estimation (training) itself.

Five different beer brands were selected in one specific European country. A number of variables were identified which should be taken into account for forecasting the market response. The variables selected were: price, numeric distribution, weighted distribution, numeric out-of-stock, weighted out-of-stock and the share of the total publicity budget (for the entire market). Marketers amongst the readers will certainly recognize these variables. With these variables a multiple linear regression model was estimated, as well as a multiplicatif model. A neural network was trained with the same variables and using the same data-set. We do not want to go in detail on the performance comparison (for detail see van Wezel and Baets, 1995) but only give some observations on the results which were obtained.

Even on the data set used for estimation (training) the neural networks perform better than the classical models, if we consider root mean square error and R^2 as quality indicators. These statistics show how much of the variance in the model is explained by the estimated form of the equation. Both absolute values and relative values have been used for comparison. The neural networks perform better, both on the absolute values of the variables and on the relative ones. For the absolute values the improvement is most dramatic. For some beer brands the difference in explained variance on the trained set was improved from 38 % explained variance to 86 %. The predictive quality of the models is of course not measured on the trained set itself, but rather on a new set which has not been used for training yet.

If we compare the performance on the data set which has not been used for estimation, then the differences in average become even more important. The extreme cases are somewhat less dramatic. Explained variance improves e.g. from 16 % to 50 % or from 29 % to 70 %. In all cases the neural network performs better for the out of sample data, which means the sample which has not already been used to estimate the equations and/or train the neural network. These observations suggest that for forecasting, connectionist knowledge nets are stronger than approaches using equations.

It is important to remind one here that equations need to be identified before we are able to estimate them, whereas neural networks only need a set of variables. During the training, the neural network structures the variables itself. Finding the exact form of the equation for market behavior is difficult and there are no ways in which one can know whether a particular form of an equation is the correct one. Statistical estimation only validates the statistical performance on a specific dataset. The fact that for market response modeling, neural networks do not need a priori forms of equations is in itself a knowledge creating force of connectionist approaches. For the readers interested in a more detailed comparison of the use of classical statistical approaches and neural networks in marketing applications, Venugopal and Baets (1994 a and b) can be consulted.

It should not be concluded out of this research that neural networks always perform better than classical methods. Performance has a lot to do with the nature of the problem. If we can isolate problems which are rather static and linear, then classical approaches will perform better (Weiss and Kulikowski, 1991). In other words, if we are convinced that we work in a static market which behaves linearly, we should not be too concerned with knowledge approaches.

Unfortunately, markets today do not seem to behave like static systems. If we are interested in developing decision support or change support, based on the dynamic properties of the economic system, then neural networks can perform support and visualization which other methods cannot. In that case we are not only interested in forecasts - or rather, we are not really interested in forecasts anymore - but we are interested in developing a system which describes the dynamic behavior of the market and our products. Such systems make the tacit knowledge somewhat explicit and allow for much better management decisions. Furthermore these systems show adaptive behavior and hence change depending on the changing market. While applying such models we are not in the business of forecasting anymore, but in the business of understanding markets in order to manage a company on that market. We are trying to get hold of the necessary knowledge inside and outside the company in order to perform better in a dynamic market. Not only the approach becomes different, so does the aim: manage knowledge and learn from it in order to work on sustainable development of the company.

5.2. Brand imaging

Another typical marketing application is brand imaging. Brand imaging has to do with the creation and the maintenance of a brand value. The brand value of a product is the perception which clients have about a product and which can be based on objective, but mostly on subjective elements. A branded product is something which the client immediately recognizes and which he relates to a set of predefined qualities or to an overall image. As an example one can take German consumer electronics. Though they are not a specific product but rather a group of products, they are branded. Most people will associate them with quality even if they have never experienced it themselves. A BMW car is a branded product. One does not speak about a car anymore, but rather about a BMW. In the past, some products have been so strongly branded that their brand name replaced the object name: Bic is used in many European countries for a pen; Perrier is used in France for a light sparkling water; Spa in Holland is the equivalent of any brand of water; Kodak is widely used for a photographic camera.

Brand images differ from country to country and from culture to culture. This should not surprise us if we know that brands are mainly based on perceptions and after what we have discussed about the contextual dependence of perceptions, it should be clear how important culture is in that respect. Any company interested in brand imaging should pay attention to those cultural aspects.

Branded products are interesting for a company in the sense that they can easily create buyer loyalty and in doing so avoid switching behavior of clients. The image of a brand is to a huge extent a perception problem. Of course, some inherent quality is necessary for a product to become a brand, but once beyond a certain point, perception starts playing an important role. Nobody really knows why loyal buyers remain loyal, but the reasons for this loyalty is part of the knowledge connected with this particular product. This knowledge can be tacit to a high degree. As already suggested earlier, some of the knowledge about your product is in the hands of the client. They know better than yourself why they buy the product, why they remain loyal to the brand and what is not up to level in other brands for them not to change. Clients know what products they want to buy and in many cases they know that better than suppliers do. Any knowledge network approach to the kind of branding problems we discuss here, hence, one has to involve the client in order to capture his input.

Once a brand is created, it is important for a company to manage this brand so that it remains distinctive from other producer's brands. While there are an important number of coffee brands on the markets, it is important to make one particular brand as clearly distinctive from all the others as possible. If two brands were to be perceived to be too close to each other, one of them risks disappearing. If we want to maintain a brand as close a possible to its brand image, we should try and get some idea of the perceptions around the brand.

For a large European coffee and tea producer some research has been done about the possibility of creating a knowledge network about a specific coffee brand in a specific country. The specific research question was whether it was possible to identify a network (connectionist structure) which could provide the company with an idea of the elements of importance for the brand image of a particular coffee brand and its relation with those variables on which the company could have an influence. The latter variables are chemical and technical factors which are variables in the production process of the coffee. The raw product coffee differs from origin. Different coffee crops are used in order to produce the same brand of coffee. Therefore, the production process becomes crucially important in order to make a brand exactly what the clients expect it to be.

A large number of coffee producers exist, but they also have each different brands. If the buyer had the perception that his preferred brand was not as good as before (and this perception can be based on any factor) he could switch brands. If a brand lost its specific brand image, it could disappear completely from the market, even if based on a purely objective analysis, the quality of the product has not changed. In some products, brands are more fashion related than in e.g. coffee. If a brand is more fashion related, this only complicates the risks which a company needs to manage.

Needless to say that in this kind of application, neural networks are used more for their specific strength, since perceptions are involved. In this specific research case only neural networks have been considered, but it was clear that a combination of neural networks with fuzzy logic would have allowed much more attractive knowledge maps. The company attempted earlier tests with classical approaches but they failed to produce output which could be used.

As said earlier, the quality of raw coffee (coffee beans) is not constant and depends, amongst other things, on the origin of the coffee. The production process can change the raw material a little, and the same production process, using the same chemical and physical inputs on different raw beans, will give a different taste. The client who buys the product should always have the perception that he buys the same brand. The only way of manipulating that brand perception is in adapting the production factors once the origin of the coffee beans is known. The origin of the coffee is a given at any specific time. In this research 27 chemical and physical factors have been considered on which the company can have an

For this particular problem a two step approach was applied. In the first stage Kohonen maps (a specific algorithm for unsupervised learning) were used in order to structure the problem. All the input variables (27 chemical-technical, 5 expert taste variables and 3 buyer taste variables) were used in order to train a network. The training created a knowledge net which was able to identify out of a set of coffees, those groups of coffees which were good, medium or bad and a number of gradations in between. The net could perform that on past coffees, as well as on new production lots. The different coffees considered would be represented in order to allow easy comparison. Figure 5.1 is an example of such a representation.

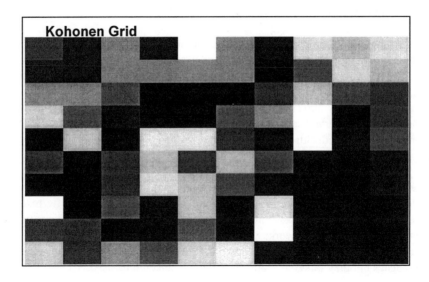

Figure 5.1: Black and white representation of a set of coffees

The pictorial representation of the classification of coffees is a colored square in which each coffee was represented by a smaller square which has a white, black or grey color. The grey color can have a wide range of different varieties, more or less blackish. The more the picture (small square) of a specific coffee appears to be blackish, the better that particular coffee was in the perception of the buyers. In this way we could classify the different coffees, basically mapping perceptions on

The pictorial representation of the classification of coffees is a colored square in which each coffee was represented by a smaller square which has a white, black or grey color. The grey color can have a wide range of different varieties, more or less blackish. The more the picture (small square) of a specific coffee appears to be blackish, the better that particular coffee was in the perception of the buyers. In this way we could classify the different coffees, basically mapping perceptions on perceptions and physical variables. This provides us with a knowledge structure about the coffee production process in respect to the buyer's perceptions.

In a second stage, supervised learning algorithms were used to improve the detail of the analysis. The aim of the knowledge network is to provide information about those variables which the company can influence, based on those observations on which the company has no impact and given the changing (dynamic) perception of the clients. At this stage of the process we are particularly interested to find the influencing factors on the buyer's brand perception with the aim of manipulating the production process in order to produce "good" coffee. Via this analysis we can identify those variables of highest importance for the perceived coffee brand quality. More detail is given in Baets (1997). Figure 5.2 shows that for each of the three brand characteristics on which the clients were questioned (overall taste, bitter, strong) how each of the 32 variables considered influenced the final client's perception. From that overall view, we then distilled those five variables which were most important. For judgment 1, e.g., we found that variable 14 (say, time of the burning of raw coffee beans) was most important and that a rise in variable 14 with one unit, would influence the taste perception of the client with -1.23. For each of the three taste perceptions we identified the five most important influencing variables, as well as its potential influence.

This application is an interesting one in respect to the creation of knowledge networks, using a connectionist approach. Based on a number of perceptions (of the experts and the buyers), combined with some quantitative observations, a picture is made of the production and branding process. This picture shows the knowledge which is involved in this particular production process, using the different perceptions where necessary, but without making the knowledge about the production process explicit. The output is a network which can tackle all new cases, but it is not a description of the production process. The company can use this picture in order to manipulate the production process. If the company feeds

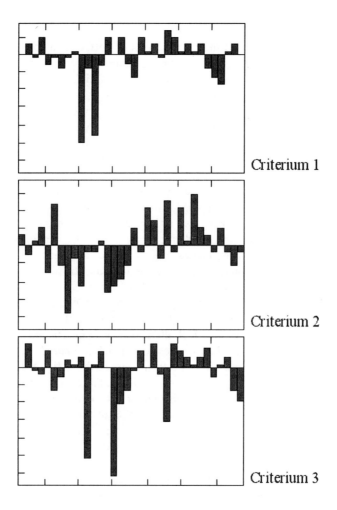

Figure 5.2: Influence of chemical and physical variables on the final client's perception

the system with new observations, it also creates a continuous learning system which shows the evolution of the brand as perceived by the market. This allows a company to react earlier than its competitors to a possible shift in the market. But the company is not able to identify why buyers perceive their brand the way they the company is not able to identify why buyers perceive their brand the way they do. That knowledge is hidden (tacit) in the network and can be used using the "reference" network. It cannot be made explicit and no other technique could dothat. This is a particular characteristic of a connectionist approach. Therefore, connectionist nets can tackle problems which other techniques cannot.

5.3. Introduction strategies in new foreign markets

Introduction strategies for new (possibly emerging) markets is a managerial concern which receives increasing interest in the more global markets of today. Classically, companies will do some market research in order to get a feeling for the characteristics of that market and they will probably combine this with some benchmarking. Benchmarking is a comparison which a company can make with other companies in comparable circumstances: either companies with comparable activities in the market they want to conquer; or companies with the same activities in comparable markets. An obvious outcome of the market research is a number of market segments which should be interested in the product of the new entrant. In approaching only these segments, the launch campaign can be limited and better targeted at the same time. However, the market segmentation approach presumes the existence of homogeneous segments which would not be influenced by the new company/product itself. No positive feed-back is assumed in segmentation approaches. It is also presumed that segments remain stable, at least over the considered time period. It can be argued that if this were the case, then the new company/service would mainly be a replacement of other existing services on that market, in which case it would be very difficult for the new entrant to acquire an interesting market position.

Most of the research undertaken for these kind of problems is qualitative research based on interviews. The analysis of these interviews is extremely difficult and does not automatically deliver an overall picture of the market which the company wants to target. The results of the interviews are often reduced to a number of variables and those variables are brought together in equations which are estimated based on variables derived from interviews. This assumes that answers on questionnaires are context free and that these answers can be reduced without losing context to a limited number of variables. Market research needs a limited number of variables which are as little as possible correlated amongst themselves.

These approaches give a static picture at a specific moment and contain rather straightforward observations.

A connectionist approach aims to train a knowledge network also based on the results of the questionnaires, but containing as many variables as possible and in doing so maintain as much as possible the context of the answers in the knowledge network. This approach implicitly presumes that context is equally as important as the answers themselves. Once the knowledge net is trained, then it is able to answer the kind of questions in which a company is interested for designing introduction strategies, based on the knowledge which the interviews contain but without making explicit the knowledge used.

For a major European airline, research was undertaken to investigate whether the US market could be interesting for its freight carrier activities. In the event that this market proved promising, it is needed to investigate how to design an appropriate introduction strategy (for detail see Baets, 1997). Via classical market research, three segments were identified. Members of those segments were interviewed. Based on the full questionnaire, using all the input from the different segments, new "virtual" segments were identified. Virtual segments are groups of people who share the same kind of thinking in respect to a specific subject, irrespective of their adherence to classical market segments. Members of virtual segments may be members of different market segments. These virtual segments have been identified using Kohonen networks.

Using the knowledge in the trained knowledge network, it could be shown that the classical segments did not really exist in respect to this particular service. They probably do exist in general when considering the freight carrier market, but when applied to the specific service which this airline intended to offer, other virtual segments appeared to exist. Instead of the 3 original segments, 5 virtual segments were identified. In total 57 variables were considered of which many were perceptions. In the questions, three different headings were targeted: the perception of the new service; the perceived weaknesses of comparable services; the switching behavior of potential clients.

Comparable to the previous example on coffee brands, and comparable to figure 5.1, the virtual stakeholder groups could be pictured. It was identified which of these virtual stakeholder groups was most promising. Also comparable to the previous example, the variables (perceptions) which most influenced a particular desired behavior were identified and it could be seen how important their influence was on the desired behavior. Those variables for which the difference between the perceived quality of the new service and the perceived quality of delivery of competitors was the largest, indicated easy entries.

The outcome of the research was in the first place a better segmented market which had an influence on the marketing campaign in order to make it better targeted at a lower price. The second outcome of the research was the identification of those arguments to be used in the marketing campaign which were those perceptions which proved to have most influence on the desired buying (switching) behavior.

A classical approach with market segmentation would have failed and would not have been cost-effective. This more targeted approach was much more effective for a lower cost. This particular research has inspired the company to adapt their introduction strategy accordingly. The real value added, however, will only appear if the company uses this system in order to create moving pictures of the market and its market penetration. In that case they would fully benefit from the dynamic character of the knowledge networks of which the embryo was created in this project.

REFERENCES

Baets W, 1997. Intelligent Decision Support: The Combination of Artificial Neural Networks and Fuzzy Logic (Dutch version). Nijenrode Management Review.

Nicolis G and Prigogine I, 1989. *Exploring Complexity*. Freeman.

Nilson T, 1995. *Chaos Marketing: How to win in a turbulent world*. Mc Graw Hill.

van Wezel M and Baets W, 1995. Predicting Market Responses with a Neural Network: the Case of Fast Moving Consumer Goods. Marketing Intelligence & Planning. Autumn.

Venugopal V and Baets W, 1994a. Neural Networks and Statistical Techniques in Marketing Research: A conceptual comparison. Marketing Intelligence & Planning. Vol. 12, Nr. 7.

Venugopal V and Baets W, 1994b. Neural Networks and their Applications in Marketing Management. The Journal of Systems Management. September.

Weiss S and Kulikowski C, 1991. *Computer Systems that learn: classification and prediction methods from statistics, neural networks, machine learning and expert systems*. San Mateo, CA: Morgan Kaufman Publishers.

6. EXPERIMENTS WITH COMPLEXITY AND DYNAMIC SYSTEMS

In previous chapter we have discussed a number of examples of the use of artificial neural networks in business applications. The aim of these examples was to show the potential power of connectionist approaches to knowledge management. However, most of the given examples were not yet knowledge oriented. For a better understanding of knowledge oriented applications, like the ones we are going to discuss in this chapter, it was necessary to understand thoroughly the functioning of connectionism.

In this chapter the reader is introduced to two different groups of examples. The first group consists of a number of well researched projects, which all aim to create and structure knowledge around business problems in which other knowledge techniques (like experts systems) did not prove to be value added. The second group consists of a number of problems which could be solved with the approaches discussed so far, but which are not yet researched. Most of them are outcomes of brainstorm sessions with companies on the subject mentioned. The aim of describing them here is to suggest a number of dynamic and non-linear situations which managers are confronted with daily. With the examples, possible consequences are suggested of a reduction of these problems via simple linear approximations, like the ones we often use today. With these examples we want to invite the reader to start thinking about his own managerial context and support him to identify interesting situations where improvement can be obtained. All the examples have to do with the consequences of the dynamic behavior of our economic environment and with the use of neural networks and/or fuzzy logic as a way to support change processes in such a turbulent environment. They relate neural networks to knowledge management and complex behavior. They concentrate on the creation and sharing of knowledge and the necessary learning attitude of the managerial environment.

6.1. Perception mapping in banking

6.1.1. Introduction

During the past few years, we have witnessed a growing interest in the topic of organizational learning and change. The idea gained ground that organizations of tomorrow, unlike today's "command and control type" organizations, more than anything else need to develop the capability to learn, adapt and change (de Geus, 1988; Senge, 1990; Leonard-Barton, 1992; Haeckel and Nolan, 1993). Different concepts of organizational learning share the view that while people are a key organizational resource, it is more appropriate to perceive them as being intrinsically motivated, curious and willing to learn and take action. In other words, and referring to previous chapters, a transition takes place from a resource-based to a knowledge-generating organization.

In banking particularly, until recently, management was concerned with the optimal use of the different resources (people, material, production capacity, etc.). These days, the core processes get more attention, since they would create the value added (Kaplan and Murdock, 1990). Eventually, a number of companies got involved in business process re-engineering or re-design and banks are very often front-runners in this. However, the business process is more than a purely logistic integration. Business processes specifically in the services is related to the body of knowledge created and managed inside the company, independent of whether this knowledge is kept implicit or explicit (Johansson et al., 1993). That is where process re-engineering and knowledge management get together. If no knowledge is available and shared on the context of a specific process and its economic environment, any re-engineering process can be considered as "out of the blue".

In this section real life applications in banking are reported. The aim of the project was to create knowledge maps about the IS strategy alignment process (MacDonald, 1991; Baets, 1992; Henderson and Venkatraman, 1993): can we identify and visualize the context of the IS strategy alignment process which makes this process a success or a failure. These knowledge maps measure and represent perceptions of managers. They can be used as tools in the process of organizational learning and change, as well as in the mere process of knowledge creation. However, knowledge creation in banking in general is still in an experimental phase, at least if we consider knowledge in the broad sense like has been discussed so far. The research project discussed here describes a specific example of such a knowledge map.

During the research project, an attempt was also made to validate a "corporate knowledge map" (see further on for a detailed description) using classical statistical techniques. Only limited success was obtained. Therefore, experiments with neural networks were undertaken. It eventually provided the common ground throughout the company in respect to the level of knowledge, necessary for an improved understanding of the business process context.

For a good understanding of the concept of "knowledge mapping", the reader should be aware of the emergent shift which takes place in strategy theories. Amongst the different schools of thought (Mintzberg, 1989, 1990), the "prescriptive" group treats strategy formation as a two phase activity of conceptual design followed by implementation. Mintzberg (1990), Rockart and Hofman (1992) and Senge (1990) argue that strategy is much more an emergent process of a learning organization and that change is ongoing: it is not an event; it is a process. The approach used for this research project adheres the latter point of view on strategy.

Since IS strategy alignment is identified as important for the decade to come in most industries, but certainly also in banking (CSC Index, 1992; Niederman et al., 1991), it appeared to be an interesting case for this application. Based on a research project in a number of European banks, data was gathered in order to create and validate a knowledge map. This map attempts to integrate in one system, issues of corporate strategy, macro-economic environment, micro-economic behavior, IS strategy and planning, organizational forms and managerial mind sets. The gathered data were all perception-like, since many of the above mentioned issues cannot be expressed in purely quantitative data.

6.1.2. Business process engineering and IS strategy alignment

Scope

IS strategy alignment aims to bring the corporate strategy and the IS strategy closer together in such a way that they mutually balance each other. In practice, this often boils down to re-engineering business processes. Therefore it can be of help to describe briefly what is understood by business process (re-)engineering (BPR) in this example. Based on actual research and publications, information technology management, organizational change and business process engineering (e.g. Ramaswami et al., 1992; Benjamin and Blunt, 1992; Rockart and Hofman, 1992; Niederman et al., 1991) are identified as the core of the same effort to improve corporate performance.

Business process (re-)engineering has to do with knowledge of companies and how this knowledge can be created and exploited inside these organizations (Johansson et al., 1993; Davidson, 1993). It might also usefully include a discussion on what information is strategic and what is not, as well as on what corporations do with this information, or, eventually, what corporate learning is really about (Senge, 1990; Leonard-Barton, 1992). Within the actual interest for business process re-engineering, one of the key issues is knowledge management for decision making, starting with a better understanding of the business processes themselves (Johansson et al., 1993; Knorr, 1991; Kaplan and Murdock, 1990).

Objectives and theoretical founding

Managers today seem to have difficulty in describing the business processes in which they are involved. This could be caused, either by a fragmented view of their own situation or the rapidly changing environment (changing strategy, increased competition in the market, chaotic behavior of markets, etc.) (Stacey, 1993). Research seems to confirm the managers' fragmented view of their own business, in the particular case of banking, in relation to IS strategy alignment (Baets, 1993). Therefore we have tested a number of maybe remarkable hypotheses in order to have a clear indication of the problems of building the appropriate contextual information for process re-engineering. Once we have an idea about the problems related to this context for business processes, we can use these inputs for our knowledge maps. The hypotheses tested and validated (Baets, 1996b) were :

> **1.** Managers have difficulty in defining their company's strengths and weaknesses, in respect to the market. They find it difficult to agree on the buyers behavior and on the influence of the market (economic environment) on the bank. They have difficulty in coping with the definition of their information needs for decision making, even if they are highly skilled professionals.

> **2.** Bank executives are unable to draw an explicit link between banking problems and their solutions using IT. Knowledge of banking issues (not skills) improves the understanding of the IS planning and strategy process.

> **3.** Most IS issues in literature are known by managers, even those issues related to organizational matters and the IS process.

> **4.** Different organizational structures produce different mindsets in respect to the IS planning and strategy process.

> **5.** Managerial mind sets are relevant to the understanding of and attitude towards the IS planning and strategy process.

The validation of these hypotheses suggested that some shared knowledge is missing and therefore a tool seems desirable to support communication between developers and users about the business processes themselves (Leonard-Barton, 1992). The eventual tool should concentrate on organizational modeling or "intellectualization of business processes" (Haeckel and Nolan, 1993). This is the process of the creation of a model of the business process, including organizational and environmental factors. In a further stage, this tool can play an important role in training (learning) of users (managers).

It is generally claimed that decision support requires a better understanding of the business processes on which decisions are based (Firebaugh, 1989; de Callatay, 1992). Representation of (tacit) knowledge is important in this respect.

The theoretical basis for the case tested here is known as the IS Strategy Alignment theory (Henderson and Venkatraman, 1993; Baets, 1992; MacDonald, 1991; Parker et al., 1988). Figure 6.1 shows the process of aligning IS strategy with corporate processes (corporate strategy). At the left of the figure, one can observe the corporate strategy and the corporate organization. At the right of the figure one observes the IS organization and the IT strategy. Those four should fit together in a process which is indicated by the arrows on the figure. The flow of the process as indicated with these arrows balances the corporate strategy through the organization after which a balance is established with the IS organization. A possible present mismatch can lead to improved IT support which in turn can boost the corporate strategy. Understanding this overall business process requires knowledge of the different parts of this process, as well as of their interaction. In addition, as Figure 6.1 shows, the corporate environment is important in the analysis of information needed. Given the many uncertainties around this overall business process and given the importance of the corporate context, a successful alignment process can benefit from a tool (a map) to facilitate the process and to improve the communication between all people involved in this process.

The creation of the corporate map, which is central to the process of alignment, is based on perceptions of the business people involved (Baets, 1992). Most of the information which managers use while taking decisions is based on perceptions.

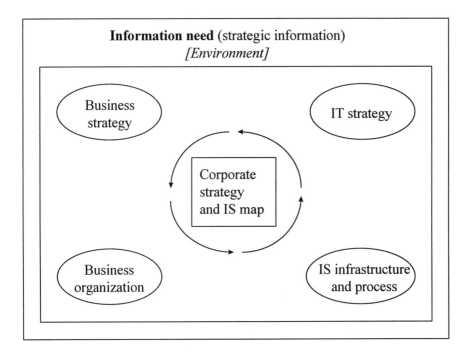

Figure 6.1: Extended Strategic Alignment Model
(Baets, 1992)

In this particular case of the banking industry, a rough example of that overall business process has been identified, based on literature and field research. Such a business process description for a bank is shown in Figure 6.2. Figure 6.2 only indicates the headings under which a series of issues of importance are re-grouped; it does not give all the detail which is inside such a map (for the full list of issues, see (Baets, 1993)). The map itself is of less importance for the example. The process of creation of the knowledge tool gets most attention, since this is the core of a knowledge creating process.

6.1.3. A case study from the banking industry

As said earlier, this research project takes the IS Strategy Alignment process of
figure 6.1 as the basic business process considered. A provisional knowledge tool
(see Figure 6.2) was designed and research validated that tool. The process of
creation of the knowledge tool is briefly described below.

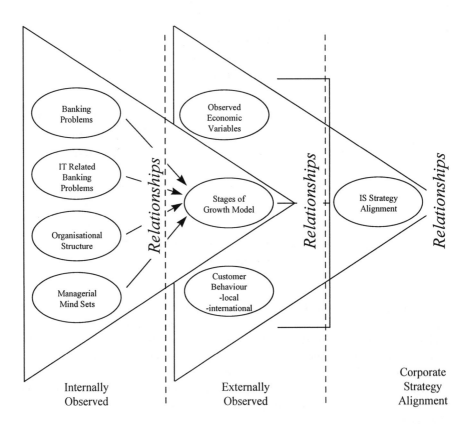

**Figure 6.2: Corporate map, describing business processes within a bank
(Baets, 1993; after Baets, 1992).**

A number of issues needed to construct the alignment map in banking were identified from the literature and through research. These key issues were described in the literature under the following headings:

- Squeezed margins on the interest rate products (Baets, 1991; PA Technology, 1990)
- Competition (PA Technology, 1990; Dockery, 1991)
- Geographic deregulation (PA Technology, 1990)
- Dilution of identity (Litan, 1991; Dockery, 1991)
- Human Resources management (Essinger and Rosen, 1989; Belgian Banking Association, 1990a, 1990b)
- Rules and Regulations (Harvard Business Review, 1991; Seidman, 1991)
- Information technology (Baldwin, 1991).

A detailed list of around 50 issues was used in a pilot research project (amongst 32 managers of one bank). The outcome of the pilot project was a ranking and regrouping in the following 8 sections :

- banking problems
- IT-related banking issues
- organizational issues
- the managerial mind set
- IS strategy planning
- economic environment
- buyer and market behavior
- IS strategy alignment process

These headings are found in figure 6.2. The map in figure 6.2 also shows the links between the issues identified and shows how they are part of the IS strategy alignment process. For the organizational structure, we referred to the Mintzberg terminology (1973, 1979; Mintzberg and Waters, 1983) and used structures like "bureaucracy", "entrepreneurial environment" and an organization based on "ad hoc management". For the measurement of the individual manager's mind set, Kolb's terminology (1983) was used which defines the analytical (reactive) and the creative (proactive) mind set as the two main ones. For the representation of the IS strategy and planning process, the terminology of a Stages of Growth Model (Galliers, 1991; Galliers and Sutherland, 1991) has been accepted as a valid one. Such a stages of growth model assumes that IS development takes place in a number of different steps in a specific order. Factors of importance for IS in such a model are e.g. skills, staff, systems.

Research in four European Banks (Baets, 1993, 1996b), in which around 60 managers participated, gathered data on manager's perceptions on these issues. Based on these data (perceptions), neural networks were trained which structured the tacit knowledge of the 60 interviewees. Figure 6.2 and its arrows was detailed in the form of a network which was able to produce and reproduce the mind sets of the different participating managers. In its capacity of doing so, the network contained the tacit knowledge which the participating managers possessed about their business process within its context. This trained network was then able to deal with new cases, new people or new situations.

The challenges

It is important that business process (re-)engineering makes use of a representation of a kind of the tacit knowledge which is key to the process considered. This knowledge cannot be considered outside its economic and organizational context. As opposed to product metrics which mainly concentrate on quantifiable issues, it is clear in the IS theory that non-quantifiable issues like organizational and human factors are of paramount importance (Baets, 1992). Only limited work has been done in this area (Norden, 1993).

This process of the creation of knowledge maps is in some kind an "intellectualization" of business processes and therefore it contributes to the creation of the repository of knowledge which we discussed in earlier chapters. If we can visualize the necessary inherent knowledge in case of a specific business process, without making it explicit and hence without loosing its tacit quality, we acquire useful information for management decisions. This is a step in the creation of a corporate IQ (Haeckel and Nolan, 1993): the body of knowledge which is the real value added of the company. It is this knowledge which differentiates one company from another. Eventually, this knowledge can have different forms:

objective knowledge, skills, adequate mind sets, adequate organizational forms, etc.

For detail on the research itself, the reader can refer to Baets (1996b).

6.1.4. Some observations based on this experiment

This project experimented with the use of neural networks for knowledge generation, with the aim to support an organizational change process. IS Strategy Alignment is taken as an example of contextual business process engineering. This research project revealed certain qualities of neural networks in case of the creation of corporate knowledge (maps).

Based on the experience of this project, we can conclude that neural networks can be used in a number of different ways. Neural networks enabled the "identification" of the corporate map. This corporate knowledge can then be used in a second stage for identifying the context of new alignment problems and/or for learning. This knowledge map could be used by individual managers who wanted to learn more about the experience of their bank in respect to IS Strategy Alignment. Therefore, an individual manager could learn from the general knowledge acquired inside a bank, independent of the fact that the particular manager himself had never been in contact with IS strategy alignment previously.

Typical of a knowledge map is the presence of both quantitative and qualitative issues. The latter issues relate to the human factors and the organizational issues. Furthermore, those soft issues should be integrated with the quantitative ones, in order to form one integrated corporate map. As has been argued, the organizational and human issues are extremely important for the success of IS Strategy, but it has always been very difficult to include these in other knowledge tools. Furthermore, the data gathered are not really physical observations, but human perceptions. Since most of management research is concerned with human perceptions, the use of neural networks for knowledge generation is promising.

Neural networks are not only a tool to generate knowledge, they are as much a tool to represent knowledge and to exploit it. Once a neural network is trained adequately, one can be sure that for any given input (case), the network will generate the correct output (how to deal with this particular case). Since neural networks generate implicit numerical connectors, one can imagine reversing these connections into an expert-type system. As is commonly known, the major problems related to the limited success of expert systems in management applications have more to do with the process of knowledge generation, than with problems related to software and development (Firebaugh, 1989).

Based on the results of this research project, some additional features of neural networks have to be mentioned. Neural networks prefer exact observations, with a clear spread (e.g. outliers) rather than observations with a strong common tendency. A second interesting feature of neural networks relates to the fact that they do not need predefined equations to be estimated. Neural networks, therefore, imply the need to concentrate on the elements (knots or neurons) of a network of knowledge building blocks, more than on equations describing knowledge (if they were in existence). This feature in particular, allows us to research into non-linear dynamic equations.

Applied to business process (re-)engineering, a tool based on neural networks can be used as a facilitator for the communication between managers (functional, line and IS managers). The "knowledge map" can make the context of the business process somewhat explicit, before one tries to engineer or even re-engineer it. As argued before, it cannot be assumed that managers are able to describe a business process clearly enough, or that they have a common idea about a particular business process. Corporate knowledge maps, based on e.g. neural networks, can bring us beyond the pure technique of business process engineering and back to corporate concerns. Business process re-engineering should be a general management concern and, hence, need to cover issues like organizational design, human mind sets, communication, alongside financial concerns and effectiveness matters.

Another observation based on this research project is that there is still important prejudice against neural networks, even though it has been argued and confirmed that neural networks are closely linked to the way managers (and people in general) think (de Callatay, 1992). Any real life application can suffer from this prejudice.

Knowledge representation is still "the" problem behind all Artificial Intelligence discussions (Firebaugh, 1989). Where information has to do with numbers, strings and Boolean values, knowledge has to do with processes, procedures, actions, causalities, time, motivation, goals and common sense reasoning. Once we try and use these alternative methods in business applications we become more aware of the necessity to include them in our analysis.

This research suggested also that there is a close link between the capacity to generate and manage knowledge on the one hand, and the IT infrastructure supporting this process on the other hand. Therefore, in the next chapter we will develop a possible IT architecture to support knowledge networks.

Once integration of quantitative and qualitative elements has been established, trade-offs can be derived between quantitative elements and qualitative elements. Based on an adequate knowledge map, one can imagine the comparison of two alternative corporate policies, which were previously impossible to compare; such as, for example, comparing internal reorganization versus external communication (publicity) in the light of an improvement in corporate strategy.

6.2. Client profiles for a more aggressive and better informed front-office

Service companies are increasingly aware of the necessity to develop closer relationships with their clients. In this example, we focus on the example of banks, but any conclusion drawn or observation made for banks can easily be transferred to e.g. consulting companies, insurance companies, etc. Banks all have a brand name and at least from the individual's point of view the difference between banks increasingly becomes the level of service, rather than pricing. If we say that the service level becomes important, perceptions become important, since service levels are based on the user's perception. Banks have observed that clients are not too brand-loyal anymore, at least compared to earlier years. Therefore, the marketing and sales force of banks has to be organized a little more aggressively. Banks should know their clients more intimately and they should offer services which perfectly fit any specific client. If banks fail to offer on time a specific service to a particular client, the client is going to shop with other banks and may find a service elsewhere better and/or cheaper. If a client switches for one product, then the risk is high that he could do the same for other services or products. If banking products become increasingly like consumer goods, then it will become difficult to continue cross-subsidizing different services. Furthermore, some banks may attract only clients with lower credit ratings or they may only be able to offer services on which they make lower margins. Reasons enough for banks to become interested in a more aggressive marketing approach. In common terms we could say: the banking market is becoming increasingly more competitive. More aggressive marketing can only be based on better information about the client base.

Banks were amongst the early investors in Information Technology and today many of them have a well established database of their clients containing amongst other things, interesting transaction data. Today, many banks use it rather passively. If we accept the appearance of positive feedback phenomena on the banking market, as described in earlier chapters, it could be extremely interesting for banks to make the first move for any particular client. In order to be able to do that, the bank should have a good idea about what the clients really want and what kind of services he would like to have next. Very practically can a bank identify amongst its clients, those clients who are close to buying a house and hence need a mortgage loan ? If they can do so, they can approach these clients with interesting offers, before these clients start shopping around for better deals with competitor banks. Another well known example where improvement is possible in the front office is the one of a person who goes into a branch of his bank which is not his, and the bank people are only able to give this person the balance of his current account. In case the client wants to discuss e.g. a loan for a boat (imagine a stand at a boat show), the bank clerk has no idea how this client is really like or what he is interested in. The bank clerk is not able to differentiate the offer and adapt it to that specific client. He can only treat all potential clients equally. If more information were available about the client in a knowledge network, this network would be able to deal with any new client profile much more flexibly, based on the experience which it has learned in the past. Limited information on the client would allow this system to position this person immediately and transform this client profile into an adequate one for the bank. Such a system could suggest better deals for good clients or for new clients or whatever seems the best at that time. It all boils down to client profiles.

A commercial system based on a knowledge network operates as follows. When a client identifies himself via answering a few questions, he can be positioned in a class of "club-members" (virtual segment) having more or less the same financial background, wishes and interests. The system suggests solutions for this client, before he even states the problem. The more the client fills in details about what he is interested in, the more specific the advice the system can provide. This process of transformation of information on the client into an adapted or refined offer takes place dynamically. These kind of applications bring the knowledge of the back-office straight into the front-office. What has to be decided today in main branches of banks, can then be decided on the spot in any local branch or on any stand on a special event (say at a boat show or holiday fair).

Which reader has not experienced the frustration of entering a branch office where nobody is able to answer any other question than those related to money transfers. Any other request has to be dealt with by the main branch and even information has to be given by that main branch. A few years ago a large bank launched a new service which was a central number to announce theft of bank and credit cards. If the client registered all his credit cards, bank cards and any other important documents like passports, etc, with the bank, one phone-call is enough to block all the cards and accounts. Furthermore, the clients are informed when their passport expires, etc. Not bad as an idea and certainly interesting given the multitude of cards which clients have today. Only, the bank was not even able to deliver an application form in which the cards which the client had with their bank were already indicated. This service was obviously developed isolated from the main database as a stand alone. Furthermore, it took 3 to 4 times sending documents back and forth before all cards were registered. Any change in address or card number (and banks do change card numbers), made a new series of document exchanges necessary. To cut a long story short, the value added of the system was lost, since no (obvious) knowledge was built into the system. Any person could have developed this service independent of the bank's prior knowledge. The general idea is one of straight forward programming. Write down all card numbers on a sheet of paper together with the phone-numbers where to cancel them. Write down all important documents you have and their expiry dates. Give this sheet of paper to your mother-in-law (any other person having some natural talent for law and order could do too). Call her whenever something happens (in many cases you will have to do that anyway). This was a missed chance to develop a more knowledge based approach which could have provided a better service at the end.

Another example of the same phenomenon are the letters which many of us receive from banks warning us that the balance we have in our current account is high. Instead of writing that the client was probably losing x-amount of money with his money sleeping in an account and what it could have produced if it had been invested, a general letter is written with no specific suggestions at all. This also seems to be a missed chance, since if the bank had client profiles it would be able to suggest solutions for the particular client, which goes beyond the classical savings accounts and which fit into the client's pattern of living and/or spending. Nowadays, a standard letter goes out to all clients.

How can we conceive a system which identifies client profiles dynamically ? A number of different information sources should be brought together and combined. First we have the information that banks posses about their clients. Furthermore, banks should get hold of behavioral information which can either be bought externally from market research companies or which could also exist or be created inside the company. But foremost they need to have their own experience base about their different clients, including a history of payments, loans, etc. Based on the combination of this information, neural networks can be trained which identify different virtual client groups. Each virtual client group can then be considered as a client profile. The use of neural networks in such a database produces a knowledge system which gives insight into the different client group's potential behavior. Such a system can position any client within its "client profile". But such a system can also identify potential new clients who best fit one or another client profile. Not all clients fit a profile of a particular bank.

Based on this information, clients can be approached more efficiently and effectively, turning passive bank marketing, mainly based on mailings into a more aggressive client approach. Existing clients can be offered services which probably correctly fit into their spending pattern of today. It fits into their logical next demand for financial services. If the client profiles are used on external databases, we can identify potential clients which fit the banks profile. Different specific potential client groups can be targeted with specific services fitting the target group with a high hit-rate.

This example of client profiles transfers the knowledge and intelligence of the back-office into the front-office. As we all remember from our visits to banks, bank clerks can seldom answer questions which go beyond the day to day business. It would minimize a lot of client anger if bank clerks could at least give some advice on a broad range of problems. Since no human being is probably able to posses all the knowledge for general purpose advice, bank clerks should be supported with knowledge systems of the kind described above. Instead of asking clients or potential clients to contact the knowledge source which is often located in headquarters, the bank decentralizes that knowledge base throughout the network of branches. Clients can consult the bank's knowledge base locally and probably in the future, from their homes.

Hence the problem is broadened from identifying different client profiles to the creation of a front-office application which contains the intelligence of the bank's back-office. Many banks these days are interested in these kind of front-office applications. Unfortunately, too often they exclusively consider expert systems. As we have discussed in earlier chapters, expert systems are not made to capitalize on this kind of knowledge in the back-office. Expert systems deal with very focused applications of a rather static nature.

Compared to expert systems, neural networks applications are adaptive techniques. They show learning behavior, comparable to learning behavior of human beings. This not only updates the application. Once this application is developed and used, the use creates continuously new or adapted knowledge on client behavior. Such a system provides the bank with a continuous monitoring system about their client's service profile.

6.3. Risk management

An important bank application in which adaptive systems can deliver important value added is risk management. For a number of years already, banks have been developing risk management systems. Of the wide spread of risk management applications, Assets and Liabilities Management Systems (ALM's) are the most exciting. Most operational applications use advanced quantitative techniques in order to calculate e.g. durations, alphas and betas and in order to match all that in a balancing system. More behavioral or process oriented elements are neglected for the simple fact that they are difficult to express in numbers. Therefore, ALM's are often considered as advanced calculation engines which do their calculations in disregard of their business environment. However, bank managers know very well that e.g. market tendencies, competitor cross-moves, market behavior (which are again perceptions), processes of positive feed-back, etc., all play an important role for risk management. Quantitative techniques have proven weak for trapping context bound deviations. Adaptive techniques, on the other hand, are conceived for that.

In order to illustrate the importance of a context bound approach in risk management, instead of a purely quantitative one, we describe the real life case of an insurance company. An important, but not top-rated, insurance company was very proud to have as one of their main clients a large petroleum/chemical company. They considered having this client as a guarantee for a long term survival. It also happened that this chemical company was doing rather well and therefore their stock value was doing well on the stock market. Hence, it was decided to invest in shares of that company for the insurance company's portfolio. Insurance companies cover the potential disaster of their contracts (which figures on the liabilities' side of their balance) by money making investments of stable quality (which are assets for the insurance company). This insurance company was very happy again to have quite a number of the petroleum company shares in their portfolio. Both facts separately can only be good news for a company. However, the combination of both in the same balance sheet was potential dynamite for this company. If anything went wrong with the petroleum/chemical company, say a major explosion with environmental and human damage, then the insurance company would be hit twice. It would have to pay for the coverage of the disaster, and on top of that their stock value in the chemical company would go down, which would affect the insurance company's balance sheet. Their ALM system did not show that. An adaptive system could have shown this, provided that it was designed to do so.

6.4. Quality management

6.4.1. Introduction

In this section we discuss a case of how knowledge creation and learning can be of importance during major change processes. Quality management is the common denominator of this set of examples. Major change processes have to do with changing the perceptions of stakeholders, who all have, in general, different aims and experiences. In the different cases, an attempt is made to visualize (map) a change process via the perceptions of the different stakeholders. In a later stage software tools are constructed which allow people to observe the different perceptions and to play around with these "knowledge maps". The aim of this tool and of this approach in general is to support a learning process. When different stakeholders use the software tool, they can observe different attitudes and learn from them. This tool allows stakeholders to get a view on how other stakeholders perceive the problem. All this takes place in a non-confrontational environment and the approach allows having large numbers of people and stakeholder groups involved. Since the outcome is a software tool, this tool can also be put at the disposal of many people via a computer network.

The examples given deal with quality control issues. The one has to do with issues of control of processes and quality of output (environmental concern), and the other deals with the quality control procedures during maintenance works at motorways. In both cases, the stakes are high and differ for the different stakeholders. In both cases, the different parties involved have a priori attitudes which are not really co-operative but rather opposed to each other. What has been attempted is to research whether one can build a software tool or a support system of any kind which has the following qualities:

1. Contain all the tacit knowledge which the different stakeholders (e.g. including "clients") have about the process to be changed.
2. Picture (visualize) a situation and its evolution via the *perceptions* of *all* stakeholders.
3. Attempt to keep as much of the initial complexity in this picture as possible, as well as attempt to keep as much variety of perceptions as possible.
4. Visualize this network of mutually connected opinions and positions in a way that the different stakeholders could "play" with the perceptions of each other and "learn" from this.
5. Via the stakeholders who question the system, create a procedure of continuous adaptation of the picture of the process. The system should learn from the questions of the stakeholders and the system should evolve based on the learning behavior of the users.

6. Translate this picture into rules which are understandable for managers; hence avoid the use of equations and mathematics. In the first place we would use terminology which is used in the brochures or leaflets for stakeholders.
7. Use the adaptive (learning) qualities of the tool to identify which rules are of real importance. Allow the tool to suggest what can be learned from this particular process and which could be of use in other comparable situations. Allow people to learn from the experience of other.

In general, this approach and the resulting tools contain a number of qualities which can be found in hardly any support systems. This approach shows learning and adaptive behavior, based on the changing perceptions and the learning of the stakeholders themselves (e.g. clients, personnel, suppliers, etc.). The system adapts gradually according to learning which takes place with the people who use it. The system learns from the users and hence the system does not force the users to think the way the application does. The system uses "vague" (fuzzy) rules which are close to the normal manager's reasoning. The research project which is commented on, suggests that such a system seems to show some intelligent behavior, somewhat close to human reasoning. However, it should not be concluded that we are close to machines which replace human thinking.

In general, the creation and development of such systems pass through a number of stages. A first stage consists of making an inventory of issues of importance for the quality process considered, which are recognizable for all stakeholders. These issues are not the same as definitions of quality. Issues are related to quality but do not define it. Some of the issues maybe related vaguely. The advantage of related issues, rather than definitions is that definitions are also excluding as much as they are clarifying. Issues are much more open ended and more people will recognize themselves more easily in issues, rather than in definitions. These issues can be mutually overlapping, but the more issues we can identify, the better this is for the eventual tool.

In a next stage, a questionnaire is built using these issues in order to be distributed amongst the stakeholders; not only the stakeholders within one's own company but also amongst external stakeholders, e.g. clients and suppliers. All stakeholders score the issues on a 1-10 Likert-type scale, considering the importance or the degree in which they are recognized by the interviewee. This process is probably the most time consuming.

With these results, neural networks are trained which in a further step are translated into visual representations, "maps" or "pictures". During this part of the process virtual stakeholder groups are identified, which often go across the original stakeholder groups. It is the existence of these virtual stakeholder groups which make it possible that things change at all. If amongst the pool of different individual stakeholders there are no groups of people sharing some ideas about the problem, than this would provide an extremely difficult starting point. Finally, this approach allows us to identify the issues of convergence and divergence amongst the stakeholders.

In general, the results of this part of the procedure have still an outcome which is not automatically accessible by all managers. Importance should be given to the development of an attractive man-machine interface. We are not going to deal with this aspect at all here, which should not suggest that this stage would be less important for overall success.

Before going into more detail in the examples, it is worth mentioning where the learning takes place in this approach. Each query to the system by a stakeholder, with the aim of learning about how other stakeholders think, in itself gives insight into how the person who questions the system thinks. Each query, hence, becomes a new piece of information for the system. It completes the database in relation to that particular problem. Comparable to how a human being learns from all experiments he experiences, a system is able to learn from each new observation it makes. In this specific case, learning takes place via the learning capacity of neural networks. The combination of the use of a tool for the creation of new individual experiments, combined with group sessions to get more insight into the problem and further combined with the learning (adaptive) behavior of the system itself, gives this approach a rather unique learning characteristic.

6.4.2. An example of an application in a chemical plant

In this section, an example is given about quality management in the chemical industry. The desired change process centers around quality management, about which a number of different stakeholders have different perceptions. The chemical company wants to innovate a production plant and introduces a new production process. The management is responsible for delivering a good quality product and, of course, there is pressure to produce this at the lowest possible cost. The management of the company is one stakeholder group and the shareholders are a distinct second one. There are at least two more stakeholder groups. First there are the environmental rules and regulations which the company should follow (the stakeholder in this is the local/central authority). It is possible and probable that these rules are in conflict with the aim of a low production cost and even maybe with the desired quality level. Furthermore, these rules are not always clear and strict and they are open to interpretation. This implies that the application of these rules is based on the perceptions on this matter of both parties involved (company and government). A fourth party involved are the people living in the neighborhood (often represented by action committees or "green" committees). The way the different parties talk about the new plant is almost exclusively based on perceptions and very rarely on facts.

This is a typical example of a situation where neural networks can be used in order to visualize the business process (introduction of a new production plant) considered, as well as the change process related to it. There are imprecise, multiple and often opposed aims expressed by a number of different stakeholders. Many of the different issues involved cannot be measured objectively. Often there is rather a mistrust between the different stakeholders. In general, the stakeholders do not even agree on definitions of e.g. quality, quality of life, and, even worse, many different definitions exist.

In such cases, it is a value added to be able to draw a "picture" of the stakes involved in a way which does not confront the different stakeholders from the beginning. Direct meetings between stakeholder groups at the initial stage of the process often lead to debates with no solutions. A consensus is difficult to find. Furthermore, in such processes it is rather difficult to define relationships between "fuzzy" variables. The stakeholders know which elements or issues play a role, but it is extremely difficult to define the relationships between the different elements. If we can construct a "picture" of the process and show it to the different stakeholders with the aim that they can discover mutual points of view without immediately going into debates on principles, then value added is created.

Via different sources (existing studies, interviews, internal memo's of the considered stakeholders) information is gathered on the possible issues of importance for the considered process. At no stage relationships or influences between issues are identified, since these are based on the individual mental maps of the different people involved (Kim, 1993). Relationships do not exist in the absolute, but they are based on the mental map (the individual internal knowledge net) of each individual. Since the ultimate aim is to influence these individual mental maps we should not take them for granted at this stage. At this stage we want to avoid existing mental maps interfering with the ultimate goal.

In order to validate the issues raised, testing takes place with people from the different stakeholder groups. After validation, a questionnaire is constructed in which the importance of the different issues can be scored on a Likert-type 1 to 10 scale. The questionnaires are distributed amongst all stakeholder groups.

Via unsupervised learning algorithms neural networks identify a number of possible structures in the data. This procedure may show not only a different set of issues then those considered beforehand, but it could also show a different structure and/or sequence of issues from those already known before. It could well be, for instance, that issues always considered as crucial by the marketing department do not prove to be important for other stakeholders. Another possible outcome is that though people do not agree on definitions of quality, in real life cases they seem to have a common understanding anyway. Eventually a representation will allow us to identify possible structures which emerged out of perceptions and not structures based on predetermined mental models.

In order to communicate this structure amongst all the stakeholders and in order to allow the emergence of common mental maps about the considered process, a visualization should be constructed. For this we can use interactive software tools of different kinds which would facilitate the use by stakeholders. Via networks (e.g. groupware) these pictures can be distributed, but also discussed amongst stakeholders. The possible impact of this approach could be much higher than with other classical communication tools (paper, workshops) (Chen et al., 1994). Specifically for change processes where many individuals and/or groups are involved, this is an additional advantage.

The map which is created in this way does not picture a common average idea, but contains the different views, the diversity and variety of opinion. Compared to other cognitive mapping techniques (Eden, 1988) this is clearly a strength of neural networks. Cognitive mapping strives for a consensus, where consensus possibly does not even exist. It is not excluded that we do not agree about change processes but that we nevertheless need to be able to work with different stakeholder groups. Specifically in such cases it is important to keep as far as possible the diversity of opinion on the problem and not to strive from the beginning to reach a consensus (an average).

The result of a trained neural network is a matrix of values where virtual groups, comprising members of different stakeholder groups are set out against the issues considered. Arbitrarily, choices need to be made about the number of issues and the number of groups. The more virtual groups one allows, the more detailed information one keeps, but the overall picture is less accessible. If one chooses for less virtual groups, detail is lost but "behavior" is easier to understand. There is no best choice in this respect and experience in any particular situation will show what is workable.

This matrix can be represented in a number of different ways. An easy example is a graph representation where the result resembles a wheel of a bicycle (see figures 6.3 and 6.4). On each of the spokes an issue is represented. The user can click on a spoke, gets the issue printed on the screen and a scale to score the issue is also printed. If a user does this for a number of issues, the system calculates which virtual group the user is most probably part of and shows all the other issues of that virtual group on the graph.

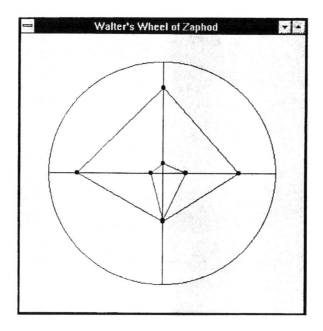

Figure 6.3: Example 1 of a simplified visual representation of issues

Figure 6.3 gives a simplified example of a system with only four issues. The difference between the outer quadrigone and the inner one can be the difference between the perception of a particular person on four issues compared to the perception of his nearest "virtual" group. In that case, the differences are highest on the northern, eastern and western axis and hence this identifies the axis on which to concentrate the change process. A tool allows at each point to compare a particular mindset with an overall one, or with the one of any particular virtual stakeholder group. In reality, these representations contain more issues.

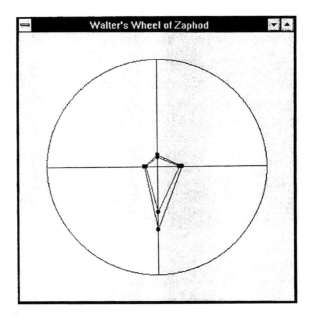

Figure 6.4: Example 2 of a simplified visual representation of issues

Figure 6.4 is a simplified example of a case which is extremely close to the virtual group's perception. Figure 6.4 could also be a picture at the end of a learning process. The particular stakeholder started from a mental map like the one of figure 6.3. Via using the system, observing and learning how other stakeholders see this matter, the individual gradually adapts his mental model. Eventually he acquires enough knowledge in order to be able to join the virtual group illustrated in both figure 6.3 and 6.4 (the inner quadrigone). The tool allows us to visualize the evolutionary path from figure 6.3 to figure 6.4. Hence the tool shows the learning path which that particular individual goes through.

In the real life case, these representations are richer (more issues, more explanations, interactive questioning, etc.) and the possibilities of the tool also allow us to visualize the learning behavior itself. This tool produces an immediate overall picture of the mind set of the virtual group in respect to a particular business process. It allows comparison between virtual stakeholder groups and individuals, or between different stakeholder groups. This picture can be commented on, discussed or simply considered for better understanding. If the problem size is large, one may need to limit the number of spokes purely for practical matters. In this example only four spokes are shown to illuminate the concept. The more that is invested in the userfriendlyness of the interface, the higher the communicative power could be.

The next step of development of such a system is to allow the system to "auto-adapt". Each request for information is then translated into a new observation and the neural network also learns to deal with the new case. In this way a pseudo-living system of evolving perceptions is created. The basics of this concept are explained in Kim (1993) and were discussed in earlier chapters. Baets et al. (1995) give some more detail on the application side.

6.4.3. An application in a major change process related to motorway maintenance

The second example is of more or less the same nature as the previous one. It deals with a change process which aims to shift the responsibility for the quality of the maintenance of motorways from the authorities onto the subcontractors. In this application, the aim was to visualize all the tacit knowledge about quality of maintenance work present amongst all different stakeholder groups. A visual representation, backed up with support information had to provoke and support a smooth change process. If in the first stage the tool is used to provoke learning and therefore to provoke change, in the second stage, the tool developed is made to support the change process itself. Supporting the change process is amongst others done by the monitoring function of the tool. The tool monitors the evolution of the virtual stakeholders' mental maps and visually compares them, roughly the way it is represented in figures 6.3 and 6.4. The learning character of neural networks makes it possible to produce such a "moving" picture. Again, the neural network structures the tacit knowledge of the stakeholders and structures it in a way that it is re-usable. It allows us to include new observations, which in this particular case means any new information coming from an inquiry. These "moving pictures" show the core of the problem which is the shared knowledge. They can support the change process and they can support the process of acceptance of the change amongst the stakeholders.

In the beginning of the process, the situation was as follows. In a specific European country, a particular civil service (public authority) was responsible for the construction and maintenance of motorways. For simplification of the example, let us call this service PAM (Public Authority for Motorways). They have quite a large responsibility, not only for the planning and construction of motorways, but also for their maintenance. The budget for maintenance only is around 25 billion ECU per year. The PAM does not do the job itself. They are only politically responsible for the management of the network of motorways and therefore they need to make sure that maintenance takes place. This maintenance is subcontracted to private entrepreneurs. However, PAM remains responsible for quality control. As can be imagined, PAM has an army of people on different construction work all over the country, physically controlling whether private entrepreneurs do the job according to the desired quality standards. Needless to say, this creates some tensions between the PAM and the entrepreneurs, but also at a lower level between the construction workers and the controllers. This approach is rather expensive and not necessarily efficient. Furthermore, an organizational structure where one party does the work and the other one controls is recipe for problems.

On a political level, it is considered as desirable to start reorganizing this quality control process and to subcontract it in one or another way to private enterprises. This is a fundamental change, given the current situation. All parties involved have major doubts about the desirability of this change and nobody really knows what direction it will take.

Different stakeholders are involved, all having different goals. Within the PAM different parties have different stakes. Headquarters are closer to the political power and therefore they are closer to the desire to subcontract as far as possible, keeping only some limited sampling control at the PAM. The regional directors, who manage the real subcontracting procedures and who organize the control themselves, have in many ways a different view. They are rather ignorant of the private sector. Needless to say within the regional offices, those control agents who risk to losing their job by a possible change process have yet another and different view. Another group within the PAM (say the internal consultants and/or study services) are responsible for designing control procedures and quality standards. They also have different views. Of course an important stakeholder group is the entrepreneurs and it is often too easily assumed that this is a homogeneous group. Instead, entrepreneurs of different industrial sectors organize themselves on corporate basis. Finally there are at least two more stakeholder groups. The politicians have certainly got stakes in this debate, as they have more reason to push for change, rather than any other of the stakeholder groups. However, politicians do not appear to be a homogeneous group either. On a local level politicians act differently from politicians on a more regional or national level. Last but not least the ultimate client is a stakeholder. In this case the ultimate client is the driver who uses the roads. They have an interest in the security of the motorways, as well as on limiting the time spent on maintenance, since maintenance causes delays and queues. These are the different stakeholder groups which have been considered in this study. One could certainly identify more stakeholder groups. To name only one example more, we could have integrated insurance companies since they have stakes both in the entrepreneurs´ side (bankruptcy, security on the workplace) and in the road users (car accidents). Many of the stakes involved in the change process are non-quantifiable and difficult to identify. Many of the stakes are based on perceptions, rather than on real objective grounds. Many of the stakeholder groups, would not be able to identify their stakes, or if they were able to do so, it is not certain they would want to communicate them. This describes the scene for this particular example.

This example is one of vague, multiple and often opposed goals of different parties in the same process. Many of these elements can hardly be measured. In many cases of the management of change, there is a lack of trust between the parties. The different stakeholders do not even agree about definitions (like in this case about what "quality" is really about).

In these circumstances, the idea of making a "picture" in a non-confrontational way, is an interesting one. One knows what is important, but one seldom knows how different issues influence each other. If we could create a "picture" and show it to all stakeholders so that they can start working with it in order to get a better understanding of each others perceptions without immediately getting involved in political debates, a value added is created.

The procedure which was followed in this project is as follows. Existing material was consulted which describes the project and the process from one or another point of view. This material might be internal reports, interviews, studies, etc.

The aim is only to identify issues, not to identify relationships between these issues at this stage. This part of the procedure is not highly time consuming, though this depends on the complexity of the problem.

In the next stage, a list of issues identified in the previous stage is validated with a number of the stakeholders. It is important to make sure that the different stakeholders use the same terminology, before launching a wide-spread questionnaire. This is a rather technical matter, since it has to guarantee comparability of results. This does not mean that different stakeholders need to agree. It only needs to be checked that they are using the same terminology. Based on this validated list of issues, a formal questionnaire is produced.

Different media can be used in order to distribute and process these questionnaires. In this research a paper-based distribution was used, which of course imposes a boundary on the number of possible respondents. One could easily produce an electronic questionnaire, which would make both distribution and processing easier and faster. It would allow the project to use much more input. The questionnaire asks for "recognition" of issues. A typical question would be "how much do you recognize issue 1 as being important in this process". Measurement takes place on a 1 to 10 Likert type scale.

We do the same with the definitions. We want to avoid giving definitions of e.g. "quality". The reason for avoiding giving definitions is that any given definition excludes immediately all other views on the same subject. Instead of making the process clearer, in many cases it divides the camp in two. Furthermore, it is arguable whether clear definitions can exist about such things like e.g. "quality". In a change process where the aim is to gather stakeholders, that would be counterproductive. Instead we give a number of statements about quality and we ask respondents to score how recognizable they are. Eventually, after training of the neural network, this approach will give us a networked version of statements which covers in its network version the definition of quality, without really giving one. It is not a straightforward definition. It gives all important aspects of e.g. "quality" and it also gives the interrelationship between the different aspects.

With the data gathered, neural networks are trained. The aim is to identify a knowledge structure. This structure does not have the form of a set of equations (or rules) but it is a network of interrelated knots. The more knots there are and

the more they are interrelated, the more they are able to picture the full complexity
of the problem. The more complex the network is, the more it keeps variety of
opinions but the more it also resembles reality: the more it allows us to show real
pictures. In order to obtain such pictures, unsupervised algorithms (see earlier
chapters) should be used. In this particular case we used Kohonen maps in order
to identify structure.

What has been observed in this particular case is that the result of such a trained
network can be different from what is conceived as the reality today. This
difference can occur both in the structure itself as well as in the direction of certain
links (which are not to be confused with equations or rules). It could be that an
issue or a set of issues which have always been claimed important by the
marketing department does not appear to be that important for the overall stakes in
the process. It could equally be the case that though different stakeholders have
different ideas about quality and definitions of quality, they could still have
opinions close to each other when it boils down to practical aspects of the quality
process. Eventually, any representation (or a number of different representations)
will allow us to identify a structure which is deduced from observations and
perceptions, rather than from predetermined mental maps. In this process, no
mental model is forced on to any of the stakeholder groups. All different
structures are a priori equally possible. Only the practical use of the different
pictures will allow discrimination of the one in favor of the other.

At this point, there are two possible ways forward. They have different aims and
could even be pursued in parallel. The first one is to analyze further with
supervised algorithms in order to get an even better, clearer and more detailed
picture. This could be considered as zooming in on a picture or rather focusing it a
little better. The second way is make a representation of the network and use it
for further learning.

The first way to proceed is to deepen the analysis. In that case we use supervised
learning algorithms in order to find more detail in the structure. We do not limit
ourselves to the structure, but we are also interested in underlying relationships and
mutual influences between knots. In this stage we try to make the process visible
as far as possible. It is important to keep in mind that this approach starts from
observations and not from predefined structures. Such a network gives the "ins",
"outs" and "throughs" of the change process as they are perceived by the different

stakeholders. In this stage we get more information on the background of the change process. It does not necessarily picture the change process in the sense of what we could call a "corporate picture". Instead, they are shots taken at a particular time, but that does not make them less interesting.

The second way we can choose to continue, is to picture the change process in order to allow learning from this picture, but also in order to create a moving and learning picture. A further advantage of this second approach is that we create a tool which allows communication (e.g. using corporate telecom networks). In order to make this accessible, we have to develop an interactive software tool. An additional advantage of this software tool is that we can distribute it inside and outside the company (amongst the different stakeholders) over any kind of telecom networks (like an Intranet or Internet). In doing so, the impact of such a tool, distributed on a large scale, can be seriously more important compared with the effect of workshops which one could organize, using such a tool as supporting material. However, if we wanted to use such a tool over networks, adequate facilitation would need to be organized. One could think about GDSS (Group Decision Support Systems) environments in order to support this. Hence, if we are dealing with change processes where many people are involved who are located in different geographical locations, this may be a very interesting alternative. More detail on GDSS is given in the next chapter.

We could now go into some detail of the procedure, but it does not differ very much from the previous example. The result of the training of a neural network is in fact a matrix of "loadfactors". The issues which are considered are e.g. indicated on the different rows and the virtual stakeholdergroups are on the columns. It is clear that in this case a choice needs to be made about the number of virtual stakeholder groups. No choice is ideal concerning numbers. In many cases it will be practice, i.e. the use of the system itself, which will give us some evidence about the optimal number of virtual stakeholder groups. It would lead us into too much of detail, but algorithms exist which can assist in identifying the "optimal" number of virtual stakeholder groups (for detail see e.g. van Wezel and Baets, 1996).

The matrix of "loadfactors" can be compared to an indication of relationship between the issues and the virtual stakeholder groups, as well as it indicates a sensitivity of each virtual stakeholder group to each issue. However, these loadfactors have a different mathematical content than say equations and coefficients. These load factors only carry sense in the overall structure which is the trained neural network. We can represent this matrix in different visual ways. Without claiming a general validity, we have chosen in this case a graphic representation, mainly for reasons of simplicity and comprehensibility. This representation can be seen as an extension of the examples shown in figures 6.3 and 6.4.

Once the network has identified the virtual stakeholder groups and represents all issues on the spokes we can start playing around with the system. This moment is very important in the learning phase. Individuals are able, not only to play around with their own perceptions and mental maps, but also with the mental maps of the other stakeholders. They can see how the different groups think, without being immediately in a confrontational situation with other stakeholders. It allows stakeholders to get much more insight into the problem, using perceptions of all different stakeholders. One can hardly imagine any other approach which pictures perceptions, but also allows comparison and representation. This software tool allows individuals to experiment and to learn. It remains each individual's responsibility to be open and willing to learn. A company can only create an environment which invites learning. As argued in earlier chapters, it is impossible to force a person to learn, one can only invite people to learn and make it attractive and interesting. Probably the big advantage of this system on this level is its capacity to allow learning in a non-confrontational environment about perceptions of different stakeholder groups without these virtual groups necessarily being the original groups. This is probably the only way to break through difficult debates of groups with long established but rather opposed interests.

On this level of individual learning that is what one can achieve. Any further development of the system will depend on the budgets available. The more money that can be invested, the better the application can be made and the more attractive it becomes for individuals to play around with. This is a known problem in software design. In the case of a large change process, or in the case of change processes within large companies one could even consider using CD ROM technology for improved interactivity. Any improvement possible will improve the communicative value of the application; it will not change the quality of the network trained. This does not mean that the interface of any software tool is not crucially important. One should keep in mind that the ultimate goal of this development remains the support of change processes. The better processes can be communicated, the more effective one can expect changes to be.

On the group level, more value can be drawn from this application. Therefore we have to consider some other possible extensions: the possibility to create "moving" pictures, which then picture the change rather than the situation; the possibility of connecting these moving pictures to policy variables via fuzzy technology.

Let us consider first the problem of creating "moving" pictures, or learning systems. One of the aims of the development described above is to provoke change in perceptions and mental maps. Hence we presume that once people are using the system for a certain time their perceptions change. Can we measure this change and can we make sure that the system adapts itself according to these changes ? One easy way of doing so is organizing workshops with limited groups of people. The tool can then be used to support the workshops. However, the chance remains that this discussion becomes a confrontational one. We have experimented with GDSS (Group Decision Support Systems) software in order to avoid this shortcoming and for limited groups this is a very useful alternative. However, in the case of targeting larger groups, a GDSS approach has the same shortcomings as any other group meeting: only a limited number of people can be involved; meetings are rather time consuming; outcomes are difficult to communicate.

If we aim to target larger groups, we can only consider working with the tool itself. If we refer back to what we have discussed about neural networks in previous chapters, one of the main qualities of neural networks is its learning behavior. Any new information can be smoothly integrated into the existing network. If we join new pieces of information or observation (new perceptions, new experiences) the neural network will integrate them and keep itself up to date with the latest information. This learning behavior is smooth and cannot be disturbed by accidental mis-information or people who start using the system "just for fun". In practice, each request made to the system as described earlier can also be considered as a new piece of information. As already stated, the way a person queries a system also gives insight into how this person thinks about this problem. If while using the system this person learns and hence slightly changes his perception, a next request would be a different one and it would show some of these slight changes. Incorporating all these changes of everyone using the system, feeds the system continuously with slightly changing perceptions. The neural network supporting the system is fed with the new observations and retrained regularly.

By doing so, the system contains the most up to date perceptions of stakeholders. If we keep old pictures and compare them with the new ones we create a kind of a log of moving pictures. This log shows us the itinerary of learning in respect to this specific change process. It shows whether learning has taken place at all, but it also shows how learning took place and about which perceptions. We should not underestimate this capacity to show learning. We do not have a lot of other ways of showing change and learning. A further advantage of this "moving picture" approach is that it gives the company insight into the "history" of its corporate mental map. In this case, of course, this mental map is limited to this specific change process. However, one could also imagine building a system where the company itself is the subject (say an interactive corporate newsletter) which then would keep track of changing perceptions on a general corporate level.

Briefly, this approach of "moving pictures" allows to show change and learning. It also allows the system to keep itself constantly updated, so that people using the system always get the latest mental maps.

Another interesting development is the connection of the moving pictures, as described above to policy variables via fuzzy logic. The aim is to connect pictures (reality) with policy (dreams) and allow the reality (the pictures) to show which of the dreams (policy) are really in any relation to reality.

The civil authority discussed here (PAM) has published a number of policy targets concerning quality control. They have been discussed in a lot of advisory councils in which many of them lost a lot of their meaning. However, they remain the official policy goals of the PAM. They are stated in normal managerial language, understandable for everybody. A last step we have made in this project is to connect the moving pictures mentioned above with the policy goals.

In practice, a limited number of issues are identified and a network is trained using these issues. The choice is made for the most accessible ones, those who make most sense in every day life for the managers. They are not necessarily the most important ones, nor the most influential. These issues are then defined as fuzzy sets the way it has been described in the earlier sections of this book on fuzzy sets. Fuzzy membership functions are defined also the way it is described in the previously mentioned section. The same is done with the policy goals. They are redefined as fuzzy sets with fuzzy membership functions. Fuzzy rules then combine the moving pictures with the policy goals.

Once the software tool gets used and the moving picture gets updated by new requests (as described earlier), the policy goals vary also via the connection with fuzzy rules. The moving pictures become the drivers for the goals, which means that the perceived reality is driver for the policy goals. The more the tool gets used, the richer the picture becomes and the more we have information about the inter-linkage of the issues (picture) with the policy goals. If we continue doing this for a number of observations and over a certain period of time, this system will show us which of the policy goals are real and based on perceived issues and which of them are of pure political and arbitrary nature. Such a system allows the PAM to update its goals but also to show the link between the goals and the issues which the stakeholders feel are important.

Useful developments in this direction need support within the company. As we have already advocated, knowledge management only makes a change within a company where the corporate environment allows learning (and hence also allows people to make mistakes). The kind of development described here is one example of such an advanced learning approach. Not every company will be able (or willing) to work with it. On the other hand, this kind of systems create a lot of new knowledge which can be added to the existing one. It can also operationalise some knowledge which at present is only tacit. Though the theoretical developments prove promising, it is not yet fully implemented.

In respect to the theory highlighted in previous chapters, this systems gives impulses to a company in the sense that it continuously confronts the company with new "observations". If an individual or a group incorporates the new experiences in the existing mental maps, learning occurs. This illustrates the single and double loop learning cycles described earlier (Kim, 1993). The learning cycle in this application is not so important, but instead the measurement of learning (change) and the knowledge base which is behind this learning process. We start with an initial picture which we are going to use to launch the change process.

During the change process, the map (picture) will change gradually further away
from the original one, at least if some learning occurs. At any point in time,
different maps of different time periods can be compared. This does not only
allow comparison, but it also allows us to draw a path of change (direction, speed,
etc.). The basis for this change process is the knowledge base which is created via
this process. This system not only creates knowledge, it also manages it and keeps
it up-to-date. It remains a choice between getting a rich picture with little detail, or
getting a very detailed picture, but probably with misleading detail. At least in this
project, this methodology has proven to be useful.

6.4.4. Some summarizing observations

Based on the two examples described here, it is impossible to draw general valid
conclusions. There is simply not enough conclusive evidence in favor or against
what has been advocated here. Only, in these examples, the approach has worked.

Knowledge based approaches accept that knowledge is held by all different
stakeholders, also stakeholders from outside the company. That is why this
approach keeps the application as "rich" as possible. Change processes need to be
recognized by all parties involved, not only by those who initiate the change
process. This approach is a *non confrontational* one. In many meetings,
unfortunately, the real agenda remains hidden. The approach described above can
avoid this to a large extent. It is comparable to one of the main advantages of a
GDSS system, which is that the procedure guarantees anonymous participation
and input. People will give their perceptions more easily if they are not
immediately confronted by an "opponent".

The approach used in these examples is based on the neural network concepts and
more specifically the idea of *the company as a (neural) knowledge network*. All
stakeholders have been involved, also the external parties. As already argued,
clients have in many cases very valuable knowledge about their supplier's
company. If we want to built a knowledge base and a knowledge network, we
have to have the courage to include the tacit and explicit knowledge of the clients.
In these particular cases, the ultimate client (the public) was not really involved,
but some other third parties were. This approach gathers in a flexible way all
knowledge knots in the commercial network of the company. It continues to

involve all these knots and tries to find structure in their interaction. Therefore, this approach is able to create knowledge of a different nature, often tacit knowledge.

Key to this approach is the role which is given to perceptions, instead of observed "facts". The disadvantage of using perceptions is that they are more difficult to visualize. Numbers can easily be presented using statistics or graphics and that is one of the main reasons why we have always paid less attention to perceptions. The approach tested here is capable of *visualizing perceptions* and therefore also of visualizing the knowledge network which can be constructed with these perceptions.

The software tool which has been designed is a tool from which individuals can learn. In some respect it can be considered as a *personal laboratory* for testing alternatives and options and in order to make new experiences at no cost or damage. This tool is also an instrument which learns itself. From new observations and/or questioning it derives additional knowledge. Therefore this tool does not only create knowledge, it also monitors the evolution of the knowledge at an individual and group level (all stakeholders together). These systems show *learning and adaptive behavior*, which gives them a unique character in the wide field of decision support. Above all, this approach attempts to visualize group mental models.

Without dealing with them in any detail, it is worth mentioning the potential applications of this approach in change processes of a political nature. If we consider major political changes (like the ones taking place in South Africa or in the CIS) there are often different stakeholder groups with different agendas and even different definitions of the same problem. Any open discussion between the different stakeholder groups will lead the different stakeholder groups very often back into their already known points of view. The approach discussed in this chapter could be considered as an alternative for supporting political change processes. It can visualize perceptions and change, without being confrontational.

6.5. Dynamic thinking

In this last section of the chapter we want to briefly introduce some areas of management in which dynamic non-linear thinking can innovate what is done today. The examples are taken from real life brain storm sessions during executive courses. These examples also describe some consequences of thinking about dynamic systems and knowledge networks. As you will see, some of them suggest dramatic impact on the way business is conducted these days. However, these examples only discuss the structure of the knowledge network which needs to be developed if we are to apply some of the ideas. Contrary to the previous set of examples, no research in any particular network has been done yet or is discussed in this section. We will take as examples: recruitment systems, reward systems, product development and project based education.

6.5.1. Recruitment systems

Contrary to the examples given in earlier sections of this chapter, the examples described here presume that knowledge networks already exist. This section attempts to analyze the consequences if knowledge is indeed networked. These examples do not suggest solutions, but rather they raise questions. It will be clear that the consequences of the knowledge based approach for a company can go far, but it also indicates the tremendous pool of potential energy which has not been touched on yet in many companies. Creative use of knowledge networks, as described here, aim to deliver the sustainable development which companies are interested in. The combination of a knowledge network approach with a learning attitude is key for sustainable development.

The first example given concentrates on recruitment of personnel. Many companies are interested in hiring the most intelligent people. They interview and test candidates as individuals. At best, some attention is given to communication skills and ability to work in groups. However, if knowledge is built up dynamically each time a problem needs to be tackled, employees need to be good at creating knowledge in variable teams. New recruits are tested on their team qualities, but the concept of the dynamic creation of knowledge over time is fundamentally different from working in groups on solutions. The knowledge worker may not be the most intelligent individual, but rather the person who contributes most to a knowledge network. A group of highly intelligent individuals, even if they are able to work in groups, are not a guarantee for the highest degree of knowledge creation. They may work together but no real additional knowledge is created. No real new ideas come out; nothing is shared. Let us have a look on an easier example.

Musicians are rather individually trained and the "best" go for individual prizes in famous music contests around the world. However, creating music in an orchestra is different. Harmony of the music and the musicians´ dependence on each others contributions is important. Small jazz combo's may show that even better than large orchestras do. The sound of a small combo, compared to a big band or compared to an individual musician is different. If we want to create a strong combo, we may want to look for a different type of musician than if we were forming a big band or needed a solo performer. Brilliant individual musicians can play with an orchestra, if the orchestra follows them.

In a corporate environment the question is not so much whether we want an individual or a knowledge worker. If we accept that in our service society knowledge workers are what we want, then we need to recruit them with that aim in mind. We then need to design recruitment criteria and tests which allow a company to interview a candidate differently from the way we do now. In a corporate environment, we are not looking for individual musicians who can play with an orchestra, but we are interested in hiring people who together form combo's or big bands. They should be able to "create" together, rather than to play tremendously nice music which has been composed by others. A company can not always imitate others (only play composers' music) but sometimes it needs to create something itself (create a new piece of music). That makes the difference between two orchestras and that equally makes the difference between two companies.

In most recruitment procedures today, companies are still interviewing to find the best possible musician, who, of course, should be able to play with an orchestra but in an individual (soloist) role. Afterwards they are surprised that all these individuals claim a soloist role and only want to become the prima donna of the ballet. They are all extremely good at playing someone else's music. They perform very poorly if they have to create music themselves in conjunction with the group. This metaphor of creating music instead of playing existing music is important to show the difference between managing a knowledge network compared with managing a (hierarchical) company. In many cases, managing means playing the music of those who compose the music on the market. Many managers are followers which does not need to be a problem if the market is not too dynamic. If the market is dynamic, success will be for those who continuously create the music; knowledge needs to be continuously created, based on a network of experience and learning. In the case of the latter we need to hire knowledge workers who are able to do that.

6.5.2. Reward systems

A logical extension of the recruitment system discussed above, is the design of a reward system in order to motivate the above mentioned knowledge workers. Performance of people is measured today against an individual target. Sometimes, teamwork is taken into account, but seldom a company tries to identify the contribution which workers make to corporate knowledge. Team performance and knowledge creation as main performance does not come into the picture. In project groups some people bring in the creative ideas whereas others are able to put them into action. Unfortunately, those who put them into action often get the credit. It is doubtful, however, that these people would ever have managed it if their colleagues had not conceived the project in the first place.

Secondly, many reward systems are static and seldom take into account the dynamics of the market, nor the dynamics of the company itself. Except for some simple linear rules - like increasing all salaries by say a few percent or giving individuals a bonus - no reward systems takes company-specific contributions into account under changing conditions. Many companies set targets for each individual worker and measure the performance against these targets at the end of the year. The targets themselves are not discussed anymore. In a dynamic system this seems rather restrictive and not really fair on the workers. It is not easy to do better, but it is necessary. Some research has been done on this subject, mainly by postmodernist economists. In one of these studies (Van der Linden, 1993) it was even suggested that it was more motivating for workers to get a pat on the back than to get a salary increase. I would not like to go that far, but the study reveals an interesting viewpoint on reward systems. It accepts that markets and companies develop chaos and it considers reward systems from that point of view. These studies suggest that classical reward systems, at the least, do not follow the reality of market and company.

Ideally, people should be rewarded for their contribution to the corporate knowledge creation and this reward system should be an adaptive one, taking into account the evolution of the market. A combination of neural networks and fuzzy logic could be a reasonable approach in order to develop such reward structures. The neural networks can picture the business processes considered (see earlier examples) and it can learn, based on a continuous input of new observations. Therefore, this system can give an up-to-date picture of reality. This picture is dynamic, just as environment is. At any given point in time it pictures the present situation of the company. This position can be compared to an earlier stage, say the moment on which the targets were set. Then, some evolutionary path can be identified. Fuzzy logic allows a vague approximation of variables. In the case of reward systems and human performance, it is extremely difficult to identify quantitative values. Fuzzy approximation is what we all do in that case and fuzzy logic could provide good vocabulary for that. It allows the reward system to deal with vague variables and it could allow us to judge people in terminology which both parties understand. This can avoid discussions about a specific number-score (does the person belong to group 5, 4 or 3 for his bonus ?) but instead concentrate on achievements.

This approach needs management which is willing to reward contribution to knowledge and not to profit margin (if indeed we could measure the latter). This approach is only realistic if the company is knowledge driven and has a learning attitude, which means that it is open to learning via trial and error and it gives employees real responsibilities. Such a company should be willing to empower people and allow them to develop creativity. Such a company will not be too hierarchical nor too bureaucratic. Given all these conditions, it is clear that we are still a while away from such a reward system. However, this is a straightforward consequence of the dynamic non-linear behavior of markets and companies. If the company understands that knowledge management and learning is the way ahead to sustainable development, something should be done about their reward system.

The combination of recruitment systems and reward systems (including a career development path) is probably one of the most challenging systems to work on in a

knowledge based company.   It could provide the competitive edge for the
knowledge company.

6.5.3. The 400 km/h car (product development)

In order to introduce the problem of product development, let us give a metaphoric
example which hopefully clarifies the problem. When I was an adolescent, I drove
a motor bike. When I recently drove a motor bike again it was astonishing that all
pedals and handles were still in the same place, doing exactly the same things as
years before. The same is very much true of a car. The design of cars and the
engines changed over the last twenty years, but the mechanical handling of the car
still takes place roughly in the same way as it was done twenty years ago. If one
compares radios of 20 years ago and the hi-fi chains of today, no comparison is
possible. New devices were invented which are part of the hi-fi chain, like the CD
player, which dramatically changed the quality of the sound. Even the design of
the "radio", if we are still allowed to call it that, is quite different, not to mention
the remote control.

It is almost impossible to conceive that the evolution which took place with the
radio and many other devices (e.g. from photo-camera to camcorder) did not take
place with motor bikes or cars. Why did nobody radically re-think the whole idea
of personal transportation. Let us consider the following simple request. Why did
we never design a car which is able to drive 400 km/h. The reader will
immediately say that this is impossible. Why ? I do not know whether it is
possible or not, but imagine a company wants to try it. Who should they hire ?
Probably most people would suggest to hiring the best auto engineers in the world.
Maybe that is why it does not yet exist. These engineers would only confirm the
fact that it does not exist because it is impossible. They would immediately tell
you that engineers have already tried over a number of years and found it to be
completely impossible. Probably this is true since they continue thinking along the
same lines. Many companies think about product innovation very much along the
same lines as what they already know. The same people have to invent new
products, implicitly denying the existing ones which they also invented or
designed previously. This may be too much for one person.

Rather than hiring the best engineers for the design of the 400 km/h car, one could advocate that we should hire the client who is willing to pay a lot of money in order to get that 400 km/h car. He will know what he wants and what it should look like. He will dream his dreams along lines which are probably unknown today to our company and which engineers have excluded from the very beginning. Once his dreams are as detailed as he can make them, then the engineers should come in. Does this not sound familiar to the way the Walkman was developed? If we want to design products, based on knowledge, we should not forget that the clients may have a lot of knowledge about our products. We should not under-estimate the amount of knowledge which is present even in many industrial products, like cars, consumer electronics, etc. For all these products, the clients know exactly what they want, what is good and bad with the present products and how they could be improved and/or reinvented.

In product development teams, clients should be involved. They can give tremendous insight into the failures of the past and the wishes for the future. If one includes the clients, one will get early feedback on the performance of the new product. One could imagine launching a product on a limited scale amongst the "friends-clients" and letting them test it. Gradually, the product would be improved and after few trial and error a good product can be put on the market. Putting a thoroughly beta-tested product on the market from the first time is extremely difficult and expensive.

The gradual development of products also fits into the picture of the dynamic market. The time from design to delivery can be very long and for many products it is extremely important to remain aware of the evolution of the market. Again, and without lots of details, fuzzy neural networks can be used in order to make a moving picture of the product/market combination, using the perceptions of all stakeholders, certainly those of the clients. These systems can evolve with the markets and give up-to-date pictures, correcting the original picture for the current situation.

6.5.4. Project based education versus knowledge transfer based

It would be too easy only to investigate industry and business and not to consider the "knowledge business" by excellence which is education. For the sake of clarity, let us limit ourselves to business education and even more specific to MBA programs. They are considered as the top courses producing the managers of the future. It should be kept in mind that whatever is said of MBA courses is partly true for other management education courses too, including company specific courses.

MBA courses are classically knowledge transfer based. Students are sitting in a class room and knowledge in transferred to them via teaching. Over the years, case studies were used more and more in order to illustrate practical examples. Case teaching, however, became a variant of classical teaching in that it still presumed that knowledge is something which exists "out there" and could be transferred easily. This approach does not take into account the fact that only mental models will drive the manager of tomorrow and in order to build these mental models, the manager has to internalize the material. Each manager creates his own knowledge. No knowledge is universal. Management education presumes that knowledge is somewhat universal, somewhat rule based. This implies that there are good and bad ways of managing companies and the aim of education is to teach the students the correct rules. These rules are found via research and in order to be able to research in enough detail, management needs to be split up (reduced) into different functional areas, say marketing, finance, accounting, human resource management, etc. Everybody knows that they do not exist in their own right in a real company, but for the sake of knowledge transfer we divide the management world into functional areas. "If God had meant the world to be organized according to the faculties of universities, he would probably have done so." In doing so we can approach any specific managerial aspect with a "scientific" approach (in many cases quantitative research).

In practice, this does not seem to respond to the real world. If we have a big elephant which is extremely difficult to clean we could theoretically say that we cut this elephant into 15 small pieces and have different teams each cleaning one of the pieces. We have made the problem accessible, we could say. But what we have really done is we have killed the elephant. You do not get 15 small elephants but one dead elephant. In management education, we unfortunately tend to do the same. We kill the elephant for the sake of accessibility and scientific detail.

Until very recently, almost all top MBA programs in the world consisted of a set of courses which were thought out in great depth and many of them heavily reliant on quantitative approaches. Integration, if dealt with at all, was covered in the strategy course. If strategy has any reason to exist as a course (Whittington, 1993) it does not deal with integration. MBA graduates upon entering companies, were either expecting the world to be organized according to the courses of their MBA programs or alternatively organized as a set of case studies. Since neither correspond to reality, frustration arose. Companies were frustrated with the MBA graduates' inability to apply theoretical knowledge and MBA graduates were frustrated to find out that the world was not divided according to their courses.

What business schools have probably been doing is considering the world as a static and non-linear system in which knowledge can be built up with (seldom changing) rules. Research approaches were linear and static and the models researched were also linear and static. Any possible disturbing loop was eradicated by splitting management into sub-disciplines. However, if real life is different, if the markets are non-linear and dynamic, then this approach does not really help.

Business schools are now changing in order to give more importance to managerial skills, which is a way of training the students to deal with dynamic environments. Business schools concentrate on skills to develop knowledge, to work in groups, to communicate, etc. which are all qualities of importance in the knowledge oriented company. Project based education is probably the best approach in order to show the students how businesses run. Students should be fed with the past experience of many people, with the aim of building up their own knowledge network. Tutoring on real life cases (field work) rather than teaching theories is what should happen in order for students to build up their own knowledge network.

No teacher can really teach anything if the student is not willing to listen. If the student listens but does not internalize into his mental model, no change in perception can ever occur. Therefore, management students should create an attitude to be able to deal with changing dynamic environments and therefore develop a knowledge and learning approach. Based on the experience of others and based on their own experience via projects, they will create their own knowledge net.

In the eighties, companies criticized business schools for their knowledge transfer orientation, but still many of them continue. Only now do we see some experiments with networked business schools which try to develop a knowledge network and support in order to be able to produce higher quality education. These schools are highly project driven and put a lot of emphasis on managerial skills. They teach theory for the sake of the past experience of so many generations of managers but aim to give insight rather than solutions. Quantitative approaches make way for more knowledge network approaches like brainstorming sessions, mental mapping, business simulations, etc.

A last remark which should be made here is that for management development within a company, this view on education fits closely with the earlier remarks on recruitment and reward systems. Complex dynamic systems should be dealt with as complex dynamic systems. One elephant, cut in 15 pieces, does not produce 15 small elephants but one dead elephant. A knowledge oriented company should integrate its recruitment, performance measurement and career development in such a way that it reflects the dynamic situation in which the company operates as well as to taking into account the internal dynamics. This is not an easy task, but it is the key for success to the knowledge driven company.

The two latter chapters have discussed a number of real life examples of experiments with knowledge management techniques. If manageable real life problems did not exist, this book would be of little value. Dynamic non-linear systems are not a theoretical concept and the use of neural networks and fuzzy logic is not an academic exercise. This should be clear in the examples. For those readers who still have some doubts, a final real life example is given in the epilogue. For those who already see the relevance to their own company of the concepts advocated here, the epilogue is a gift.

The next chapter discusses in detail what infrastructure is necessary for a company, in order to be able to become a knowledge networked company. Roughly speaking, there are two necessary conditions which are not necessarily sufficient. Sufficiency can only be guaranteed by the management which should be and remain devoted to this approach. The necessary conditions are: a learning attitude and an information network able to support a knowledge network. The latter is dealt with in next chapter.

REFERENCES

Baets W, 1991a. Coincidence: A business simulation... Users guide and Technical Notes. Lovanium International Management Center, La Hulpe.

Baets W, 1991b. The Strategic Use of Information Systems and Information Technology: A Methodology for Strategic IS implementation (Russian original, English translation available). Bi-monthly Journal of the All-Union Society for Informatics and Computer Science, Union of the Scientific and Engineering Societies of the USSR. Moscow. November.

Baets W, 1992. Aligning information systems with business strategy. Journal of Strategic Information Systems. Nr. 4, September.

Baets W, 1993a. IT for organizational change: beyond business process engineering. Business Change and Re-engineering. Vol. 1, Nr. 2, Autumn.

Baets W, 1993b. Information Systems Strategic Alignment: A case in banking. Working Paper. Nijenrode University, The Netherlands.

Baets W, 1996b. Some Empirical Evidence on IS Strategy Alignment in Banking. Information & Management. Vol. 30, Nr. 4.

Baets W, Brunenberg L, van Wezel M and Venugopal V, 1995. Corporate Cognitive Mapping: Mapping of corporate change processes. Fourth International Conference on Artificial Neural Networks. Cambridge, UK.

Baldwin C, 1991. What is the future of banking: Rescuing banks may mean reinventing the banking system. Harvard Business Review. July-August.

Belgian Banking Association (BVB/ABB), 1990a. Jaarverslag.

Belgian Banking Association (BVB/ABB), 1990b. Het investeringsgedrag van de banken. Aspecten en Documenten. Nr. 116.

Benjamin R and Blunt J, 1992. Critical IT issues: The Next Ten Years. Sloan Management Review. Vol. 33, Nr. 4, Summer.

Chen H, Hsu P, Orwig R, Hoopes L and Nunamaker J, 1994. Automatic Concept Classification of Text from Electronic Meetings. Communications of the ACM. Vol. 37, Nr. 10, Oct.

CSC Index, 1992. *Critical Issues of Information Systems Management.*The Netherlands: CSC.

Davidson W, 1993. Beyond re-engineering: The three phases of business transformation. IBM Systems Journal. Vol. 32, Nr. 1.

de Callatay A, 1992. *Natural and Artificial Intelligence: Misconceptions about Brains and Neural Networks*. Amsterdam: North-Holland.

de Geus A, 1988. Planning as learning. Harvard Business Review. March/April, pp. 70-74.

Dockery E, 1991. The strategic use of Information Systems Technology in banking firms and building societies. City University Business School. Working Paper 117, April.

Eden C, 1988. Cognitive mapping. European Journal of Operational Research. Nr. 36, pp. 1-13.

Essinger J and Rosen J, 1989. *Advanced Computer Applications for Investment Managers*. Canterbury: Financial Technology Publications.

Firebaugh M, 1989. *Artificial Intelligence: A knowledge-Based Approach*. Boston: PWS-Kent.

Galliers R, 1991a. Strategic information systems planning: myths, reality and guidelines for successful implementation. European Journal of Information Systems. Vol. 1, Nr. 1.

Galliers R, 1991b. "Choosing Appropriate Information Systems Research Approaches: A Revised Taxonomy." In *The Information Systems Research Arena of the 90s,* Nissen H, Hirschheim R and Klein H (eds.). Amsterdam: North-Holland.

Galliers R and Sutherland A, 1991. Information Systems Management and Strategy Formulation: The 'Stages of Growth' Model revisted. Journal of Information Systems. March.

Haeckel S and Nolan R, 1993. Managing by wire. Harvard Business Review. Vol. 71, Nr. 5, Sept.-Oct.

Harvard Business Review, 1991. What is the future of banking: Rescuing banks may mean reinventing the banking system. July-August.

Henderson J and Venkatraman N, 1993. Strategic Alignment: Leveraging information technology for transforming organizations. IBM Systems Journal. Vol. 32, Nr. 1.

Johansson H, McHugh P, Pendleburry A and Wheeler W, 1993. *Business Process Reengineering - Breakpoint Strategies for Market Dominance*. Whiley & Sons.

Kaplan R and Murdock L, 1990. Core Process Redesign. The McKinsey Quarterly. Nr. 2.

Kim D, 1993. The link between Individual and Organizational Learning. Sloan Management Review. Fall.

Kolb D, 1983. "Problem Management: Learning from Experience." In *The Executive Mind: New Insights on Managerial Thought*, Suresh Srivastva and Associates. Jossey-Bass Ltd.

Knorr R, 1991. Business Process Redesign: Key to Competitiveness. The Journal of Business Strategy. Nov./Dec.

Leonard-Barton D, 1992. The Factory as a Learning Laboratory. Sloan Management Review. Vol. 34, Nr. 11, Fall.

Litan R, 1991. What is the future of banking: Rescuing banks may mean reinventing the banking system. Harvard Business Review. July-August.

MacDonald K H, 1991. "Business Strategy Developments, Alignment, and Redesign." In *The Corporation of the 1990's*, Scott Morton M (ed.). NY: Oxford University Press.

Mintzberg H, 1973. Strategy Making in Three Modes. California Management Review. Winter.

Mintzberg H, 1979. *The Structuring of Organizations: A synthesis of the Research*. Englewood Cliffs, NJ: Prentice Hall.

Mintzberg H, 1989. *Mintzberg on management: inside our strange world of organizations*. NY: Free Press.

Mintzberg H, 1989. "Strategy formation: Ten schools of thought." In *Perspectus on Strategic Management*, Fredrickson (ed.). New York: Ballinger.

Mintzberg H, 1990. The Design School: Reconsidering the basic premises of Strategic Management. Strategic Management Journal. Vol. 11, pp. 171-195.

Mintzberg H and Waters J, 1983. "The minds of the Strategist(s)." In *The Executive Mind: New Insights on Managerial Thought*, Suresh Srivastva and Associates. Jossey-Bass Ltd.

Niederman F, Brancheau J C, and Wetherbe J C, 1991. Information Systems management issues in the 1990's. MIS Quarterly. Vol.16, Nr. 4, pp. 474-500 .

Norden P, 1993. Quantitative techniques in strategic alignment. IBM Systems Journal. Vol. 32, Nr. 1.

PA Technology, 1990. Banking on Survival. The situation in The Netherlands. July.

Parker M, Benson R and Trainor E, 1988. *Information Economics: linking business performance to information technology*. Prentice Hall.

Ramaswami S, Nilakanta S and Flynn J, 1992. Supporting strategic information needs: An empirical assessment of some organizational factors. Journal of Strategic Information Systems. Nr. 2.

Rockart J and Hofman J, 1992. System Delivery: Evolving New Strategies. Sloan Management Review. Vol. 33, Summer.

Seidman W, 1991. What is the future of banking: Rescuing banks may mean reinventing the banking system. Harvard Business Review. July-August.

Senge P M, 1990. *The Fifth Discipline: The Art & Practice of the Learning Organization*. NY: Doubleday.

Stacey R, 1993. Strategy as Order Emerging from Chaos. Longe Range Planning. Vol. 26, Nr. 1, Feb.

Van der Linden G, 1993. Een Essay over en Empirisch Onderzoek naar Betekenissen van Loon en Beloning. Casus van een postmoderne visie op   bedrijfsbeheer. PhD thesis. Rijksuniversiteit Groningen.

van Wezel M and Baets W, 1995. Predicting Market Responses with a Neural Network: the Case of Fast Moving Consumer Goods. Marketing Intelligence & Planning. Autumn.

Whittington R, 1993. *What is strategy - and does it matter ?* London: Routledge.

7. IT SUPPORT FOR ORGANIZATIONAL LEARNING: THE ORGANIZATION OF KNOWLEDGE NETWORKS

In the first few chapters of the book, we have discussed the theories and concepts of knowledge management. A deeper understanding of the knowledge generating process in an economic or managerial environment will make it easier for the manager to introduce knowledge management within a company. The previous chapters described real life examples of different size, complexity and focus which all had to do with knowledge management in a managerial context. These examples gave some insight into the possibilities of knowledge management. This chapter deals with the corporate "environment" necessary to create the knowledge based company. If a company understands the crucial role which knowledge plays for its future sustainable development, how can it tackle the introduction of knowledge based management. As is argued in this chapter, the mentality of management (the learning attitude) and the support architecture (information and knowledge technology) of the company make or break knowledge management.

7.1. The necessary and sufficient conditions for designing and using knowledge networks

Until now we have discussed advantages of some knowledge approaches. Interesting features of these knowledge approaches are e.g. their self-learning capacity, their adaptive behavior, their network structure, etc. However, we have also mentioned a number of times that knowledge approaches can only flourish in companies having a learning attitude. Though we have already mentioned what learning is about in respect to knowledge management and though we have highlighted some aspects of a learning attitude, this chapter is going to describe this in more detail. In the following section we concentrate on what we understand by a learning attitude and what we understand when we use terms like organizational learning (learning on an organizational level). This is one aspect of successful knowledge management. Moreover, it proves to be the necessary condition. Successful knowledge management is only possible with an adequate learning attitude within the company. However, it is a necessary condition, not a sufficient one.

The sufficient condition for organizing knowledge networks is the adequate use of Information and Knowledge Technology (IKT). IKT is a combination of techniques and technologies which all relate to what is commonly known as IT, telecommunications and Artificial Intelligence, often brought together in a physical network. It is not the aim to become too technical in this book, but the interested reader finds enough in the second part of this chapter which allows him to see how to support knowledge management with an adequate IKT infrastructure.

An example is given of a company in the financial services business using such an IKT approach nowadays. This is only to be considered as a practical illustration of the concepts developed in this chapter. It is in no way an example which needs to be copied.

However, above all, knowledge management and learning is an attitude and a way of working with management. It is an overall approach which goes beyond the addition of a number of functional tactics. One could even say that it is a kind of philosophy of management, rather than a science. It uses scientific approaches and Information and Knowledge Technologies, but only to make the overall picture much richer than the addition of the separate building blocks can provide. The building blocks themselves (functional tactics) lose importance and even disappear as goals in themselves. Still due importance is given to marketing or finance, but within a much broader managerial framework with much broader managerial goals. The subjects fade away as individual subjects. The technologies do not limit the manager but instead give an environment which easily allows experimentation and learning. Therefore, this process is one of redefining the target of the company from a profit-making or share-value increasing entity to a knowledge creating unit. The first type of organization has a rather short-term focus, whereas the latter type has a rather long term one. The ultimate aim of the company no longer is growth, but it becomes sustainable development. In the long run, that is what a company will need to survive and what will allow it to contribute to wider economic development.

Some parallels can be drawn with ideas of quality management. Many companies, and increasingly those in the services sector, pay a lot of attention to quality management. Quality management is not another discipline in itself, nor is it a pure integration of different disciplines. It is a way of conducting business, from its very conception through to the marketing , sales and after-sales activities. Total quality management is often considered a philosophy rather than a science, but many companies which have experienced it can witness the contribution it makes to overall performance. Quality management invites people to get closer to their business process and to pay attention to detail. So does a corporate learning culture. People put more of their soul and faith in their work and feel much closer to the business. Today, quality management is dealt with in many handbooks but many of them deal with it as if it were a new discipline. A scientific approach, based on rules, standards and procedures is advocated in many handbooks. The reader who wants to understand the conjunction between quality management and a learning culture is referred to a book which has seldom been considered as a management book but which many of us already read : Zen and the art of motor cycle maintenance (Pirsig, 1979).

Pirsig's book describes in much detail and in an approachable way the attitude which we are advocating in this book. It argues for an openness to the outside world and to the tools which we work with. It advocates listening to problems and reflecting on possible evidence; rather than using our automatic pilot mechanism which we have developed. It argues strongly against an attitude which became common in many companies: managers need to know answers to all questions, and if they do not, then they are bad managers. Pirsig's book advocates another managerial philosophy, which in many aspects introduces the sufficient conditions for knowledge management. Managers should manage as if they were part of the environment. It is like driving a car. When a person drives a car, he looks at nature through a window. Nature passes by as if the driver was looking at it on a TV screen, while seated in his chair. The driver is no part of the environment. Nature becomes distant and we do not really have any feeling for it anymore. Management becomes a movie which we are watching. On a motorbike, Pirsig argues, the driver is part of nature. He feels and smells nature and is able to react much faster to changes in nature. This analogy suggests that managers should be more in touch with the environment (riding their bike), getting a close feeling for how the markets are and how their employees work, learn and share their experiences, rather than staying in their offices, looking outside as if they were watching to a TV screen.

From a knowledge based perspective, the process of doing something is probably more important than the ultimate goal. The process of moving somewhere and of learning about the situation is a process which initiates knowledge. If the ultimate goal becomes too important and central to a company, what does the company do when it reaches the goal (if possible) ? Should it stop operating ? Can one conceive that at a point in time a company chooses to change course ? The process of corporate survival, or call it sustainable development, is therefore more important than the ultimate goal which could be share-holders value or short-term profit.

We should not operate on automatic pilot, but instead remain attentive to any minor changes which could snowball at a later stage. Self-criticism is a quality which many managers lack. They have already experienced it all and they immediately jump to conclusions. Maybe reality, or we can also call it the problem in managerial terminology, is slightly different. Maybe reality hides a dynamic movement which is going to grow very fast. We should pay attention and be alert in order to see. When we have seen, we can start to learn and know.

Instead of over-emphasizing procedures and rules, we should allow people to have fun in their job. Knowledge is created by people who share experiences. When people have fun in their job, they identify with the job and they put their soul in the job. They are willing to learn and to adapt since they do not feel threatened by rules and regulations. They can come up with an idea or a proposal. They will pay attention to detail since they will observe things they have not seen before and they will enjoy it. Sense for detail is a basic attitude for quality improvement. Furthermore, quality is also the ability to "listen" to the problem. Managers should take time in order to take distance. If one "listens" to the problem, on many occasions the problem itself suggests solutions. Quality ends up to be a healthy combination of men and machine. So knowledge management ends up being a healthy combination of a learning culture and an IKT network.

7.2. The necessary condition for knowledge networks: a learning culture

In order to apply this learning culture in a company, we have to make the previous introduction a bit more formal. Therefore in this section we further develop what we understand by a corporate learning culture. What are different aspects of this corporate learning culture and what can we expect to happen if we go for a corporate learning culture ? Roughly, we have to expect things like experiments, empowerment and knowledge creation from bottom-up. Organizational learning is what this attitude is called.

In today's competitive world, no organization can afford to stand still. Organizations have to run very fast even just to stay where they are. The success of an organization in the global competitive race depends on the *knowledge* of its members and their ability to make right business moves to keep up with the environment. Organizations not only need *knowledge;* they also need the skills to dynamically update and put knowledge into practice . This results in the need for organizations to *learn continuously* and to look for *continuous improvement* in their actions through the acquired knowledge. Hence, to survive in the global competitive environment, organizations transform themselves into *learning organizations* . *Organizational learning* is the name of this process.

A learning organization enables each of its members to learn continually and helps generate new ideas and thinking. By this process, organizations continuously learn from their own experience and that of others and adapt themselves so as to improve their efficiency towards the achievement of their goal. In a way, learning organizations aim at converting themselves into "knowledge-based" organizations by creating, acquiring and transferring knowledge so as to improve their planning and actions.

In order to build a learning organization, or a corporate learning culture, companies should be skilled at systematic problem solving, learning from their own experience, learning from the experiences of others, transferring knowledge quickly and efficiently through the organization and experimentation with new approaches. Developments in Information and Knowledge Technologies make it increasingly possible to achieve these competitive needs and skills. Intelligent IT tools which are capable of supporting certain aspects of learning processes are commercially available as we discuss in the next section.

Practice has shown us that we cannot easily separate the learning culture from the
IKT base. Therefore, we want to go one step further and propose here a
conceptual framework for integrated intelligent systems with the aim to support
organizational learning and knowledge networks. All managers who are interested
in the concept of learning and knowledge management cannot avoid following up
the evolution in the IKT world. In the next section we discuss organizational
learning as a concept followed by a discussion of different learning processes and
the available Information and Knowledge Technologies to support knowledge
networks. Eventually, a conceptual framework of an integrated support system
for organizational learning and knowledge management is presented and the
example of a company is given which experiments with such a framework.

7.3. The sufficient condition for knowledge networks: the integration of Information and Knowledge Technologies

Learning Processes and Information Technology Support

"Creating a learning / knowledge-based organization is simple but not easy"
(Honey, 1991). A new wave of information technology (IT) can support in
creating knowledge-based / learning organizations. New developments in IT such
as Case-Based Reasoning System (CBRS), Expert Systems (ES), Group Decision
Support System (GDSS), Cognitive Mapping and Artificial Neural Networks can
support some aspects of organizational learning processes and organizational
transformation. This section overviews different learning/change processes, more
from a planning perspective and the corresponding IKT tools for supporting the
learning process. More detail can be found in Venugopal and Baets (1995).

Learning through Case Studies (LC)

Human beings find it easy to use case studies / analogies in handling an uncertain
situation in a complex and dynamic environment. In the context of organizations,
managers are often interested to learn how other companies approach certain
problems. Especially while making strategic decisions, managers often look for a

similar case from other industries to get an idea / insight on the experience of one firm to resolve a particular problem (e.g. benchmarking). The objective here is not to follow a "me too strategy" but to look for an "analogous" strategy. Rarely, managers will find something that is exactly similar to their current situation. When managers do not find a similar case, a "nearly similar" case is identified and adapted to the existing situation of the organization so as to establish a strategy/ solution that is relevant and feasible (Sullivan and Yates, 1988). Even when they do not find "nearly similar", the process generates new ideas and facilitates "learning from the experience of others". The ability to use and manipulate cases is important for learning organizations. A Case-Based Reasoning (CBR) system, a recent development in Artificial Intelligence (AI), is a tool that can support the learning processes through cases.

A Case-Based Reasoning System (CBRS) essentially consists of a case-library and a software system for retrieving and analyzing the "similar case" and its associated information. The case library may have cases covering a broad range of ideas across different industries and business functions. Each case may contain a description to capture the underlying competitive situation, the environmental condition, management priorities, experience, values that allowed a certain strategy to succeed. A software system helps indexing each case in such a way that a search yields a modest number of "analogous cases". The system can supply a complete explanation of reasoning leading to each recommendation (Sullivan and Yates, 1988; Lewis, 1995). If there is no case that exactly matches the given situation, then it selects the "most" similar case. An adaptation procedure can be encoded in the form of adaptation rules. The result of the case adaptation is a completed solution but it also generates a new case that can be automatically added to the case library.

Exposure to prior cases/experiences and the steps taken to arrive at a decision can often be richer and more useful as it encodes the important learning and thinking that went into the decision. As CBR can generate details regarding justification for particular decision and explanation for failures, it could be a support tool for a learning organization. It can be used as a learning device, but also as an input device for a knowledge base.

Another tool with the same purpose are *knowledge-based systems.* As knowledge-based organizations also rely on their specialists, replacement of the specialist often causes difficulties due to the nature of the work. Intelligent systems such as a *Knowledge-Based System (KBS) / Expert System* can serve as "knowledge-base" or "organizational memory" to counteract their dependency on the expertise of their individual members. Expert systems differ from CBRS with respect to Knowledge representation, inference and control. KBSs are valuable for, but often limited to particular managerial handling. One would expect the use of KBSs to be less widespread than CBR systems for the purpose of knowledge networks.

Learning through Participative Strategy Formation (LPSF)

Changes in organizational culture have led to increased use of participatory management methods. For instance, Japanese management methods stress the importance of management by consensus. As a result, organizations form committees or working groups in which members of the organization meet and share their knowledge so as to solve complex and ill-structured problems. Due to the uncertainty and complexity prevailing in the environment, sometimes even a "normal" well-defined problem requires participative / group decision making. Hence, it is a common phenomenon in a contemporary organization.

Participative strategy formation always constitutes a learning process as there are always differences in perceptions and understanding among various interest groups in organizations. Some group members may have more knowledge, competence and experience. Group learning occurs as the interaction among members takes place. As one shares knowledge with the other members in the organization, they gain information / knowledge but their feedback instantly adds value for the sender. As each group learns and creates from its new knowledge base, the base itself grows. Exponential growth occurs in the value of each sharing group's knowledge base (Quinn, 1992).

Sometimes, participative / group planning fails due to a lack of proper participation, communication and understanding among the members in the group. Recent developments in Information Technology have provided systems such as Group Decision Support Systems (GDSS) which can support participative / group planning. These systems are certainly not a cure for all afflictions in participative / group planning. However, there is a growing interest in using such systems in participative / group planning (Richman, 1987).

Group Decision Support System (GDSS) - A tool for LPSF

A Group Decision Support System (GDSS) is a computer-based system consisting of software, hardware, language components, procedures and tools (Huber, 1984) which can support participative strategy formation. There could be many different configurations of a GDSS.

A GDSS enables a group of people to work interactively and simultaneously using the networked hardware and software to complete the various aspects of the planning process. For example, automated brainstorming tools can be used to address the question, "what should the company do to become a knowledge-based / learning company in the next five years?". Using the system, group members can interact to generate and evaluate relevant ideas from their terminals. The group facilitator can then prioritize the ideas they have generated and can select one for further electronic discussion. Finally, the group can work together using a text editor to formulate a policy statement regarding the goal they have selected. This is how a GDSS can support a learning process (Jessup and Kukalis, 1990).

The capabilities of existing GDSS vary. Essentially, they reduce communication barriers by providing technical features such as the display of ideas, voting, compilation, anonymous input / interaction, decision modeling, electronic mail and the bulletin board function. Also, they act as group experts by providing advice in selecting and arranging the rules to be applied during the decision making process. The ultimate aim of this technology is to bring people together and facilitate efficient and effective interactive sharing of information among group members.

Learning through Sharing Individual Knowledge (LSIK)

Needless to say, no one has perfect and complete knowledge about a large and complicated world. Each member of the organization has his own views/ knowledge/mental models about the happenings in the organization and business environment. Expertise from each member is usually limited in both quality and scope. Hence, sharing of knowledge and unification of knowledge is essential for any organization to be a knowledge-based organization. In such organizations, learning occurs when they are dynamically utilized and updated. This shared and pooled knowledge can be viewed as the knowledge corpus for the organization and could be useful in many ways. For instance, the pooled knowledge could lead to effective policy decisions. When the knowledge is stored on an appropriate medium, sharing of knowledge can take place without any problem. However, the problem arises while pooling the knowledge. A tool which can support pooling of knowledge is a Cognitive Mapping System.

Cognitive Mapping System - a tool for LSIK

A Cognitive Map (CM) is a representation of relationships that are perceived to exist among any attributes and / or concepts. It is a tool which can be used to represent "thought / knowledge / mental model " of different individuals. The components of cognitive maps are nodes and signed directed arcs. Nodes represent concepts or variables. Signed directed arcs represent causal relations between concepts / variables. The sign + in the directed arc represents a direct relation and the sign - represents an inverse relation. The process of constructing cognitive maps for a given environment is called cognitive mapping. Cognitive mapping has been employed in different fields such as cognitive science and decision analysis. A computerized cognitive mapping system can be used to pool these ideas to get a "pooled knowledge".

Dynamic Learning of the Relationship among Organizational / Environment Factors (DLROF)

In a learning environment, if an organization has to be adaptive and responsive, it has to sense the present situation and predict the future environment both inside as well as outside the organization. For predicting the future environment, organizations have to dynamically learn the relationship among several factors and business processes. The dynamic learning of the relationship among business processes and other factors is essential for various purposes such as strategic / long-range planning and benchmarking. Often, top management has found that strategic and long-range planning has created problems which they were supposed to prevent. Although there could be several reasons for these failures, an overriding reason is due to the assumptions that there are specific / identifiable relationships among the factors. For instance, use of quantitative models for long range forecasting make the simplifying assumption of linearity in their underlying structure, which enables models to be built more easily. But, linear models are bad in absorbing turning points in the business processes. It is no longer advisable to make assumption about the relationship among various factors and business processes; it is essential to "learn" the relationship. Neural Networks offers exciting possibilities for " dynamically learning" the relationship among various factors / business processes as already discussed in much detail (Baets, 1995, 1996, 1997 and 1998; Baets et al., 1995; Venugopal and Baets, 1994 and 1995; van Wezel and Baets, 1995).

Artificial Neural Networks for DLROF

We want to summarize Artificial Neural Networks (ANNs) in this section as a learning technique within the context of IKTs. ANNs are a new information processing paradigm which simulates the living human brain. When the knowledge is in the form of quantitative information, ANNs play the role of Case Based Reasoning Systems. ANNs consist of many simple elements called nodes. The nodes are densely interconnected through directed links. Nodes take more than one input information, combines them in a particular way for reasoning purpose. The power of neural computing comes from connecting artificial neurons into artificial neural networks. The simplest network is a group of neurons arranged in a layer. Multilayer networks may be formed by simply cascading a group of single layers. The nodes of different layers are densely interconnected through directed links. The nodes at input layer receive the signals (values of the input variables) and propagate concurrently through the network, layer by layer.

ANNs have the ability to learn and identify complex patterns of information and to associate these with other information. ANNs can recognize and recall information in spite of incomplete or defective input information. They can also generalize learned information to other related information. These abilities form the basis for supporting learning of the relationship among business factors / processes . ANNs can take this information from corporate databases and can help in learning the relationship. Once the relationship is learned, it could be used as an early warning system for corporate failure. Though statistical tools could also be used for this purpose, they are constrained by their assumptions and other technicalities.

Though ANNs lack the ability to give explanation at intermediate stages, integrating them with expert systems can remove this deficiency to some extent and therefore can support a learning process. Efforts are being made both academically and commercially in this direction.

Integrated Intelligent Support System for Learning: a Conceptual Framework

From previous sections it is clear that different IT tools can independently support different organizational learning processes. For instance, some aspects of inter-organization learning and intra-organization learning can be supported by CBRS. Similarly, GDSS supports learning through participative policy-making. As organizational learning is viewed as integrated and collective learning, it is necessary that existing IT tools should enlarge the scope of their supporting roles and have greater capability or they should be integrated in an appropriate way so that it can support organizational learning and knowledge networks.

Intelligent support tools such as CBRS, KBS, GDSS, ANN together with a knowledge-base , case library and data base can be loaded on to a fileserver which is connected to other computers/ terminals through a local area network where all members have equal access to the different tools and are able to communicate freely. New technologies such as electronic brain storming, group consensus and negotiation software and general meeting support systems can be integrated in the GDSS for supporting group learning. Computer mediated communication systems and wide area networking would enable the companies to store, process, retrieve external information and provides an electronic learning environment where all members can communicate freely. Public domain databases can be incorporated. Technologies such as voice mail, E-mail and video conferencing can be made available for an efficient and effective communication. All these together can serve as environmental scanners. Companies' computers can be networked through Wide-Area-Networking with a relevant external system. Thus, remote access to business environmental knowledge can be made available within the company at any time. Venugopal and Baets (1995) discuss a conceptual framework for integrating these intelligent tools which could facilitate efficient and effective learning processes and support knowledge networks. However, the implementation of such a prototype integrated system will require a fundamental rethinking of the organizational design and transactions. Figure 7.1 shows this conceptual framework.

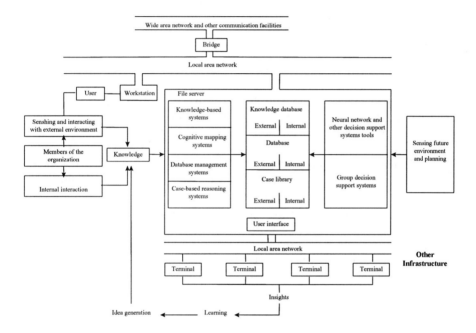

Figure 7.1: The conceptual framework of the integrated intelligent system of organizational learning.
(after Venugopal and Baets, 1995)

Figure 7.1 gives an overall integrated picture. It is clear that companies do not need to start from a complete architecture from the beginning. In many cases they can start off with the creation of a knowledge base using e.g. CBR (Lewis, 1995). This will create a first knowledge base which can be analyzed using ANNs. These

ANNs, in turn, feed back more knowledge to the knowledge base. Not only does a knowledge base exist, but there also exists an integrated tool to continue creation and the management of knowledge. The process of continuous learning, improvement and knowledge building is begun. Such a system can be built for a specific aspect of management (e.g. quality management; personnel management), but it could also incorporate the wide managerial scene of the company. The combined use of CBR and ANN for input, consulting, analysis and comparison is often a first stage of a knowledge network.

The experiences of a major financial holding

Companies start experimenting with this kind of alternative IT architectures and approaches for knowledge management, which they often put on top of their classical Information Systems. They do not replace systems, instead they build new systems based on new IKT techniques and architectures which retrieve part of their information in existing computer systems. This decreases the risk of re-opening or re-programming often badly documented programs. If this trend continues, IS architectures may look rather different in companies a decade from now. In order to clarify these concepts, we want to describe the example of a particular company which is experimenting with such an architecture. This example only describes one example of one particular company and its possible application of knowledge networks. It should not be seen as a prototype example which could be easily transferred to another company.

The company

The considered company is a Dutch financial holding which has its main activities in the insurance business. They cover a number of different insurance activities, like general risks, life insurance, pension funds and medical care. They have different brands in each of the activities and almost each activity in itself has a legal corporate structure. Furthermore they provide banking services, mainly in the private sector and they have portfolio companies running large financial portfolios. Their total annual revenue is around 10 billion Dutch guilders (2 Dutch guilders equal roughly 1 ECU), their assets value 4 billion and they employ 6,700 people. Over the past ten years, this holding was very active in acquisitions, which partly explains the existence of the large number of branded products. They never attempted to integrate and rationalize the newly acquired companies. The company has almost 10 % market share which makes them the second largest insurance company in the country: the largest has a 20 % market share. This company is by nature a physically networked company already.

The financial market can be characterized by a growing instability, which implies stronger competition, a growing number of mergers and low profitable companies leaving the market. Efficiency becomes an issue strengthened by the Third European Guideline on deregulation of the insurance sector. Different from other insurance companies, this company heavily relies on direct writing. Where the averages in the market are 22 % direct writing and 50 % via intermediaries, this company produces 86 % via direct writing and only 10 % via intermediaries. In view of a total number of clients of around 2.5 million and the large number of different brands, the IT architecture for this company is of paramount importance. This company has lots of fragmented and dispersed knowledge inside its different brands, but it is crucial for them to share that knowledge and build a knowledge based network for the complete holding.

The management culture

The corporate structure and philosophy is based on the "fleet" philosophy. The **ship** is the business unit. The **captain** is the manager who has overall responsibility. The **admiral** of the fleet is the executive board and the management board. They determine the overall strategy. The **course** is set out by each individual business unit. They have their own agreed targets. Mutual competition is allowed, but conflicts are not. This takes care of the **collision** problems at sea. The **fleet** itself is characterized by "small is beautiful" and "big is strong". However, in the maritime insurance business they are not strong, which is probably what inspires them to use this metaphor.

We can translate this vision in a number of down to earth assumptions. They decentralize the result responsibility and in line with that, they also delegate entrepreneurship. They deliberately did not opt for the one-firm concept; rather they adhere to a network organizational structure. The necessary synergy is not targeted via integration but through co-operation. The holding gives due

importance to interface management. Japanese innovation strategies are what the
company is interested in. Eventually, co-ordination should take place on product
platform level which should allow them to keep a unity in the diversity.

Clearly, in this industry and with this management culture, many of the classical
approaches would fail. Therefore, the company experiments with alternative
approaches.

Their experiments

Figure 7.2 gives an overview of how the company considered trends inside the
company and trends in the overall environment.

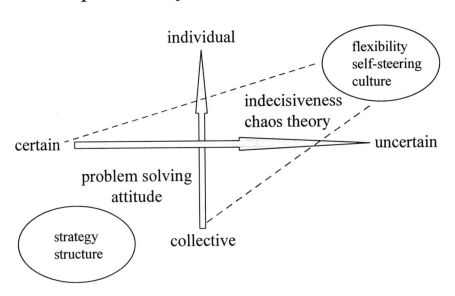

Figure7.2: internal focus

The focus of the company was mainly internal. They fostered flexibility and a self-steering culture where the individual was confronted with uncertainty. This led in certain cases to indecisiveness. On the certain and collective side, they had, as almost any other company, a strategy which was translated into a structure. The managerial attitude could be identified by a problem-solving attitude. Probably the only difference with modern managerial theories would be the importance they always gave to what we discussed earlier in the book as chaos theory. This approach led to the well known dilemma between flexibility and synergy. On the flexibility side of the equation they chose multi-labelled products via multi-distribution channels. They decentralized management control. They preferred to give flexibility a decisive role, unless arguments in favor of synergy changed the balance: low cost strategies and economies of scale are probably the best known examples of the latter.

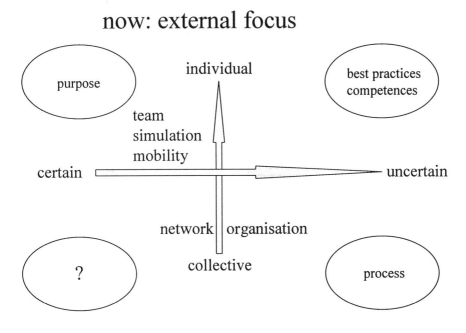

now: external focus

Figure 7.3: external focus

In order to solve this dilemma they now chose another approach which is described in figure 7.3. They refocused the company to become more outward looking. In the individual-uncertain quadrant they fostered a best-practices approach and they gave their employees additional training in order to make them aware of the crucial importance which managerial competencies play as a support for each individual as a manager. They opted for a networked organization and gave due attention to the managerial process in the many situations of uncertainty. With this purpose they introduced team technologies, scenario planning and program management. The rationale of the company was to focus on the individual. Team building was fostered, together with an enhanced mobility. Simulation techniques allow employees to be an active part of the definition of the corporate purpose itself. Where before strategy and structure were in place to manage the "collective certainty", almost no importance is given to this today: process and competencies is where the attention is focused today.

It is this new approach which necessitates a creative use of IKT in the way described earlier in this case study.

Their IKT approach

They explored a number of IKT developments, positioning what is available against the added value and the maturity of the technology. Their analysis of IKT techniques for distribution is summarized in figure 7.4.

IT: distribution & product innovation

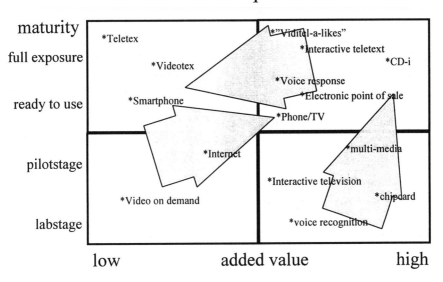

Figure 7.4: IT: distribution & product innovation

For the distribution of services and product innovation, they are exploring those mature techniques promising a high added value. But in order to support the new managerial focus described before and shown in figure 7.3, specific team technologies were introduced. In a new network environment, experiments are taking place today with a number of these technologies of which some have been described in detail earlier in this chapter: group decision support, team memory, knowledge networks, neural networks and data warehousing. A personal workspace concept supports these experiments. New IT competencies had to be acquired in respect to e.g. client-server architectures, groupware, office automation, data mining, multimedia and neural networks.

This resulted in a number of remarkable changes in the IT management of the company itself. This approach seems to have created a convergent IKT infrastructure, certainly on the decision making level. Within the **fleet,** economies of scale and synergies are used more efficiently. This shows via vendor management, pick and mix strategies and co-makership of many applications. IT-entrepreneurship and IT-management are located within the operating companies. IT performance reports are established. IKT-strategic platforms for co-ordination and overall prioritizing includes members of the Executive Board, IT-directors and group information managers. In a completely different way are IT service centers empowered. Needless to say that this has created a much more stimulating climate for the IT professionals. People work more together on projects and key people are exchanged. Competence centers are created in order to support these changes, but also in order to capitalize on the acquired experience.

Observations based on this case

Conclusions can not yet be drawn on the experience of this company but some observations are worth summarizing.

This company has a view on IKT and this view clearly differs from what we see today in many other companies, not limited to the financial world. This view is rather experimental and the company accepts that this approach has some inherent risks. Being a good insurance company, they probably estimate the potential benefit to be higher than this inherent risk.

The view of this company is initiated from its overall corporate strategy. This view seeks to integrate the corporate strategy and the IKT strategy and to create a mutual balance. This approach is a good example of IS strategy alignment in an operational setting, on a corporate wide level.

This case is an interesting example of IKT enabled knowledge management on a corporate level. To the author's knowledge, these kinds of experiences are still rather rare. Real experience is built up today inside this company and in a few more years this has the potential to be a "showcase".

In this case, the company uses new IKT developments (e.g. GDSS ana neural networks) for a fundamental long term development of its corporate strategy and not merely for fashionable reasons on specific projects. This should provide different insights after a longer period of time.

This experiment only started recently and it is still continuing through a lot of trial and error. Important, however, is the potential experience which this company is building up today. The interesting question in this case is whether this approach (or a comparable approach) could give a company a real advantage in the insurance/finance market. Only the future will tell.

7.4. From organized Information Technology to a non-structured emergent knowledge environment: the role of Intranet technologies

With the arrival of the Internet and Intranet technologies, a whole new range of possibilities have become available to us. For the majority of applications, Internet is considered solely as a powerful resource for structuring and navigating information space. People regularly describe most communication technologies in conduit terms, talking of information as "in" books, files, or databases as if it could just as easily be accessed or "out-sourced". We are asked to put ideas "down on paper", to "send them along", and so forth.   But equally, Internet could be a powerful resource for constructing and negotiating social space. Consequently, as never before, scattered groups of people, unknown to one another, rarely living in contiguous areas, and sometimes never seeing another member, have nonetheless been able to form robust social worlds. In the professional environment we have not seen this kind of self-created and self-organizing groups very often. A different appraisal of the working-learning-innovating triangle, supported by an informal IT platform, can lead to the development of "community-based knowledge refinement": an emergent knowledge environment. This section investigates into this interesting development, using the examples of service technicians in a copy-machine company (Brown, 1997).

Working

Orr's (1987a, 1987b, 1990a, 1990b) ethnography of service technicians ("reps") in training and at work in a large corporation paints a clear picture of the divergence between espoused practice and actual practice, of the way this divergence develops , and of the trouble it can cause. Bourdieu (1977) and Ryle (1954) have already emphasized the importance of a "work in progress" approach. They distinguished the "modus operandi" from the "opus operatum": the way a task, as it unfolds over time, looks to someone at work on it, while many of the options and dilemmas remain unsolved, as opposed to the way it looks with hindsight as a finished task. The "opus operatum", the finished view, tends to see the action in terms of the task alone and cannot see the way in which the process of doing the task is actually structured by the constantly changing conditions of work and the world. The "opus operatum" inevitably smoothes over the myriad decisions made with regard to changing conditions. As a journey becomes complex, a road-map increasingly conceals what is actually needed to make the journey. "Thick description", by contrast, ascends from the abstraction to the concrete circumstances of actual practice, reconnecting the map and the mapped.

Orr's study shows how an organization's maps can dramatically distort its view of the routes its members take. Many organizations are willing to assume that complex tasks can be successfully mapped onto a set of simple, Tayloristic, canonical steps that can be followed without need of significant understanding or insight and thus without need of significant investment in training or skilled technicians. But as Bourdieu, Suchman (1987a) and Orr show, actual practice inevitably involves tricky interpolations between abstract accounts and situated demands. People are typically viewed as performing their jobs according to formal job descriptions, despite the fact that daily evidence points to the contrary (Suchman, 1987b).

Directive documentation, which is amongst others used in order to support "reps", does not deprive the workers of the skills they have: rather, "it merely reduces the amount of information given them" (Orr, 1990a). The burden of making up the difference between what is provided and what is needed then rests with the reps, who in bridging the gap actually protect the organization from its own short-sightedness. As a result, a wedge is driven between the corporation and its reps:

the corporation assumes the reps view the overly simplistic training programs as a reflection of the corporation's low estimation of their worth and skills.

The training of and documentation for reps are, of course, about maintaining machines. However, a large part of service work might better be described as repair and maintenance of the social fabric of the company (Orr, 1990b). If a major breakdown occurs, a rep cannot simply replace a machine. That would undermine the trust of the client in the rep and its company. Orr's research describes the successful use of another technique which reps use (and people can use in general): a long story-telling procedure. It shows that the process of forming a story is, centrally, one of diagnosis. The key element of diagnosis is the situated production of understanding through narration, with a primary criterion of coherence. A story, once in possession of the community (e.g. the reps), can then be used and further modified in story telling diagnostic sessions, like the one used for its creation in the first place: yet another knowledge technology.

Central to the reps' practice are the three overlapping categories "narration", "collaboration" and "social construction". Those categories get to the heart of what the reps actually do which, significantly, may have no place in the organization's abstracted, canonical accounts of their work. First of all, telling stories helps to diagnose the state of a troublesome machine. The quality of narration is that stories have a flexible generality that makes them both adaptable and particular. The reps try to impose coherence on an apparently random sequence of events in order that they can decide what to do next. What the reps do in their story telling is develop a causal map out of their experience to replace the impoverished directive route that they have been furnished by the corporation. The second characteristic of story telling is that the stories also act as repositories of accumulated wisdom. In particular, community narratives protect the rep's ability to work from the ravages of modern idealizations of work.

Shared narratives are obviously communal and thereby collaborative. A story goes through a collective, not an individual process. The insight accumulated is not a private substance, but socially constructed and distributed. The activities defined by management, on the contrary, are those which one worker will do. Work as the relationship of employment is discussed in terms of a single worker's relationship to the corporation. Orr's studies show how reps trade stories back and forth throughout the day while meeting for coffee or for meals.

Story telling constructs a shared understanding out of bountiful conflicting and confusing data. This constructed understanding reflects the reps' view of the world. They constructed a rep's view of the machine and not a trainer's. Such an approach is highly situated and highly improvisational: it is a social construction. A further feature is that in telling these stories an individual rep contributes to the construction and development of his or her own identity as a rep and reciprocally to the construction and development of the community of reps in which he or she works.

Learning

Concepts of knowledge or information transfer have been under increasing attack. In particular learning theorists (e.g. Lave 1988; Lave and Wenger, 1990, 1991) have rejected transfer models, which isolate knowledge from practice, and develop a view of learning as social construction, putting knowledge back into the contexts in which it has meaning (Pea, 1990; Brown, Collins, and Duguid, 1989). What is learned is profoundly connected to the conditions in which it is learned. Lave and Wenger (1990) propose in this respect the term Legitimate Peripheral Participation (LPP). Learning, from the viewpoint of LPP, essentially involves becoming an "insider" process. Learners do not receive or even construct abstract, "objective", individual knowledge; rather they learn to function in a community. In short, they are "enculturated" (Brown, Collins and Duguid, 1989). Learners acquire the embodied ability to behave as community members.

The central issue in learning is becoming a practitioner, not learning about practice. This approach situates itself in the practices and communities in which knowledge takes on significance. In such communities of peers, a specialist cannot hope to exert hierarchical control over knowledge that he or she must first construct co-operatively. As Orr (1990a) says: "Occupational communities ... have little hierarchy; the only real status is that of member. The communities that we discern are often non canonical and not recognized by the organization. They are more fluid and interpenetrative than bounded, often crossing the restrictive boundaries of the organization to incorporate people from outside (and that can include both suppliers and customers)."

First, work practice and learning need to be understood not in terms of the groups that are ordained (e.g. "task forces" or "trainees"), but in terms of the communities that emerge. Second, attempts to introduce "teams" and "work groups" into the workplace to enhance learning or work practice are often based on an assumption that without impetus from above, an organization's members configure themselves as individuals. The process of working and learning together creates a work situation which the workers value, and they resist having it disrupted by their employers through events such as a reorganization of the work. This resistance can surprise employers who think of labor as a commodity to arrange to suit their ends. The work can only continue free of disruption if the employer can be persuaded to see the community as necessary to accomplishing work.

The question arises: how is it possible to foster learning-in-working ? If learners need access to practitioners at work, it is essential to question didactic approaches, with their tendency to separate learners from the target community and the authentic work practices. If training is designed so that learners cannot observe the activity of practitioners, learning is inevitably impoverished. Learners need legitimate access to the periphery of communication (to computer mail, to formal and informal meetings, to telephone conversations, etc.) and of course to war stories. They pick up invaluable "know how" - not only information but also manner and technique - from being on the periphery of competent practitioners going about their business.

Innovating

Canonical accounts of work are not only hard to apply and hard to learn, they are also hard to change. Communities-of-practice (like the reps) continue to develop a rich, fluid, non-canonical world view and the challenge of changing practice. This, it has been argued (Hedberg, Nystrom and Starbuck, 1976; Schein, 1990), drives innovation by allowing the parts of an organization to step outside the organization's inevitably limited core world view and simply try something new. The organization presupposes an essentially pre-structured environment and implicitly assumes that there is a correct response to any condition it discovers there. By contrast, the enacting organization is proactive and highly interpretative. The source of innovation lies on the interface between an organization and its environment.

Enacting organizations differ from discovering ones in that in a reciprocal way, instead of waiting for changed practices to emerge and responding, they enable them to emerge and anticipate their effects. An enacting organization must also be capable of reconceiving not only its environment but also its own identity, for in a significant sense the two are mutually constitutive. By asking different questions, by seeking different sorts of explanations, and by looking from different points of view, different answers emerge. Indeed, different environments and different organizations mutually reconstitute each other dialectically or reciprocally.

In some sense it was necessary both for Haloid to reconceive itself (as Xerox) and for Xerox's machine to help bring about a reconceptualisation of an area of office practice for the new machine. What people failed to see was that a copier allowed the proliferation of copies and of copies of copies. The quantitative leap in copies and their importance independent of the original then produced a qualitative leap in the way they were used. They no longer served merely as records of an original. Instead, they participated in the productive interactions or organization's members in a unprecedented way.

If an organizational core overlooks or curtails the enacting in its midst by ignoring or disrupting its communities-of-practice, it threatens its own survival in two ways. It will not only threaten to destroy the very working and learning practices by which it, knowingly or unknowingly, survives. It will also cut itself off from a major source of potential innovation that inevitably arises in the course of that working and learning.

Organizations as communities-of-communities: an integrated view on working, learning and innovating

The complex of contradictory forces that put an organization's assumptions and core beliefs in direct conflict with members' working, learning, and innovating arises from a thorough misunderstanding of what working, learning and innovating are. The corporate tendency to downskill can often lead to non-canonical practice and communities being driven further underground so that the insights gained through work are more completely hidden from the organization as a whole. Then later changes or reorganizations, whether or not intended to downskill, may disrupt what they do not notice. The gap between espoused and actual practice may become too large for non-canonical practices to bridge. To close that gap, an organization needs to reconceive itself as a community-of-communities, acknowledging in the process the many non-canonical communities in its midst.

Size of the company is not the single determining feature. Large atypical, enacting organizations have the potential to be highly innovative and adaptive. Within an organization perceived as a collective of communities, not simply of individuals, in which enacting experiments are legitimate, separate community perspectives can be amplified by interchanges among communities. Out of this friction of competing ideas can come the sort of improvisational sparks necessary for igniting organizational innovation. As Von Hippel (1988) argues , sources of innovation can lie outside an organization, among its customers and suppliers.

Any design of organizational architecture and the ways communities are linked to each other should enhance the healthy autonomy of communities, while simultaneously building an interconnectedness through which to disseminate the results of separate communities' experiments. In some form or another the stories that support learning-in-working and innovation should be allowed to circulate. The technological potential to support this distribution (e-mail, bulletin boards and other devices that are capable of supporting narrative exchange) is available. Working-class groups (like the reps) are remarkably open with each other about what they know. Within these communities, news travels fast. Community knowledge is readily available to community members.

This view of communities-of-communities contrasts strongly with the perspective of the conventional workplace, where: work and learning are set out in formal descriptions so that people (and organizations) can be held accountable; groups are organized to define responsibility; organizations are bounded to enhance concepts of competition; peripheries are closed off to maintain secrecy and privacy.

Stolen knowledge

Whilst Information Technology has now become widely available and, in particular, the Internet has grown exponentially, the use of IT has not progressed, often simply reinforcing the classical metaphor of knowledge being poured by a teacher into an empty vessel (the student). Little attention has been given towards the reconceptualisation of prevalent notions of teaching, instruction, the learner, subject matter, technology and system, transforming these into something quite different. A situated approach contests the assumption that learning is a response to teaching. Even if a learner did not learn what a teacher, or educational technology, or workplace instructor attempted to teach, it is not just justifiable to conclude that nothing was learned. The process is not, then, like the addition of a brick to a building, where the brick remains as distinct and self-contained as it was in the builder's hand. Instead, it is a little like the addition of color to color in a painting, where the color that is added becomes inseparably a part of the color that was there before. What is learned can never be judged solely in terms of what is taught. And this is a severe problem for the operationalisation of situated learning, based within a framework of educational technology.

Rabindranath Tagore quoted in Bandyopadhyay (1989:45) introduces an interesting metaphor of "stolen knowledge".

> *A very great musician came and stayed in (our) house. He made one big mistake ... (he) determined to teach me music, and consequently no learning took place. Nevertheless, I did casually pick up from him a certain amount of stolen knowledge.*

Tagora "stole" knowledge by watching and listening to the musician as the latter, outside his classes, played for his own and others' entertainment. Part of the need to "steal" arises because relatively little of the complex web of actual practice can be made the subject of explicit instruction.

Compared to abstracted, explicit knowledge the implicit aspects of practice, while occasionally very difficult to get in perspective, have a dynamism by virtue of their very implicitness. More generally, abstractions become problematic when their own historical and social locations as practice are ignored. Work on expert systems suggests that technologies whose representation of the complexities of practice are misleadingly partial may make that practice difficult or even impossible. Any decomposition of the task must be done with an eye not to the task or the user in isolation, but to the learner's need to situate the decomposed task in the context of the overall social practice. The presence of the full context gives the learner the chance to "steal" whatever he or she finds most appropriate.

The work of Lave and Wenger, discussed earlier, unfolds a rich, complex picture of what a situated view of learning needs to account for and emphasizes, particular the social, rather than merely physical nature of situatedness. Legitimate peripheral participation (LPP), which is their understanding of learning, clearly distinguishes between learning and intentional instruction. The richness of interpersonal interaction is usually either overlooked or deliberately disrupted in the classroom. In the workplace, learners can, when they need, steal their knowledge from the social periphery, made up of other, more experienced workers and ongoing, socially shared practice. The classroom, unfortunately, tends to be too well secured against theft. Information Technology should not reinforce the limitations of the class rooms, but rather allow for participative learning.

Community-Based Knowledge Refinement

Web technology (http + html) made the network-of-networks which Internet is, accessible for a wider population. Within the view that innovation is in itself a joint activity of a number of "Complex Adaptive Systems" (CAS), Internet and the web can provide a medium for innovation.

Technology companies do not focus on products anymore, but on product platforms. These designed product platforms also tap the tacit knowledge inside the company. Each product platform can put a number of product variants on the market. Product variants rapidly evolve from those platforms. Furthermore, platforms themselves evolve through discontinuous changes in technology components. The role of the product platform can be compared to the role of the chromosome in the human being. All companies have in their "peripheries" a number of occurring "experiments". But very often we do not see them and therefore we cannot learn from them. In the first place, we need learning in order to see the learning which takes place in those peripheries. As has been argued before, let the world do the work for you; do not abstract the world.

In the case of the reps, the instructions for troubleshooting an intermittent copy quality fault is to place a test pattern on platen, to run 5000 copies, sort throughout for bad copies and then compare the bad copies with a certain chart. But what a rep often does is pick from the paper basket the last copies which were made, after which the rep was called, and which immediately shows the problem for which the rep was called. As Orr's research shows, an important, non-documented error will be dealt with via "story-telling". Since telling stories seems to be how people learn, then the task for Information Technology is to create a "learning space" which allows self-learning via exchange of stories. In IT terminology one would think about collaborative software.

Within Xerox, a process of Community-Based Knowledge Refinement is put in place. This systems filters from 25000 calls per day to 300 cases per product. The production of the cases (the stories) is done by the reps, but so is the filtering. On level 1 (hotlines, etc.) the story is created by the authors. On level 2, a number of these cases are submitted to editors (reps themselves) and they are examined. If they are rejected (on level 5; after examination on level 3 and validation on level 4) then additional refereeing takes place in order to limit the waste of knowledge. The retained cases are then refereed by referees by the community of product leaders before they get integrated in the Case Base. This mechanism leverages both the social and the technical. It is a social way to create and award good ideas.

Though this case base is of immediate interest and use of the reps, it also allows further learning using learning algorithms. Genetic algorithms (based on sources of variability) are used in order to create a "community mind". A complex fitness scheme is created which is using the following sources of variability :

  Machine placements (temperature, humidity, dust, ...)
  Market niches (copy shops, ...)
  Print shops (wide range of paper stock)
  Operator profiles
  Heterogeneous field force (urban specialists, rural multi productists)
  Evolving failures (machine age,...)

Further track is kept of the network of field engineers and their ongoing conversations. Learning and adaptation, also in the "community mind", takes place via critique, cross coupling and combining "tips". Via this approach, a vast space boils down to "knowledge".

The important question for a company is: how to facilitate this process; how to honor the emergent ? Precisely in leveraging the small efforts of the many (people) in order to drive learning and innovation, web technology can be useful. However, web technology should be organized in a way to facilitate this learning and seldom organizations facilitate this. Fortunately, "emergent practice" can be identified through "authorized practice". It is only a different sub-set.

The real work gets done by "emergent practice". Emergent practice is based on co-operation of people in Communities of Practice (CoP) (Brown, 1997). How can we identify the difference between a group or team or task force and a CoP ? One can talk about a CoP, when members know what other members really know and how to provoke that know-how for their own purposes. CoPs facilitate the group in using new processes, tools, language, models, etc. to do the work to which outsiders have to be introduced. CoP members' identities have changed in their own and others eyes. CoP members have two identities: the "authorized" identity in product groups; the "emergent" CoP member identity. It is the participation in CoP which helps them do their "real job". CoPs bridge silos and focus on practice.

A company's attempt should be to identify the emergent faster. A rumor takes 48 hours to go through a company; a mission statement takes years to get communicated. The organization should recognize that the "authorized" has to create the strategic intent and the enabling processes. The "emergent" contains the core competencies, the reservoir of capabilities. The interaction between the authorized and the emergent creates a "generative strategy": this is the sense making process of the company. This way of looking to a company considers the organization as a platform, rather than as a (fixed) structure.

The way to support the emergent or "the social fabric" throughout companies is the use of hypertext technology within the framework of a "knowledge refinement server".

The knowledge refinery server aims to allow all people to contribute as well as to reflect and learn from experiences and from each other. The advantage of hypertext links is that it allows to continue building on existing things, giving comment, describes ones own experiences, suggesting new possibilities, etc., comparable with the "story telling" approach described earlier. Linking comments, or cross-linking comment or giving comments on comments is what people allow to learn, but is also what hypertext is possible to produce.

The formal organization and the formal IT support deal with classic documents and is based on a classic client/server document management system.   The informal IT support deals with html-type documents, new expressive forms and a WWW-like community document system.

The Internet protocol is used for the backbone.   The Intranet could even use synchronous multicast. Broadcast, midcast and narrowcast could be used in a synchronous and asynchronous mode, both symmetrical and asymmetrical.   Rather than an infrastructure, a new (work) medium is born.

Some lessons learned from the Xerox experience

The challenge for companies is situated in getting the formal organization and the informal one to work together and where possible to leverage each other. Identifying and recognizing "Communities-of-Practice" and supporting them in their operations will lead to constant evolution.   Web technologies can be used particularly for that but certainly more experimenting is necessary and we must recognize that this process of technical evolution has only just got underway.

A company consists of two worlds: one built on strategic capability and the other built on strategic exploration.   This duality is reflected in the research and development activities of a company.   Research should be at the same time grounded and radical, catering for both the strategic capability and the strategic exploration of the company.   The duality of the two is detailed in the following table (Brown, 1997).

Strategic capability	**Strategic exploration**
Strengthens	Uncovers
Broadens	Discovers
Enlarges	Undermines
Advances	Destabilizes
Couples	Makes new
Builds, supports	Recreates
Relates, frames	Reframes
Is Predictable	Is Unpredictable
Enables definitions	Creates

These two worlds should be bridged productively. The serious "scientist" catering for the strategic capability should engage in deep scientific knowledge, grounded, analytical, focused on trenches, predictable and disciplinary. The "young artist", catering for the strategic exploration, will be playful, grounded also, artistic, transcending boundaries, unpredictable and multi-disciplinary. For a company, this is not an either/or situation but a both/and situation. Bridging these two cultures is not always easy but it can be made easier via IT today.

The practice of bridging the authorized and the emergent requires a different management style. Individuals should be committed to a problem (grounded). They should go to the roots of the problem (radical). A problem should be followed wherever it goes and should engender a cross-disciplinary approach, if need be. People should honor the world and make sense out of it. No attempt should be made to reduce the world to some canonical procedures. It is everybody's responsibility to engage each other and in doing so to create communities. It is a little like bringing together the seemingly impossible combination of deep structured science and art.

In summary, Xerox has experienced a shift in thinking and practice which offers a promising model for companies seeking to manage a complex adaptive system to consider, operating from inside the company a set of complex adaptive systems (Brown, 1997). The shifts which have been observed in Xerox are summarized in the following table.

Old paradigms	New paradigms
Push/Pull	Co-evolution
Products	Designed product platforms
Authorized	Authorized/emergent
Teams	Communities of practice
Strategy	Generative strategy
Managing for efficiency	Managing for knowledge formation

Based on the Xerox experience one can expect to see in the coming 5 to 10 years most products (not to say every product) "Internet-enabled" and in parallel we will see distributed innovation platforms emerging as well.

7.5. The corporate mission: sustainable development via knowledge networks

Before drawing some general conclusions in the next chapter it is worth repeating that the goal of the above mentioned companies is somewhat different from what we observe in many companies. This illustrates that the corporate mission has to go hand in hand with a possible choice for a knowledge based approach. Still many companies target (short term) growth, until reality forces them into restructuring. Many companies move from one restructuring into another, keeping the growth myth as the one and only valid one. Companies experimenting with knowledge approaches observe that the overall goal is different. Growth is no longer an objective, not in the short term, nor in the long term. Sustainable development replaces growth as a target. Sustainable development is based on the acceptance of the chaotic behavior of markets and aims to ride the waves of change, rather than to fight them. Riding the waves with a decent level of comfort replaces the absolute pressure to arrive at any price in harbor X. This price sometimes proves to be disappearance.

Sustainable development has to do with, amongst others, accepting evolution; keeping an open mind for new activities and developments; innovation of products and services; exploration of new markets. These are interesting activities for the survival of a company in which knowledge can play a decisive role. Knowledge based companies are not interested in developing an irregular schedule of development with fantastic successes but also many failures. Rather they are aiming for sustainability. If it is not the level of the development that is important but its overall rhythm. Sustainability accepts that profit margins vary from year to year, since it is no main target anymore. Sustainability does not exclude from the outset that a company ends up in a different market than the one planned. Sustainability as an aim gives the company the capacity to remain an interesting company for the market and its employees, which is contributing to the knowledge development of its workers, as well as to the overall knowledge development in the market. These developments result in new products and services.

Knowledge management and learning as a corporate strategy can support a company to manage in the chaotic markets in which they are active. However, this changes the focus of the company from a short-term profit perspective to a longer term sustainability target. A knowledge network based approach, in combination with short term corporate goals, probably fails. For the readers who still doubt or do not completely see the difference yet, the epilogue should help. It describes a last real life case which integrates all aspects dealt with in this book. Different from many other cases "Sailing by(e)" is made to illustrate either effective or ineffective handling of an administrative situation in a chaotic world, rather than for (class room) discussion only. Nevertheless, the case has proven to be useful in classroom discussion also.

REFERENCES

Baets W, 1995a, "Artificiele neurale netwerken: het in kaart brengen van veranderingsprocessen en het meten van leren", Handboek effektief opleiden, 4.131

Baets W, 1995b. Ecosip study day on Business Process Reengineering and Information Technology (Paris): Business Process Re-engineering: A corporate mind set.

Baets W, 1996a. "The corporate mind-set as a precursor for business process (re-)engineering: About knowledge, perceptions and learning." In *Information Technology and Organizational Transformation: Innovation for the 21st Century Organization,* Baets W and Galliers R (eds.). Wiley.

Baets W, 1996b. Some Empirical Evidence on IS Strategy Alignment in Banking. Information & Management. Vol. 30, Nr. 4.

Baets W, 1996c. "Gestion de l'intelligence organisationelle." In *L'organisation apprenante: l'action productrice de sens*, Jeanne Mallet (ed.). Université de Provence.

Baets W, 1997. Intelligent Decision Support: The Combination of Artificial Neural Networks and Fuzzy Logic (Dutch version). Nijenrode Management Review.

Baets W, Brunenberg L, van Wezel M and Venugopal V, 1995. Corporate Cognitive Mapping: Mapping of corporate change processes. Fourth International Conference on Artificial Neural Networks. Cambridge, UK.

Bandyopadhyay P, 1989. *Rabindranath Tagore*. Calcutta: Anglia.

Bourdieu P, 1977. *Outline of a Theory of Practice* (translation out of French by R Nice). Cambridge: Cambridge University Press (first published in French 1973).

Brown J S, 1997. Communities-of-Practice: the example of Xerox. Conference on Complexity and Innovation. April. London.

Brown J S, Collins A and Duguid P, 1989. Situated cognition and the Culture of Learning. Education Researcher. Vol. 18, Nr. 1, pp. 32-42.

Hedberg B, Nystrom P C and Starbuck W H, 1976. "Designing Organizations to Match Tomorrow." In *Prescriptive Models of Organizations*, Nystrom P C and Starbuck W H (eds.). Amsterdam: North-Holland Publishing Company.

Honey P, 1991. The learning organization simplified. Training & Development. Vol. 9, pp. 30-32.

Huber G P, 1984. Issues in the design of Group Decision Support Systems. MIS Quarterly. Vol. 8, pp. 195-204.

Jessup L M and Kukalis S, 1990. Better Planning Using Group Support Systems. Long Range Planning. Vol. 23, Nr. 3, pp. 100-105.

Lave J, 1988. *Cognition in Practice: Mind, Mathematics and Culture in Everyday Life*. New York: Cambridge University Press.

Lave J and Wenger E, 1990. Situated Learning: Legitimate Peripherical Participation. IRL report 90-0013. Palo Alto, CA: Institute for Research on Learning.

Lave J and Wenger E, 1991. *Situated Learning: Legitimate peripheral participation*. New York: Cambridge University Press.

Lewis L, 1995. *Managing Computer Networks: A Case-Based Reasoning Approach*. London: Artech House Books.

Orr J, 1987a. Narratives at Work: Story Telling as Cooperative Diagnostic Activity. Field Service Manager. June, pp. 47-60.

Orr J, 1987b. Talking about Machines: Social Aspects of Expertise. Report for the Intelligent Systems Laboratory. Xerox Palo Alto Research Center. Palo Alto, CA.

Orr J, 1990a. Talking about Machines: an Ethnography of a Modern Job. PhD thesis. Cornell University.

Orr J, 1990b. "Sharing knowledge, Celebrating Identity: War Stories and Community Memory in a Service Culture." In *Collective Remembering: Memory in Society,* Middleton D S and Edwards D (eds.). Beverley Hills, CA: Sage Publications.

Pea R D, 1990. Distributed Cognition. IRL Report 90-0015. Palo Alto, CA: Institute for Research on Learning.

Pirsig R, 1979. *Zen and the art of motorcycle maintenance.* Penguin.

Quinn J B, 1992. *Intelligent Enterprise.* New York: The Free Press.

Richman L S, 1987. Software catches the team spirit. Fortune. June.

Ryle G, 1954. *Dilemmas: The Tarner Lectures.* Cambridge: Cambridge University Press.

Schein E H, 1990. Organizational Culture. American Psychologist. Vol. 45, Nr. 2, pp. 109-119.

Suchman L, 1987a. *Plans and Situated Actions: The Problem of Human-Machine Communication.* New York: Cambridge University Press.

Suchman L, 1987b. Common Sense in Interface Design. Techné. Vol. 1, Nr. 1, pp. 38-40.

Sullivan C H and Yates C E, 1988. Reasoning by Analogy - A tool for Business Planning. Sloan Management Review. Spring, pp. 55-60.

van Wezel M and Baets W, 1995. Predicting Market Responses with a Neural Network: the Case of Fast Moving Consumer Goods. Marketing Intelligence & Planning. Autumn.

Venugopal V and Baets W, 1994a. Neural Networks and Statistical Techniques in Marketing Research: A conceptual comparison Marketing Intelligence & Planning. Vol. 12, Nr. 7.

Venugopal V and Baets W, 1994b. Neural Networks and their Applications in Marketing Management. The Journal of Systems Management. September.

Venugopal V and Baets W, 1995. An integrated intelligent support system for Organizational Learning - A conceptual framework. The Learning Organization. Fall.

Von Hippel E, 1988. *The Sources of Innovation.* New York: Oxford University Press.

8. A ROADMAP OF MANAGEMENT IN A DYNAMIC ENVIRONMENT

As suggested a number of times, one cannot expect firm conclusions on this subject. The book has attempted to share a number of experiences and experiments and took very much a learning stance. A number of comments have been given and documented. Some ideas have been suggested and some exercises in creative thinking have been described. At no point, rules have been identified or given or even suggested. The book aims for comments or suggestions, rather than for rules. In this complex material, suggestions instead of prescriptions can be of assistance. But in the end, it will all depend on what the manager does with these suggestions.

In this last chapter we construct a kind of a road map or a tourist guide. A tourist guide describes some of the places of interest, as they have been perceived by others and it suggests visiting these places. Of course, many of the suggested places are of general interest, but it could still be the case that a specific person does not share the general experience suggested at a particular tourist spot. This does not make the road map of little value, nor does it make the person who does not like a particular spot an exception. That is only the reality of life. It is the freedom of each individual to follow the advice of a guide book and afterwards to have his or her own feelings or perceptions about the place, even if these are different from the description in the book. Probably, the guide book which we offer here is of use to you. It is in no way a guarantee for a successful "holiday".

In this book we have aimed to give a deeper insight into three different aspects of management which have become increasingly important today. If the evolution of markets and economies continues to show non-linear dynamic behavior, we will observe a shift away *from a profit making orientation of companies in favor of an orientation on sustainable development*. The latter has to be understood as a flexible development of a company along its own core competencies, dropping those competencies which it no longer needs and creating continuously new competencies in line with previous experience. The company, as well as its core competencies and its corporate goal will be changing flexibly. It will be increasingly difficult to stick to the company's original core business. Development will replace profit as a target and sustainability will become more important than growth. This summarizes the changing arena in which companies operate today. This is a consequence of the dynamic and non-linear behavior of markets: chaos and complexity.

In order to be able to manage for sustainable development in a dynamic environment, the climate inside a company should be one of empowerment, initiative, acceptance of failure and mistakes and experimentation. The corporate culture should be one of (corporate) learning: allowing people to take initiatives and to learn from these initiatives. But learning is not a holy grail in itself. Learning has to be supported by knowledge networks. *If learning is the necessary condition for management of sustainable development, then knowledge infrastructure is the sufficient one.* Learning is not only aimed at an individual level; therefore a company should support individual and corporate learning. This book is focused on the discussion of knowledge creation and management as a way of supporting learning. Knowledge management is the tool which supports the environment (a learning attitude) in order to reach the corporate goal (sustainable development). Knowledge management and learning will support the management of the chaotic behavior of markets and people.

A knowledge infrastructure needs adequate IKT tools. The optimal combination of IKT tools with an adapted managerial attitude and aim is what this book tries to identify for the company operating today. An IKT architecture, in its most simple configuration, will probably be based on a combination of CBR and ANNs. From this basic infrastructure, the IKT infrastructure can easily be built.

Some more detail on this summary leads us to a number of suggestions which the reader has to decide whether he wants to "visit" or not. We have the feeling that the suggestions made are most probably of importance for each manager. They do not suggest solutions, since no typical solutions can be found for complex problems. They mainly identify "places of interest to visit", before a manager takes some of his decisions. They suggest a check-list to be used before starting off for the important "crossing of the Rubicon".

1. Market behavior observed suggests that markets react with a positive feed-back behavior on (new) products. In many markets, and increasingly so if much information is involved in a product or service, "lock-in" phenomena or "snow-ball effects" appear. The first mover may get an increasingly bigger share of the market, based on the behavior of the economic system, rather than on intrinsic quality. The classical market mechanism does not appear to describe the generic market behavior, but it seems instead to describe a special case of positive feed-back behavior. This market behavior has important consequences for the manager's marketing strategy. If we want to understand the non-linear behavior of markets, we should use non-linear methods to analyze markets. Market research methods may need some revision.

2. The more products or services become knowledge based, the more it is important for the company to get hold of all information. For complex products and services, and specifically so for industrial (one-off) products, a lot of that knowledge is with the customer. Customers know better what they want than the producing companies do. If we claim that companies should be client oriented, than this means today that they should involve the knowledge of the clients in the product (service) design phase. This needs an important change in management behavior in many companies. It implies a shift from a production driven company to a market driven one, but market driven in this case means much more than what is described in marketing text books. Clients should be part of the company's knowledge network if a company takes knowledge management seriously. It is suggested that clients become partners, rather than opponents.

3. It is a serious simplification to state that information is freely available these days and known to all market players and that all information is discounted in the market price. Instead, too much of data and information is available, but companies do not succeed in using it in their favor. Furthermore, information is only information in a specific context. The same data in the hands of different companies becomes different information. The context sensitivity, together with the overload of information today, should be an incentive for companies to re-focus their information management. That is where knowledge management comes into the picture for the first time. Another consequence of the evolution of our information society is that it is a simplified theoretical statement to say that a market price contains all available

information on the market. The pricing issue deserves some further attention and cannot be dealt with in a classical way anymore. The assumptions have changed dramatically; the concepts used are still the same.

4. In information technology we have observed a shift from individual IT in the direction of "group" IT, and from structured IT to emergent IT, including the introduction of knowledge technologies. Until recently, users downloaded information and did some manipulation with that information. In some cases, the result of those manipulations were up-loaded again in the database for use by other people. It is only recently that we have seen information technology which supports and improves group decision making. As is advocated in the book, knowledge networks are networks of people, possibly in different services and different locations. Only recently, IKT allows us to support group work. Therefore only recently, IKT is able to support knowledge networks. In turn, IKT support of knowledge networks can magnify the impact of the networks for the company. IKT approaches in many companies do not yet take this evolution into account. IKT development but also IT architectures and Decision Support Systems may need some up-dating.

5. The growing use and increasing capacity of Information Technology, and specifically the appearance of networking, has forced the "here" and "now" focus of management into a new speed and magnitude. This development re-enforces the dynamic behavior of markets and makes it also more visible. The speed of changes increases but the dynamics of the changes also differ. "Here" and "now" becomes "where ?" and "when ?". Management becomes increasingly an art of making choices, rather than the craftsmanship of project management.

6. For many years, management education has suggested that management was a science, which could be taught and measured. For many years, management has denied the social dimension of corporate behavior. A company is composed of a set of individual human beings. The more companies become knowledge based, the more people move into the center of the company. Perceptions, feelings and social interaction become important elements in corporate behavior. We no longer can assume that managerial phenomena are easily measurable or that it would be easy to express behavior in equations. We have to accept that management education should slightly re-focus from

"describing and managing reality" towards "getting hold of a kind of a reality". The latter implies a continuous adaptation and learning, rather than execution of carefully made plans. Adaptive behavior should get more focus than prescriptive management.

7. Once we have identified markets and companies as non-linear dynamic systems, then some consequences should be accepted. The future behavior of a dynamic non-linear system depends on the initial state and the dynamic behavior of the system. It does not directly depend on the past. It is important to have a clear picture of the present, rather than of the past. Though the present is based on past experience, neither the present and certainly not the future can be understood out of an extrapolation of the past. More attention should be given to the understanding of the complex structure of the present (the up-to-date present) instead of the past and its extrapolations.

8. A further consequence is the acceptance of the irreversibility of time in a non-linear dynamic system. The consequence of this is a re-enforcement of the previous observation. If we could forecast the future out of the past, this would imply that past and future are reversible. The knowledge on dynamic non-linear systems proves the contrary. Instead of concentrating on extrapolations of the past, we should get a clear picture of the present (as said above) but we should also make an effort to picture the dynamic behavior of the system. A present focus in conjunction with an attempt to understand the dynamics of systems would mean in many companies a new way of management and of design of Management Information Systems.

9. For a long time we have presumed that knowledge is something we create and store somewhere in our memory. We know today that this is not true. Knowledge is made each time over and again, based on the capacity of a "knowledge network". For the individual, this knowledge network is his neural network (the brain). For the company these knowledge networks exist of different and flexible combinations of people which should be created and managed. Hence, knowledge management is not a question of learning as much as possible and storing it in a kind of a memory. Rather, it is a question of creating and managing knowledge networks which are able to re-create knowledge and further create knowledge at any point in time. The consequences of this are important for companies. This has consequences for

the criteria on which people are hired in a company; on the criteria for rewarding them; but also on the way management uses its people. Acceptance of the power of knowledge networks implies the restructuring of hierarchical companies into "knowledge networked" companies. Creating knowledge networks without giving them the necessary freedom of initiative is a waste of the investment. Acceptance to working with knowledge networks has consequences for the role of specifically middle management.

10. We have observed that dynamic systems behave differently when far from equilibrium in comparison to being close to equilibrium. Management has to be aware constantly of this property of dynamic systems, in order to be able to react in a correct manner to on an observed change.

11. We have observed in the discussion of "artificial life" applications that a set of very simple elements can produce very complex behavior. The bee colony as well as the human neural network are two well known examples. Therefore it is not true that a group of people who individually are not able to solve a problem, should not be able to solve that problem as a group. Group behavior can be extremely complex (and hence also innovative) despite the fact that the composing individuals are not up to the desired level. This sheds a new light on the discussion of "unskilled" labor. If people are losing their jobs, since they are under-skilled, this should not automatically mean that they should leave the company. Companies could try to be more creative with groups of "under-skilled" people than they are today. Of course, management should allow them then to work in knowledge teams and this may sound for some managers as a "contradiction in terms". Science does not support the impression that this would be possible. Another consequence is that in order to build knowledge networks and to have these networks solve complex problems, we do not need necessarily "smart" people. A good knowledge network of "average" people may perform better than a group of "highly intelligent" people.

12. We have observed in organizations (e.g. biological colonies) that they always get to a kind of self-organization. There is no reason to assume that a group of humans would not obey this intrinsic behavior. In that case, any structure which a company puts onto a group of people and which is seriously different from the auto-organized form which the group would reach itself, will cause

disturbance. Needless to say that this is a potential cause for lots of inefficient group (project) work in companies. This should, however, not be interpreted as if all guidance is wrong. Guidance is different from imposed structure. However, in case the aim of certain groups is the creation and management of knowledge, the discrepancy between self-organized structure and imposed structure is even more dangerous.

13. Knowledge creation has a dynamic nature. It never stops and it can never be started on command. If a company opts for a knowledge approach, it should understand the consequences, allow it to develop at its pace and allow freedom for its development. Knowledge management is in that respect probably completely opposed to project management if one considers the degree of dynamic property. Knowledge creation is not something which should be attempted as a one off exercise. It will probably not deliver a lot. A knowledge approach should be sustainable if a real impact is desired.

14. As much as the brain (human neural network) is the knowledge network of the individual, networks of people within a company can operate in the way a neural network does on individual level. Different people can be considered as the knots in a neural network. Each individual has a tiny little part of the overall knowledge. Each time a problem arises, the network starts operating and it produces out of the combination of the different knots (people) the answer. The knowledge is not stored with one of them and it is extremely difficult to identify who contributed what to the final solution. The knowledge creation which appeared shows a dynamic behavior which implies that by doing this exercise, the network has become better able to tackle any other future problem. The knowledge network continuously re-enforces its capacity to create more knowledge. If companies drew on the consequences of these observations, they would be dramatically better organized and probably able to tackle problems more efficiently.

15. As much as our human brain shows learning behavior, so do knowledge networks. Networks of neurons (brain), people (companies) or animals (colonies) all show learning behavior. This capacity to provide adaptive behavior and, in doing so, create more and more knowledge is what companies should try to manage. If it were not for the learning and adaptive qualities of networks, knowledge networks would not be so interesting.

16. Learning takes place on different levels in different ways. All learning has to go via an individual cycle of observation, assessment, design and implementation. Only new experiences (which could be reconsidering an earlier experiment) can create learning. If learning gets transformed into an individual mental model, then some knowledge gets created (double loop learning). This individual mental model will direct the individual. On a group level, another mental model gets created based on the interaction inside the group (see earlier points). We call this the shared mental model, or the corporate culture or the corporate knowledge. We cannot work directly on the corporate (group) level. All knowledge creation is based on this three step procedure: individual action and evaluation; individual mental model; shared mental model. If a company wants to do something about the shared mental model (the corporate knowledge), they will always have to go via individual new experiences. Therefore, IKT can be extremely helpful to address a large network of people. Therefore also, no quick results should be expected of any action addressing the corporate learning issue on either the wrong level (group) or using a short cut approach. Knowledge is based on experience, but experience is not automatically knowledge.

17. The strength of the company is the way in which it can work with tacit knowledge, without making it explicit. We already have good procedures to deal with explicit knowledge. However, it is tacit knowledge which makes the difference between two companies or two individuals. It should be kept in mind that if implicit knowledge is made explicit, it loses its character and hence its force.

18. A business process does not exist in the absolute. Any person who takes part in any business process has his own perception of that process. The context and the mindset are equally important for good decisions about a particular business process. Knowledge about business processes has a lot to do with perceptions. Business process engineering should not deny that.

19. Learning appears stepwise. Any knowledge based approach should take this into account. No fast results should be expected, and knowledge networks need time to get started. It all relates to the nature of knowledge. If knowledge

were rule-based, we could force learning via expert systems. Since knowledge proves to be parallel (based on a network structure) we cannot force learning.

20. Artificial neural networks can be used to visualize mental maps and to picture change. In the way that neural networks show adaptive learning behavior, they can also be used as instruments to measure change and learning. Measurement of change has always been a problem, since we have presumed that change is something which can be objectively measured. Once we accept the learning cycle (described above) we can also see that it is extremely difficult to measure learning.

21. Quantitative methods are only of limited use when we want to measure perceptions and change in perceptions. Therefore, quantitative modeling can not be used successfully in most aspects of knowledge management. Companies should pay attention to the underlying assumptions before using quantitative techniques.

22. It is extremely difficult to externalize knowledge and if we tried to, we would change the nature of the knowledge. The only solution to that problem is not to attempt to externalize it at all. Instead, companies should create the networks which can deal with knowledge and continue creating new knowledge, instead of investing in attempts to externalize knowledge.

23. In general, connectionism (networks for problem solving) appears to be an interesting development for companies. We are only at the discovery of the power of connectionism. Though we have given a number of examples, it should not be considered as proof of its quality for general use.

24. Learning is, more than anything else, a culture which allows people to experiment and create knowledge on the basis of their experiments.

25. Artificial neural networks (ANN) are interesting techniques for knowledge management. They picture and visualize knowledge without making it explicit. Specifically their learning and adaptive behavior is a quality which needs to be discovered by management.

26. Fuzzy logic is an interesting approach to logic which is tailored on what human beings and hence managers are doing each day. It is in opposition with our Cartesian management theories, but it coincides with our day to day style of decision making. The choice should be made whether we appreciate a sound theoretical concept (classical logic) with limited applicability or rather we prefer a more human kind of reasoning approach which has proved it is able to tackle complex problems in an easy and efficient way.

27. The holy grail for intelligent decision making is probably the combination of artificial neural networks and fuzzy logic. It combines the human language and understanding, the vagueness of language and the smoothness of human behavior with a learning and adaptive behavior. Can anything describe better the qualities a manager should have ?

28. Knowledge management is as much an attitude as a method. A supportive culture of learning is a necessary condition for a knowledge based approach. Knowledge management implies a different corporate goal.

29. Knowledge management in the company of today can only be done successfully if it is supported by the correct IKT tools. IKT networks should support the knowledge networks of people. Without being exhaustive, IKT tools like Case Based Reasoning, Group Decision Support Systems, Cognitive Mapping and Artificial Neural Networks should be integrated. "Intranet" technology will increasingly support the emergent organization. In so far that the IKT backbone network and the human knowledge networks match, companies can tackle problems which they cannot tackle today.

EPILOGUE: SAILING BY(E)

This case is intended to illustrate either effective or ineffective handling of an administrative situation, rather than to be used as a basis for class discussion only.

Clive is sitting on a terrace of a pub in the yacht harbor of Scheveningen. He just accepted an offer to join a company in the South of Spain and he is questioning himself whether he would keep his sailing boat in The Netherlands, or sail it down to Spain. It is not an easy consideration, since he only has a short term contract down in Spain, so it could be that after a few years he will move it back to the North. It is fortunate that Clive has a management background and therefore he is used to dealing with this kind of strategic choices based on limited information. He analyses the pro's and con's of the alternatives. He has a lot of sailing experience and has seen most countries which one can reach from Holland in a normal holiday period. He spent some nice holidays sailing in Germany, Denmark, Sweden, England, Ireland, France, the Channel Islands and he even once sailed a boat to the North of Spain. There are not a lot of new areas to be visited, but of course, each trip is an interesting one in its own right. One does not sail in order to reach a goal or a place, but rather the process of sailing is what is interesting. If he decided to sail the boat down to Spain, he could leave it there even when he returns to The Netherlands and in doing so he could benefit from a completely new sailing area: The Mediterranean. Even if he returned to the North, he could still spend his holidays and even some long weekends down in the Spanish sun. He decides to investigate the latter possibility and makes inquires about harbors in Spain.

Weeks later and after a few visits to potential marinas, he was made the offer of a berth for sale in a nice, rather new harbor, close to Almería in the South of Spain. Renting a berth is rather expensive, so the initial strategic choice is only re-enforced: either buy a berth with the intention of leaving the boat in Spain for the rest of his life; or leave the boat in The Netherlands. Clive discusses it with many of his friends, drinks a number of beers and eventually decides to buy and sail

South. Only the future will tell whether this was the correct decision, if indeed a correct decision exists.

Since Clive is an experienced sailor, he knows he has to prepare this trip very thoroughly. He starts reading books about the possible ways to go, based on the experience of other people who have already convoyed boats to the Mediterranean. Clive knows a lot of people who are interested in accompanying him. After quite a while of assessing all the alternatives he decides to go via the Channel and the South of England until Falmouth. From there he would cross the Bay of Biscay to La Coruña (the North of Spain), continue along the coast of Portugal, pass Gibraltar and into the Mediterranean. As a crew he finds a couple with impressive experience. Paul is a professional with the merchant navy and his friend Mary has been sailing for years on different yachts. Her experience even includes a transatlantic crossing. Clive knows them well and he feels comfortable with this crew. The trip is planned and they schedule four weeks of holiday for it. It is estimated that 14 sailing days are necessary, hence another 14 days are either a safety margin if things go wrong, or it provides some time to visit interesting places.

Preparation takes place. Sea charts and pilot books are bought for the entire route. Food and drinks are stored. Insurance is expanded to cover this trip. The weekend before, Mary and Paul are coming down to help him load the boat as Clive plans to leave of the Monday. Needless to say the Saturday was one of these exceptionally beautiful days and hence it all starts in the pub of the sailing club with a morning coffee.

When Mary leaves the pub, she does not see a little step and falls. She seems to hurt herself seriously. She cannot get up and they decide to take her to hospital immediately. There they identify broken ligaments. Normally she should get a plaster and that means that she cannot go for the trip. This is not only a personal drama for her, but of course also a little problem for Clive. Fortunately, the doctor on duty is a sailor himself. After some discussion about the big plans ahead he agrees to give her a flexible plaster which she can put on and take off when she wants. However, he warns her that she should not take it off and that even with the plaster, it is stupidity to think about crossing the Bay of Biscay. If they had bad weather, she would not be able to be an active member of the crew. And why else does one participate in a crossing like this one, if not to be an active member of the crew ?

Needless to say that the atmosphere was not really very cheerful. What could be done ? A number of alternatives were considered like delaying the start date, finding another crew member, or changing the itinerary. Eventually, Clive in agreement with his crew, decided on the last option. They would follow the French coast of the Channel, which would allow them to enter a harbor in case the weather changed. Past Brest they would head for Bordeaux in order to go via the "Canal du Midi". This is a canal which crosses France and brings the boat via more than 100 locks to the Mediterranean. The mast has to be taken off to cross the canal which would cause some problems. Clive had a radar installed just before this trip. He had asked the radar cable to be installed in one piece without connectors on the deck, since he judged that it was better for the quality of reception and he would never take his mast off anyway. As a famous Dutch writer wrote: "Things can change", can´t they ?

The plan was then, once they were in the Mediterranean, they still had to reach Almería. In case this was impossible, they could then leave the yacht anywhere at any Spanish harbor and Clive could sail it further down at weekends. Some joy re-appeared on their faces and eventually on Monday they left Scheveningen with a light north-westerly wind.

As usual with such kind of distance trips, the very start is a mixture of joy and anticipation for what is ahead, but equally the crew had to get used to the sea again. Most people struggle a little with an initial feeling of unease, which often disappears after a few hours. In front of the Belgian coast the wind shifts and turns to the south-west, which is, needless to say, the course of the yacht. The engine is started and sailing against the wind using the engine again proves to be rather uncomfortable. When a few hours later the current also turns against them, sailing becomes increasingly uneasy. Suddenly Mary observes water in the galley. The crew starts looking for possible holes or malfunctioning of the engine, but they do not find anything at first sight. Further research leads to a "useless" extension on the engine, which is installed in one of the coffers, with the aim, if ever desired, to connect a warm water system. It should be maintained with the annual engine maintenance, which Clive pays a Volvo-dealer for each year. However, this particular (hidden) part of the engine seems never to be maintained. Water pours out and no other solution is found than to enter the Calais harbor for repair.

That same evening nobody can be found to repair the engine. The day after it appears that the nearest dealer is in Gravelines (20 km away from Calais) and they have to come especially for Clive. Not only does it take some time, but it also causes an additional cost. Clive feels a little sour about it, since he pays for maintenance each year and he will have to pay yet another amount for the maintenance not done. The time to wait for the repair people and the repair to be done, takes the entire day. Calais harbor only opens its locks twice a day, so they will not be ready in time to leave that day.

As one expects from an experienced crew, they regularly check the weather forecast. The entire day a south-westerly storm is announced. Since this pre-occupies the crew, they go and find more detailed information about the expectations for the rest of the week. This south-westerly storm is expected to last at least 5 or 6 days. There is no way of going against it in order to reach Brest. What can be done?

Calais is used by a lot of British sailors as a starting point for a trip to the Mediterranean via the canals of France. They take off their mast in Calais and it takes them between 3 and 4 weeks to reach a place close to Marseille. It is an easy way to get to the South for those who do not want to use the Ocean. Clive always felt that sailing boats should sail and not be used as power boats. But of course, it remains an alternative. It dramatically changes the entire idea of the trip and it necessitates other charts and pilot books. Furthermore, the boat has to be prepared for that and they have no material with them to do so. Other alternatives are considered. They can wait and see whether the storm remains for the entire week. In that case and if the storm continues, they may not have time to get to Canal du Midi. If anything would happen, they would have to leave the boat somewhere on the Atlantic coast, and sailing it further from there would be a major problem (time wise as well as technically) for Clive. Another solution might be to try and sail out, cross to the South of England and see how far they get. If they feel it is not going to work, then they could still return to Holland and put the boat on a truck. Again Clive feels that sailing boats are not made to be transported by trucks, but the trip had started and he feels he should make the best out of it. They inquire about the price of road transportation, which brings this alternative slightly out of reach.

The discussion which takes place is more animated than the previous one in Scheveningen. Everybody in the harbor is willing to give good advice, but that does not make it any clearer which is the best decision, if indeed a good decision exists. Eventually Clive opts for the lowest risk. He takes off the mast, which he feels very bad about. Then he plans to go via the canals of France in the hope that he can do it in less than three weeks. He would have some more time to get the boat at least to Barcelona. From there, he can sail the boat further South with his wife Jana or single-handed. He is sure he will not be able to get any further than Barcelona, but he is equally sure he will get there. All other alternatives could take him further, but equally they might not. Clive is not proud of his decision and feels particularly bad when the mast is taken off. He feels it as if his boat has had an amputation. He needs another few days to overcome that decision mentally. With a very friendly and helpful person at the local wharf, a solution is found to prepare the boat for its trip through the canals. A new adventure awaits them, but the anticipation is much less.

When the mast is taken off, it is observed that a part of the mast is broken. This could not be detected while the mast was standing and it could have caused major problems. If they had sailed via the Ocean and the weather had turned bad, it is not certain that the mast would have stayed, it would probably have broken. This can cause major problems of a kind which no sailor really looks forward to. One can call it good news with the bad news, though the good news remains bad news too. A new piece has to be ordered. The wharf which constructed the boat (in Belgium) is contacted and they seem able to order a new piece in Sweden (where the mast originates). How different the world would look these days if one had no GSM phone system ! The wharf agrees to mail the new piece straight to Jana, so that she can take it with her when she comes down to visit the crew around the time they are expected to be in Marseille. The crew needs the piece in order to put the mast up again. It looks a little like a Just-in-Time operation between different parties, of which some are mobile and no fixed time schedule is available. Fortunately, Clive has dealt with these theories in one of his previous jobs.

The crew considers this broken piece as a sign from heaven that they took the right option. Not that it really helps to raise the moral, but if one considers it objectively, this damage could have caused really serious problems. Thinking about all this, Clive steers his boat through the first of the 210 locks they are facing. He has to pay tolls for the use of the canals and while doing so he questions how many days he should calculate for the trip. The clerk estimates it to take 3 weeks easily. Clive panics a little, since that would imply that they might probably not even reach Barcelona. Therefore he decides that each day they start sailing at 6.30 am, when the locks start operating and they sail each day till 8.30 p.m., the time when the locks close down.

A routine is established on board. None of the crew members had sailed on canals before and they do not even know the rules and regulations. In Calais they buy a number of new charts and pilot books, as well as a book about the navigational rules on canals. The charts and pilot books look completely different from what they are used to, but after a few days they feel at ease with them. In the beginning the locks cause tension on board, since the crew has no previous experience, but after a few days even the locks become routine. Everything is new for them and they learn fast via trial and error. Fortunately, this does not cause a lot of damage to the boat.

Though France makes a lot of publicity about trips along their canals, Clive, Paul and Mary are not impressed by the accommodation. There are no harbors and there are hardly any places to moor. If a place is indicated on the chart, it is either not there, or it is used by commercial boats. Sometimes they have to moor along a grass digue. Sometimes they have to "park" alongside a commercial vessel. The depth of the canals is not always as indicated on the charts, especially when going away from the center. 1200 kilometers later, passing the 210 locks and 5 tunnels (of which some are a few kilometers long and have no lighting), they eventually arrive close to Marseille.

During the last days of the trip, contact is made with Jana in order to coordinate her trip to deliver the new piece of the mast. She will arrive at Marseille airport and she should be picked up by car. There is no way to reach the harbor where they are: no busses, no trains, no nothing. Needless to say that each of these little tiny problems take lots of time to solve. Probably that is what one should expect when managing projects of this kind.

The mast is set up again on a wharf and it does not take them too long: they are experienced. The problem is then to reconnect all the electricity, specially the radar cable. The crew is very happy to see that the radar is operating again. One always seems to feel sorry if something new does not operate, certainly if one causes the defect oneself. After a full day of work, the boat is ready to sail again. Clive feels extremely happy. They succeeded getting through the canals in a record time of 2 weeks. It was rather awful and it resembled more a slave journey than a holiday. But he is happy that he is eventually in the Mediterranean, the mast is up again, the radar operates and Jana is there. Life looks just that little bit brighter.

The crew decides that for the last week of the period scheduled, they deserve some holidays. Instead of trying to reach a place past Barcelona, it is decided to sail only during day time and try and enjoy the last part of the trip a little. Tension on board had risen considerably over the three weeks and that also needed some attention.

Except for some of the ongoing small problems which can suddenly seem important, Clive, Paul and Mary reached Barcelona without major mishaps happening. They have to leave the boat there and rent a car to drive to the South of Spain, since, they had booked plane tickets back to Holland from Almería. It takes them a full day of driving in very hot weather, but at last they reach Almería, though not by boat. But in general, they feel that they have achieved at least part of the goal.

The rest of the trip from Barcelona to Almería will be sailed by Clive and Jana, using some (long) weekends, operating from their new home base in the South of Spain. Since berthing in Spain is expensive, they are planning how to sail, as fast as possible, down to the South. Two weeks later they fly back to Barcelona for their first trip. Since Jana is not that experienced, it is decided to sail only in day-time. It limits the radius, but it also makes the trips more enjoyable.

Clive knows that the Mediterranean is different from the Atlantic. He had read a lot about it and in earlier years he rented boats in the South of France. In summer there is little wind but also almost no storms. However, when a storm comes up, it comes up fast. Therefore he decides to follow the weather forecasts very closely, certainly in the beginning. Despite the announced force 2 to 3 from the north-east, in the afternoon of the second day a South 5 to 6 comes up. During one of these wind-shifts, Clive wants to take the Jib in, but the roller-jib fails to operate. The sail is blocked and on a wobbly sea this is extremely uncomfortable. The roller-jib system seems to be broken close to the mast and it has destroyed a part of the sail. Clive cannot lower the sail and therefore decides to make a number of circles with the boat in order to role in the jib in mechanically. Then he heads for the closest harbor and starts looking for a mechanic. He hardly speaks Spanish, which of course does not facilitate the task. Eventually he finds a mechanic who can fix the system the next day, but this mechanic also warns them of a severe storm to come. Though it is summer, and the weather forecast expects a force 4 to 5, the local people warn him not to go out. After long consideration Clive decides to believe the locals. In the afternoon a gale force 11 comes over, something which had never happened before in the history of that part of Spain. Clive and Jana feel very frightened but they decide to stay on board in the harbor. Who would ever have imagined Clive being scared on his boat in the harbor ? In the meantime two more days are lost. Clive and Jana need to return and they have to leave the boat in the harbor again.

They plan to come down a week later and take another week off to progress a little more. When they arrive on board, to their great surprise, they have rats on board! Clive was not aware at all that this could happen on a modern sailing yacht. The rats had gone mad. They had bitten into all the milk cartons so milk was everywhere. They did the same with the orange juice. The smell is unbearable. Furthermore they have appreciated the biscuits, the chocolate, etc. But they also have eaten some of the sleeping bags and even some of the clothes. More out of anger than with the aim of doing something intelligent, Clive starts looking for the rats. After a long while he finds one and is very happy to be able to get it overboard. He completely ignores that rats can swim and never live on their own and during his first night on board again, he hears the brothers and sisters running through the boat. The next day he buys poison and puts it in different places in the boat. Sometimes, problems need immediate action of a disastrous nature. Sometimes the "enemy" needs to be attacked head on.

The week goes well. Each day the weather forecast gives a gentle 2 or 3 out of a northerly direction (which is interesting going South) and each day they get a 4 or 5 out of the South. After all, Clive and Jana start thinking that the world is probably organized in a post-modern way, and this is may be the first real proof of this. At least this experience teaches them to ignore the weather forecast for the rest of their trip. The roller jib breaks down again and it appears impossible to get it repaired in the next harbor. Where the first time this happened they were very concerned, this time they are used to it and they just continue their voyage. Eventually, three harbors further on, they find somebody who can repair it. At the end of that week they have to leave the boat again in another harbor, but the final goal is nearer. They would only need two more weekends to get to Almería.

The first weekend goes well. It appears that no further rat activities took place in their absence. The weather forecasts remain equally bad. The best news is that they arrive at the end of the weekend in a harbor where no harbor duties are due. It is so exceptional that they wonder whether they should leave the boat there. They suddenly get the strange feeling that if you pay harbor duties, your boat is "protected" against e.g. theft and if you do not pay, it is not protected. They cannot rationalize that feeling, but nevertheless it exists. Services for which one does not pay are no services, are they ? On the other hand paying for a specific service gives it a status, independent of its quality.   However, after long consideration they decide to leave the boat there "unattended". It did help as they did not really have an alternative.

One week later they go back for what should be their last weekend of sailing their boat down. They only need three more days and they sail along one of the nicest coast-lines of Spain, i.e. the province of Murcia. There are very few harbors in that part of Spain and you have to make sure not to miss them. Of course, in many cases, they are overcrowded. The first night they can get a place at the very end of a pontoon. It is not really a place, but if it brings in some additional money, why should the harbor not be creative ? The second night there is no place in the harbor at all and they decide to anchor. Their last night should be a romantic one, anchored in a nice bay.

What a mistake they made. That very night is the night of the local fiesta. Loud music until 6 in the morning, together with fireworks at around 3am. It seems that they are in the middle of one of these old pirate movies and they feel as if they are the target of the shooting. Nothing is less true, but imagination can do quite a lot. Around 5 in the morning, Clive suddenly hears a few people swimming around the boat, discussing how to get in the boat. He jumps out of his bed and most probably due to his bad night he shouts louder than necessary that if they do not disappear immediately, he will do "God knows what". It works.

Tired but happy they arrive in the morning of the next day in Almería. They moor at the berth which they bought months before. They leave the boat and they have a pleasant drink in one of the many bars around the harbor. At last they have arrived.

They have arrived at the place they intended to be months ago. The strategy which Clive had decided on was still valid. He had to admit that the way he achieved it dramatically differs from the way he planned. Fortunately he kept the ultimate goal in mind each time he encountered another problem. Clearly, he changed his tactics often and sometimes very drastically. He bought lots of sea charts and pilot books which are still brand new and not even touched. He bought a number of new charts and books along the way. He arrived almost two months later than foreseen and the trip had cost him probably around 30 % more than he originally budgeted for. He lived through a completely different experience, not necessarily better or worse than the planned one, only different.

While drinking his sangria on yet another terrace of another bar in another marina, now in the sun, he felt he had achieved what should have been achieved. However, he also kept in mind that this particular day was only the very first day of the rest of his sailing life.

Assignment questions

1. How much of this case do you recognize in any management case of your own experience ? Identify those specific parts of this case which are comparable to your own corporate experience (case). Highlight them.

2. Can you draw some general observations out of these highlighted parts of the text ? How do these general observations coincide with those identified in chapter 8.

3. Can you identify the moments in this case where Clive applied in one way or another some of the concepts dealt with in this book ?

4. Discuss the methods and attitudes which could have helped Clive in his decision making process at each of the different moments you identified in the previous question. Do not apply this discussion to Clive's case, but rather to your own corporate case.

5. What can you learn from this case with respect to your own management style ?

6. Take any management case you are familiar with and try to structure it into a case/story, either related to sailing, or to a music performance (depending on which of the two you are more familiar with). Does this shed new light on your managerial case ? Is it easier to discuss this sailing/music case than to discuss the management case ? Discuss.

7. Why do we have that feeling that the discussion of this sailing/music case is less serious and that we would learn less from it than from using "real" management cases ? What does this tell us about our perception of management ? Discuss.

ANNEX : AN EPISTEMOLOGICAL VOYAGE THROUGH CONNECTIONISM AND POSITIVISM (CO-AUTHORED BY GERT VAN DER LINDEN)

Along with growing activity in the field of IS research, IS research methodology in itself is developing into an independent subject of enquiry (Mumford et al., 1985; Cash and Lawrence, 1989; Benbasat, 1990; Nissen et al., 1990; Kraemer, 1991; Galliers, 1991b; Galliers, 1992). It seems relevant, at this point, to discuss different approaches and methodologies and explain what their underlying assumptions are. It is also important for the practitioner to get a really "close reading" of what to expect from research, both the more traditional IS research approaches, as well as the perspective this book offers: neural networks and connectionist approaches. It shows how selecting a particular methodology implies a fundamental position or epistemology.

We also attempt to outline how methodology is related to the aims of science. Indeed, as Bachelard (in Merquior, 1988) stresses, a research proposal and a hypothesis are developed within the framework of an evolving scientific environment and never in an intellectual and cognitive vacuum. Sartre (in Daudi, 1986) points out that a research method is a philosophical question via which research expresses itself.

Indeed, science is greater than the object that it studies. It is a voyage of discovery. It is trial and error, guessing and arguing. Hence, science can be considered as a "verb". Given the particular relationship that the researcher - the explorer - has with his object, science can be seen as a dialogue. "Science" is a reflection of a relationship with existing praxis. It is working with language and working with the self.

It is this dialogue, or reflection, which is of special interest to the practitioner wishing to gain greater insight into the philosophy behind IS research projects. It is also relevant to those, practitioners and scholars alike, who are interested in how a research project is designed and how it comes about, how the outcome of a particular research project is related to the foundations on which a particular methodology is based, its epistemology. Please note that some paragraphs are aimed at scholars rather than at more practically-minded readers.

A.1. Science and scientific action

Traditionally, research methods, including IS research methods, are categorized into two groups: scientific and interpretive. Scientific approaches may be defined as those that arise from the positivist tradition, characterized by repeatability, reductionism and refutability (Checkland, 1981). It assumes that observations can be made objectively and rigorously (Klein and Lyytinen, 1985). In terms of questioning perceptions (as is often the case in management research), it is arguable whether objective measuring is possible at all.

In juxtaposition to the scientific method, interpretive approaches argue that the scientific ethos is misplaced in terms of scientific inquiry because it fails to account for the numerous possible ways of interpreting the same phenomena, the personal impact the scientist has as an individual crafting a research project, as well as problems associated with forecasting future events concerned with human activity (Galliers, 1985a, after Checkland, 1981). According to positivists, a qualitative approach to research also has a number of limitations (Bryman, 1988). Firstly, the researcher does not have the ability to see through other people's eyes and thus interpret events from their point of view; secondly, there needs to be a strong relationship between theory and research, and lastly, there is the extent to which qualitative research deriving from case studies can be generalized.

Recent research practice suggests that the dual opposing categorization does not really reflect developments which have taken place in science, in the field of IS, and in the area of knowledge management in particular. The duality is principally still rooted in the classical view of science, in notions of "truth" being shaped and defined by scientific methods.

According to Popper (1963), the "philosophical father" of positivism, science approaches truth by identifying and eliminating wrong theories and by replacing them with better theories. The replacement process is one of trial and error. The most successful scientific theory is thus only a hypothesis that temporarily represents truth. Only via the critical study of hypotheses, can truth be approached;

the rejection of a hypothesis indicates an error (Popper, 1989). According to Popper, one can never claim that science results in proven and unarguable knowledge: science is a masterpiece created by man and, as such, can have failures. Popper argues that a scientific hypothesis cannot directly be proved true. It is assumed to be true, as long as no other observations contradict or falsify it. The criteria of scientific status are given by its capacity to be falsified, to be counter-argued, and to be tested. One comes closer to the truth by searching for theories that are wrong, by replacing them with better ones. Hence, the status of a scientific truth is dependent on a later statement; thus, scientific claims need to be institutionalized (Gutwirth, 1993).

Applying this logic, simulation as a means of reproducing or duplicating a fact to be falsified, is a technique with drawbacks in terms of "time": duplication can never take place under exactly the same time conditions. Even to Popper, falsification is not really or strictly possible: one can never falsify the same given theory since a theory evolves in terms of growth, structure and context. Again, this shows how self-referential, self-grounded, and self-contained the positivist tradition is, with its emphasis on techniques and technicalities grounded in the fundamental quest for proof. Its central focus switched from interpretation to being a technical debate on representation.

The positivist approach to science stems from the division between subject and object, the presumption of a strong single rationalistic idea, from causality and determinism. Human rationale and order are projected onto the world, in the hope of justifying a claim that reality is in line with that human rationale. Facts represent reality; there exists some universal knowledge that is valid for everybody; the Cartesian view, in which the over-riding power of man is a fact of nature, is protected. Such an image of reality considers the world as mechanistic, in which an absolute (but not a total) truth exists.

Prigogine and Stengers (1988) argue against this. These "founding fathers" of chaos theory have shown that minimal changes in the initial conditions of a model (e.g. the assumptions), which could be minor mistakes, can provoke non-proportional consequences for a particular theory. Therefore, any given model is only of limited validity: it reduces reality to one of its aspects; it attempts to understand the uncertainty of a complex system, without the final result ever being a certainty. The limited precision of numbers causes deterministic theories to be unpredictable (Prigogine and Stengers, 1988). Their view on truth stems from a primary interest in the "true" complexity of simple systems amidst local chaos, which differs from more classical approaches in terms of the equations of the models used. These equations accentuate a non-linearity that is in contrast to classical equilibrium models, and in which the dynamic character of "truth" appears via positive feedback phenomena.

The postmodernist perspective goes one step further. Postmodernism argues for the existence of a multitude of truths in which the central focus is on openness to the other, on diversity and complexity, on coincidence and chaos, on non-linearity and non-causality, on non-determinism, uncertainty, inconsistency and all other aspects which are beyond man's control (Lyotard, 1988). Postmodernism envisions no demarcation between subject and object, while content refers to mental content(s). The mental content refers to the alliance between "truth" and "claims of truth". Truths have the connotation of stability, transcending the temporal, the moment, the contingency of the singular. As Foucault (1966) states, only via text (language), can one grasp the truth: "Les mots sont les choses" ("Words are the objects"). Claims of truth are subject to the position an individual has within a network that is produced through knowledge and action. As such, "claims" refer to the local and temporal, to flux. This results in there being no absolute rationality or irrationality: experiencing is not based on simple and distant information processing. As Latour (1988) explains, the construction of meanings represents a social network. Meanings are not to be seen as individual constructs or precepts that are then socially evaluated and corrected, but rather, they can be perceived as socially created. Hence, one can no longer argue in favor of "science" having one main story-line: rather, one recognizes a multitude of stories. Science becomes a network in itself, a differentiated universe.

As mentioned above, claims of truth are subject to the position an individual has within a network that is produced through knowledge and action. In other words, the researcher takes an active part in his research act. His behavior is multiple and produced in a connectionist way, based on what is and happens at that particular moment and which can always be multiply interpreted. A scientist becomes a "constructionist"; there is no such thing as a division between object and subject. The researcher constructs the content of knowledge in relation to what happens. Or, as Latour (1988) puts it: "Les faits sont fait" ("Facts are made up"). And later, the reader himself may in turn become the author of a text, allowing objects with which he identifies to speak for him. The positive and productive element of science then is that it acts as connector with the reader and the critic. The latter attempts to identify what has been forgotten or omitted. Why are some authors neglected, or some themes not mentioned ? In the same sense, Lyotard (1988) refers to science as a language game. A document is scientific if statements are no longer isolated and if a relatively large number of peers are associated via references in the text. This mechanism reinforces a line of articles, it attracts and obtains attention. If anybody becomes isolated, it is the reader: he can stop reading, agree or continue. Research becomes "re"-search: searching for the same. As such, scientific theories are instruments of intelligence, networks of discovery which are visualized as chaotic and turbulent until a pattern emerges.

The above discourse sums up what motivated our approach in writing the book; it tells the story of a voyage of discovery, the sharing of experiments and experience, in an attempt to avoid the misleading argument between the positivist and the interpretivist school of thought regarding how to apply objectivity and how to conceptualize. To whatever school a scientist wishes to adhere, interpretation will always be his main activity.

A.2. The tradition of IS research

The aim of this section is to elaborate on how connectionist approaches and, more particularly, the use of artificial neural networks fit within the larger tradition and practice of IS research. The section develops thoughts based on prevailing theoretical concepts in IS research, and also presents arguments regarding the practice and practicalities of IS research more specifically within a business context.

Galliers (1991b) developed a taxonomy, arguing for the need to integrate to a greater degree the two approaches to scientific research methodology. His taxonomy ranged from the more traditional, empirical approaches to the newer interpretivist ones (with obviously some overlap). This classification does not suggest that the two groups are mutually exclusive. In research practice, however, they sometimes seem to be. Galliers started by organizing existing research approaches into two groups: the scientific and the interpretivist, based on a number of pre-set criteria.

Scientific	**Interpretivist**
Laboratory Experiments	Subjective/Argumentative
Field Experiments	Reviews
Surveys	Action Research
Case Studies	Descriptive/Interpretative
Theorem Proof	Futures Research
Forecasting	Role/Game playing
Simulation	

Galliers then argues that one needs to set out the possible approaches against the object of the research, which could be society, groups, individuals, methodology etc. For the study of a different object, or for a study with a different aim, or an object with a different context, a different method or combination of methods could be more appropriate. Galliers assessed the strengths and weaknesses of the various research approaches in the context of each particular aspect of IS under study. For example, in terms of theory building, Galliers proposes the traditional empirical approaches. Case studies are helpful when the object is "organizations" and for theory testing. Laboratory experiments, on the other hand, are not useable for research on a societal level.

Without going into further detail, it can be said that, besides its polarization (which is not discussed in Galliers' taxonomy), the subdivision of the taxonomy is not free of dispute. Criticism of its limitations expressed by Smithson (1991) for example, questions whether particular methods, such as case studies, should appear under the scientific label. Galliers' categorization could also be criticized because it does not include more recent connectionist or other approaches. Furthermore, authors such as Mansell (1991), regard the taxonomy as too limiting; for instance, there are four possible methodologies that can be applied to action research: Operations Research, Soft Systems Methodology, Socio-technical Systems Design (Susman, 1983), and Viable Systems Diagnosis (Beer, 1980, 1985).

Let us take a step back and look at how a typical academic IS research project is structured, and what to expect from its outcome. For this purpose, two research articles are used, published in the MIS Quarterly (considered to be the top research journal in IS): J. Hunton and J Beeler, "Effects of User Participation in Systems Development: A Longitudinal Field Experiment" (Vol 21, Nr 4, Dec 1997); D. Gefen and D Straub, "Gender Differences in the Perception and Use of E-Mail: An Extension to the Technology Acceptance Model" (also Vol 21, Nr 4, Dec 1997).

A typical academic research project starts with a *problem statement*. In the Hunton and Beeler case, it is something like "What are the benefits of user involvement ? Is user participation always desirable? How exactly should users be "involved". In the Gefen and Straub article, the problem statement is "How well is E-mail being utilized? Have employees institutionalized it within the fabric of their day-to-day work lives? How often do employees misuse it?"

The next step consists of *embedding the problem statement in existing literature and ongoing research*. The first article investigates *embedding* in terms of two sections called "Introduction" and "Research Context". The second article examines "Gender Effects in IT - Analogous Circumstances" and "The Role of Gender in Related IT Research".

Both articles proceed with the *identification of research hypotheses* of which we cite just two per article as follows. The Hunton and Beeler article gives, among others, the two hypotheses: "There is a positive relationship between pre-development, user-involvement with, and user-attitude toward the present information system" and "There is a positive relationship between pre-development, user-attitude toward the present information system, and the user's desire to participate in the development of a new information system". The second article identifies as research hypotheses: "Women will perceive the social presence of e-mail to be higher than will men" and "Women will rate the perceived usefulness of e-mail higher than men will".

In order to validate these hypotheses, *data gathering* needs to take place. Often, this happens via field research, in particular using surveys and interviews. The Hunton and Beeler article used small groups of employees who met once a week a few hours for briefing. Data gathering itself took place using a survey questionnaire with Likert-type scales. The Gefen and Straub article also used a research questionnaire. Both articles attempt to measure perceptions.

The next step consists of *analysis,* often *using statistical tools* (in the US even more so than in Europe). Both articles use statistical tests on the data gathered e.g. the Cronbach Alpha test, (M)ANOVA analysis, F-tests, fit indicators of different types, Partial Least Squares.

This leads to *acceptance or rejection of the research hypotheses.* All hypotheses in these two articles were completely or partly accepted. Though this cannot be generalized, it often happens.

The last step consists of *more general conclusions and suggestions for wider application and further research.* Though prudence is suggested, articles often generalize beyond the tested hypotheses. This introduces a further research agenda required in order to test the "extended" hypotheses.

As shown above, typical IS methodology can be categorized as "scientific". By using surveys, forecasting, and simulation techniques, IS research aims at analyzing by deduction. This is anchored in positivist epistemology based on determinism, causality, linearity, and a mechanical representation of social realities. Captured by the notions of "systemhood", the essential feature of organizations focuses both on the internal determination of behavior and on its external determination. Concepts that are a reification of experiences are expressed in static, linear, substantive norms such as structure, culture, quality, etc. while at the same time processes have become objects (Van Gils, 1997).

It is clear that in the research perspectives described above, the researcher takes a distant position and attempts to "objectify" rather than being close to the research object and involved in it. He seems to be part of the toolbox necessary for research and, as such, he does not play a role of real significance. Tools are there, particularly in the data analysis phase. The researcher acts as a "tool" when designing the survey questionnaires, validating the research hypotheses and while formulating more general conclusions. This illustrates the demarcation between subject and object: researchers are independent observers. Most of the time the researcher's non-involvement is not questioned; however, it is arguable whether drawing conclusions can be done without any "interpretation". In other words, knowledge becomes a distant information processing system that can be built up independently of the observer or the "knower".

From a practitioner's point of view (rather than from the point of view of the academic output or the published article), a research project has quite a different form. There is no clear *problem statement* at the beginning of a research project; the problem statement itself is constructed during the process of defining the area of research. Rough research directions are given within certain (corporate) boundaries, but it is from the interaction between the researcher (the explorer) and the company (the research arena) that a problem statement emerges, if it emerges at all, at the starting phase of a research project.

Given the emergent nature of the *problem statement*, research hypotheses are difficult to formulate. Research into the business environment is much more exploratory in nature: the availability of data, its interpretation and ordering, and its transformation into information (contextualisation) will also gradually clarify possible research hypotheses. This process implies that choices need to be made regarding data gathering, its interpretation and its contextualisation, aspects which will inevitably influence, not only the results, but also the *research hypothesis* itself. Of course, while management research is not value-free, as argued above, it would be somewhat cynical to argue for the separation of subject and object given the nature of the research process.

Specifically in this Information Age, the first choice which needs to be made is whether to use existing data or whether to gather new data. The multitude of existing data often results in a badly-informed guess. It is easier, if the aim is to validate research hypotheses, to reproduce one's own data. If we accept that the creation of the research hypotheses goes hand-in-hand with *data gathering* (and analysis) a number of "strategic" choices need to be made about the data gathering phase. Furthermore, management mainly deals with perceptions, feelings and ideas, which are all very difficult to measure in the first place. Whereas quantitative data are available to a certain degree, data on perceptions are rarer and can also only be measured within a specific context.

Many examples exist within the business context of the important role which perceptions play, suggesting that quantitative measurement may have drawbacks. A PC which advertises "Intel inside" is perceived to be of better quality than a PC which does not advertise it, although this does not rule out the possibility that Intel may be installed inside the second computer, at least for those who know what Intel is. In Holland and the Scandinavian countries, leadership is perceived to be effective if the manager is able to communicate with his employees and to evolve with the group towards consensus. In Latin countries, such as France and Spain, leadership has a lot to do with hierarchy. Consultative management is not practiced and would not be understood by employees. Employees would probably consider the consultative manager as weak. Hence leadership is heavily dependent on the cultural context of the company and the country in which it operates. With respect to the coffee-brand example discussed in chapter 5, the taste of coffee is a perception which depends, amongst other factors, on the time of the day that one tastes the coffee, the way in which one makes coffee (which everybody does differently), what food and drink are taken with or before the coffee. The same clients, in the same physical environment (at home), have a different perception of the taste of coffee each time they drink the same coffee: the same object (coffee) provokes different perceptions of the same reality (drinking coffee). In the case of quality control of road repair works, discussed in chapter 6, quality control procedures are considered by subcontractors as delaying procedures and as an unnecessary proof of mistrust on behalf of the contracting authority; according to the controlling agents, however, the same quality control procedures are the best way of guaranteeing good quality at the right price. Both points of view are equally valid when seen from their respective perspectives. In fact, they are only two perceptions of the same reality.

Perceptions are only the perceptions one can observe within a given context. Isolating perceptions from their context and measuring them does not make sense. Positivist methods, however, have difficulty dealing with a series of combined observations whereas connectionism deals with this naturally.

In a classical academic research project, data are gathered in order to be, more often than not, quantitatively analyzed (see, for example, the two earlier examples). When data are of a qualitative nature (such as perceptions), *quantitative analysis* performs weakly. In view of the exploratory nature of management research in general, research projects in this field tend to be emergent, where object and subject, explorer and nature, are involved in a smooth interactive process.

Lately, there has been a shift with certain IS methodologies attempting to "pay attention" to the role of "the subject" in research. The Soft Systems Methodology (Checkland, 1981), for example, aims not only at structuring and understanding problems in a company, but also strives to guide the process of improvement afterwards. Intrinsically user-dependent, it wants to leave the decision as to what should happen as a result of the analysis to a debate between the key stakeholders or actors.

More generally, Bakos and Treacy (1986) argue that, as the field of Information Sciences matures, the primary focus of academic research should move to a deeper level of analysis, characterized by specific, explanatory models connected to broader general theory. As well as aiming to create tools, a more abstract approach to tool-creation needs to be adopted (Avison et al., 1993). Most research gets trapped in the paradox that it should be aiming for abstract and quantitative results, but any abstraction, by definition, loses some aspect of the rich, multifaceted reality it represents (Kreher, 1993).

It is this paradox that causes argument in the academic research community. The duality between abstraction and/or reductionism in order to gain greater insight on the one hand, and a holistic approach in order to maintain the full picture on the other hand, causes argument. If we continue to claim that only an abstract and reductionist approach, based on pre-set assumptions and working on repeatable experiments, can deliver scientific validity, we are very much researching the same things over and over again. Repeatability and the idea it implies of generality causes us all too often to think that solutions for one management problem can easily be transferred to another management problem. In practice, this is not only shown to be unrealistic, but it illustrates the "recycling" of the positivist debate on validity, accuracy, and rightness.

A.3. The ontological and epistemological foundations of neural networks

Since the early 1950s, two opposing visions of what computers could be and do have struggled for recognition (Dreyfus and Dreyfus, 1988). One seeks to use computers to instantiate a formal representation of the world; the other to simulate the interactions of neurons. One takes problem-solving as its paradigm of intelligence; the other, focuses on learning. One school stems from the rationalist and reductionist (positivist) school; the other views itself as idealized, non-linear, holistic and oriented on the basis of neuroscience.

The connectionist perspective, based on complexity and chaos theory, aims at approaching research from the holistic paradigm, although it still struggles with ideas first introduced by the positivist tradition. Indeed, the ontological and epistemological basis of the connectionist approach can be questioned: the terminology used to describe organizational dynamics and the language used within the connectionist framework still refer to a great extent to objectivity, functionality, and a purposefulness resting on a well-defined input to the system, a conveyance, and an output. As such, the "problem" of prediction and control of the system's behavior is balanced against a sensitivity to the unavoidable disturbances of environmental origin present in the real world. Environmental determinism and a mechanical representation of social reality are key aspects. In essence, non-linearity is simplified into a so-called "workable" non-linearity that actually is a well-defined linearity with given sets of laws. Although a strong awareness of non-linearity, dynamic behavior, and disequilibrium exists, one can perceive the heritage of the Cartesian anxiety for paradox in which duality is brought back to a dilemma in which there is no real room for non-linearity.

Neural networks can be seen as an illustration of the connectionist perspective. They provide a means of mapping a set of inputs onto a set of outputs in a manner that allows the network to perform the same mapping on new data that has not been seen before, i.e. it introduces the concept of learning. Learning is more than the accumulation of knowledge: it is the operationalisation of representations and experiences in a given framework. During the training stage of neural networks, examples of the mapping of the input domain onto the output classes are presented to the network. Once successfully trained, and hence when learning has taken place, the network can generalize the learned mapping and tackle new cases.

Neural networks match much better the practitioner's expectation and experience of research, as described earlier in this annex. The practitioner's research project seldom has a clear problem statement at the onset; rather, a problem is first vaguely identified and then, during the research process itself, the problem statement acquires greater definition. As a first step, the researcher merely defines the context and tries to grasp the problem in its entirety including all its tacit complexity. Neural networks, in this first stage of the research process, do nothing more than create a context from all possible experiences. Neural networks do not need a problem statement; they serve only to structure the context. The researcher can use this context at a later stage to explore, in his role as "explorer", different possible problem statements and then use new insights in order to crystallize a clear problem statement as an involved researcher. Neural networks can be set up without the pre-requisite of a defined research hypothesis; this suits the practitioner rather well as pre-defined research hypotheses are rarely available in his line of work anyway.

As argued earlier, the data gathering phase of the research process is very often a case of "data mining", or filtering through all existing quantitative data which may be of interest. Most data, however, are perceptions and hence they are difficult for quantitative methods to deal with. The main strength of neural networks is their capacity for pattern recognition, an interesting property in terms of filtering data. Furthermore, their fault tolerance and their iterative, adaptive nature allow them to deal with "vague" perceptions.

A research project in practice is an emerging venture of an exploratory nature, where researcher, context and problem (statement) continuously interact and evolve during the research process. The research approach used should allow, even better, should support the emergent and interactive character. As discussed in the book, the neural network paradigm is a learning paradigm. The holistic picture, which in a first stage helps the explorer to draw the context, helps the "embedded" researcher to define hypotheses and to analyze "data" at a later stage. The research context evolves with the researcher, mirroring at each moment in time the present conjunction of researcher, context and problem. The learning character of neural networks guarantees the researcher that his context and research material evolve with the research project itself.

A.4. Some comparative properties of artificial neural networks

An important effort has been made by positivist scientists to position neural networks as a particular type of classifier amongst the statistical approaches (White, 1989; Geman et al., 1992; DeStefano, 1990; Juang and Katagari, 1992; Han et al., 1989; Wan, 1990; Ruck et al., 1990; Baum and Wilczek, 1988; Kanaya and Miyake, 1991; Perlovsky and McManus, 1991; Poggio and Girosi, 1990).

Little work has been undertaken in order to compare performances however. Our own research into performance of marketing models shows that neural networks can outperform regression techniques in comparable conditions (van Wezel and Baets, 1995). In most comparative research (Huang and Lippman, 1988; Lippman, 1989; Weiss and Kulikowski, 1991; Shavlik et al., 1990; Kattan et al., 1993; Thrun et al., 1991; Bonelli and Parodi, 1991; Schizas et al., 1992; Atlas et al., 1990), only operational issues are considered, such as the amount of memory required for computation, training time, classification time, complexity and cost of implementation. The capability of the resulting classifier is analyzed in terms of error rates, rejection rates (where no decision can be reached), ability to adapt to new classes, performance with noisy data, performance with missing data, ability to use outputs for higher level decisions and ability to identify outlier patterns.

Weiss and Kulikowski (1991), believe that backpropagation has many characteristics that make it an excellent learning system (in the class of non-parametric methods): it is extremely powerful; theoretically capable of representing any mathematical function; the learning rule is very effective; no simplifying assumptions need to be made. Most interesting is their claim that the future will be one of combined learning and expert systems. The rules will be created by a learning system (*cf.* black box idea). Though this seems to violate the rules of knowledge engineering in respect to understandability, any source of knowledge that enhances performance (and neural networks is one) will be used in rule-based systems.

Scholtes (1993) researched additional qualities of neural networks (specifically the Kohonen feature maps) and identified "self-organization" and "context" as the most important qualities. Both are strongly connected to organizational learning as described in this book. Eberlein and Yates (1991) stress the interesting quality that neural networks can be trained to solve a problem for which specific formula or algorithms do not exist. Franklin and Garzon (1991) even prove that artificial neural networks are at least equivalent to Turing machines (classical sequential computing). Besides our own research into the applications of neural networks, increasing interest has resulted in application-driven publications. Lodewijk and Deng (1993) experiment with neural networks in end-user development. They remark that the potential of neural networks for high-level cognitive tasks, such as planning and decision-making, has rarely been explored. They explicitly use neural networks as a technique for knowledge acquisition, since they generate a different knowledge base from the classical methods. They also view the learning algorithm as the driving force. Fletcher and Goss (1993) experiment with neural networks in analyzing (and even forecasting) bankruptcy cases. They also apply neural networks to generate knowledge, although their experiments are only based on a limited number of cases.

Absolute, factual evidence comparing neural networks and statistics cannot be given. However, from our experience it is clear that extreme care should be taken when analyzing neural networks in terms of statistical criteria. Neural networks are knowledge tools. They attempt to picture a holistic view of managerial problems. They accept the limited measurability of management and they imitate the adapted learning process akin to that of human brains with which we are familiar. In this respect, the success of neural networks is an implicit challenge to the reductionist and quantitative approaches, still common today in managerial research.

*

* *

* * *

Despite the fact that neural networks still partly make use of positivist terminology, they extract their main strength from the holistic paradigm on which they are based. They reach their "weltanschauung" via learning and self-organization within a changing context. Both context and subject are part of the same holistic view. Connectionist approaches are able, not only to reconstruct an "observation within context", but also to explore "new evidence within context": both the evidence and the context can change. They can assist the researcher/explorer in his voyage through a business experience as a sparring partner, raising some of the implicitness of fact and context. They are, however, not able to change the explorer into on objective researcher, but neither do they attempt to do this.

If Popper and Prigogine had met up with Columbus in Babylon, the destiny of management could have been changed irrevocably.

REFERENCES

Atlas L et al. 1990. Performance Comparisons Between Backpropagation Networks and Classification Trees on Three Real World Applications. In *Advances in neural information processing systems 2*, Touretzky (ed.). Proceedings of the 3rd IEEE conference. Nov. 27-30, 1989. Denver, CA: Morgan Kaufmann.

Avison D, Shah H and Golder P, 1993. Tools for SSM: a justification - a reply to 'critique of two contributions to soft systems methodology. European Journal of Information Systems. Vol. 2, Nr. 4.

Bakos Y and Treacy M, 1986. Information Technology and Corporate Strategy: A Research Perspective. MIS Quarterly. June, pp. 107-119.

Baum E and Wilczek F, 1988. "Supervised Learning of Probability Distributions by Neural Networks." In *Neural Information Processing Systems,* Anderson D (ed.), pp. 52-61. American Institute of Physics, NY.

Beer S, 1980. *The Heart of the Enterprise*. John Wiley.

Beer S, 1985. *Diagnosing the System of Organizations*. Chichester: Wiley.

Benbasat I (ed.) 1990. *The Information Systems Research Challenge: Experimental Methods*. Boston: Harvard Business School Press.

Bonelli P and Parodi A, 1991. An Efficient Classifier System and its Experimental Comparison with two Representative Learning Methods on three Medical Domains. In *Genetic algorithms,* Belew R and Booker L (eds.). Proceedings of the 4th International Conference. Univ California in San Diego, July 13-16. San Mateo, CA: Morgan Kaufmann.

Bryman A, 1988. *Quantity and Quality in Social Research*. London: Unmin Hyman.

Cash J and Lawrence P (eds.), 1989. *The Information Systems Research Challenge: Qualitative Research Methods*. Boston: Harvard Business School Press.

Checkland P, 1981. *Systems thinking, systems practice*. Chichester: Wiley.

Daudi P, 1986. *Power in the Organization. The discourse of power in managerial practice*. New York: Blackwell.

DeStefano J, 1990. Logistic Regression and the Boltzmann Machine. Proceedings of the IEEE International Joint Conference on Neural Networks. Vol. 3, pp. 199-204.

Dreyfus H and Dreyfus S, 1988. "Making a Mind versus Modeling the Brain: Artificial Intelligence Back at a Branchpoint." In *The artificial intelligence debate: false starts and real foundations,* Gravbard S (ed.). MIT Press.

Eberlein S and Yates G, 1991. "Neural Networks based Systems for Autonomous Data Analysis and Control." In *Progress in Neural Networks* (Vol. 1), Omidvar O (ed.). NJ: Ablex Publishing Corp.

Fletcher and Goss, 1993. Forecasting with neural networks. Information and Management. Vol. 24, Nr. 3, March, pp. 159-167.

Foucault M, 1966. *Les Mots et les Choses. Une archeologie des Sciences Humaines*. Paris: Gallimard.

Franklin S and Garzon M, 1991. "Neural computability." In *Progress in Neural Networks* (Vol. 1), Omidvar E (ed.). NJ: Ablex Publishing Corp.

Galliers R, 1985a. "In search of a Paradigm for Information Systems Research." In Research Methods in Information Systems, Mumford E, Hirschheim R, Fitzgerald G and Wood-Harper A, 1985. Proceedings of the IFIP WG 8.2 Colloquium. Manchester Business School.

Galliers R, 1991b. "Choosing Appropriate Information Systems Research Approaches: A Revised Taxonomy." In *The Information Systems Research Arena of the 90s*, Nissen H, Hirschheim R and Klein H (eds.). Amsterdam: North-Holland.

Galliers R, 1992. *Information systems research: issues, methods and practical guidelines*. London: Blackwell Scientific Publications.

Gefen D and Straub D, 1997. Gender Differences in the Perception and Use of E-Mail: An Extension to the Technology Acceptance Model. MIS Quarterly. Vol. 21, Nr. 4, Dec. 1997.

Geman S, Bienenstock E and Doursat R, 1992. Neural Networks and the Bias/Variance Bilemmna. Neural computing. Vol. 4, pp. 1-58.

Gutwirth S, 1993. *Waarheidsaanspraken in Recht en Wetenschap (Claims of Truth in Law and Science)*. Brussels-Apeldoorn: V.U.B. Press-MAKLU.

Han J, Sayeh M and Zhang J, 1989. Convergence and Limit Points of Neural Networks and Its Application to Pattern Recognition. IEEE Transactions on Systems, Man and Cybernetics. Vol. 19, Nr. 5, September/October, pp. 1217-1222.

Huang W and Lippman R, 1988. "Neural Net and Traditional Classifiers." In *Neural Information Processing Systems*, Anderson D (ed.), pp. 387-396. American Institute of Physics, NY.

Hunton J and Beeler J, 1997. Effects of User Participation in Systems Development: A Longitudinal Field Experiment. MIS Quarterly. Vol. 21, Nr. 4, Dec. 1997.

Juang B and Katagari S, 1992. Discriminative Learning for Minimum Error Classification. IEEE Transactions on Signal Processing. Vol. 40, Nr. 12, December, pp. 3043-3054.

Kanaya F and Miyake S, 1991. Bayes Statistical Behavior and Valid Generalization of Pattern
Classifying Neural Networks. IEEE Transactions on Neural Networks. Vol. 2, Nr. 4, July, pp. 471-
475.

Kattan M, Adams D and Parks M, 1993. A Comparison of Machine Learning with Human Judgment.
Journal of Management Information Systems. Year 9, Spring, pp. 37-57.

Klein H and Lyytinen K, 1985. "The Poverty of Scientism in Information Systems." In Research
Methods in Information Systems, Mumford E, Hirschheim R, Fitzgerald G and Wood-Harper A, 1985.
Proceedings of the IFIP WG 8.2 Colloquium. Manchester Business School.

Kraemer K (ed.), 1991. *The Information Systems Research Challenge: Survey Research Methods.*
Boston: Harvard Business School Press.

Kreher H, 1993. Critique of two contributions to soft systems methodology. European Journal of
Information Systems. Vol. 2, Nr. 4.

Latour B, 1988. *Science in Action* (Dutch Translation). Amsterdam: Bert Bakker.

Lippman R, 1989. Pattern Classification Using Neural Networks. IEEE Communications Magazine.
November, pp. 47-64.

Lodewijk and Deng, 1993. Experimentation with back-propagation neural networks. Information and
Management. Vol. 24, Nr. 1, Jan., pp. 1-8.

Lyotard J-F, 1988. *Postmodern Knowledge* (Dutch Translation). Kampen: Agora.

Mansell G, 1991. Action Research in Information Systems Development. Journal of Information
Systems. Vol. 1 Nr. 1.

Merquior J G, 1988. *The Philosophy of Michel Foucault* (Dutch). Utrecht: Het Spectrum.

Mumford E, Hirschheim R, Fitzgerald G and Woo-Harper A, 1985. Research methods in Information
Systems. Proceedings of the IFIP WG8.2 Colloquium. Manchester Business School. 1-3 September,
1984. Amsterdam: North-Holland.

Nissen H, Klein H and Hirschheim R (eds.), 1990. Proceedings of the IFIP TC8 WG8.2 Working
Conference on The Information Systems Research Arena of the 90's. Copenhagen, December 14-15.

Perlovsky L and McManus M, 1991. Maximum Likelihood Neural Networks for Sensor Fusion and
Adaptive Classification. Neural Networks. Vol. 4, Nr. 1, pp. 89-102.

Poggio T and Girosi F, 1990. Networks for Approximation and Learning. Proceedings of the IEEE.
Vol. 78, Nr. 9, September, pp. 1481-1497.

Popper R K, 1963. *Conjectures and Refutations. The growth of scientific knowledge.* London:
Routledge.

Popper R K, 1989. The Critical Approach versus the Mystique of Leadership. Human Systems Management. Nr. 8, pp. 259-265.

Prigogine I and Stengers I, 1988. *Entre le Temps et L'eternite*. Paris: Fayard.

Ruck D, Rogers S, Kabrisky M, Oxley M and Suter B, 1990. The Multilayer Perceptron as an Approximation to a Bayes Optimal Discriminant Punction. IEEE Transactions on Neural Networks. Vol. 1, Nr. 4, December, pp. 296-298.

Schizas C et al., 1992. Neural Networks, Genetic Algorithms and the K-means Algorithms. Proceedings of the international workshop June 6. IEEE Computer Society. Baltimore.

Scholtes J, 1993. Neural Networks, Natural Language Processing and Information retrieval. PhD thesis. University of Amsterdam.

Shavlik J, Mooney R and Towell G, 1990. "Symbolic and Neural Learning Algorithms: An experimental comparison (revised)", TR 955. Computer Sciences Department, University of Wisconsin-Madison, August.

Smithson S, 1991. Combining Different Approaches. Nissen H, Klein H and Hirschheim R (eds.), 1990. Proceedings of the IFIP TC8 WG8.2 Working Conference on The Information Systems Research Arena of the 90's, pp. 365-369. Copenhagen, December 14-15.

Susman G, 1983. "Action Research: a sociotechnical systems perspective". In *Beyond Method*, Morgan G (ed.). London: Sage Publications.

Thrun S et al., 1991. The MONK's Problems - A Performance Comparison of Different Learning Algorithms. via ftp form gogol.cenatis.cena.dgac.fr:/pub/neuron, called thrun.comparison.ps.Z.

Van Gils M, 1997. Social Constructionism, Non-Linearity, and the Significance of Language. Groningen: University of Groningen Paper.

van Wezel M and Baets W, 1995. Predicting Market Responses with a Neural Network: the Case of Fast Moving Consumer Goods. Marketing Intelligence & Planning. Autumn.

Wan E, 1990. Neural Network Classification: A Bayesian Interpretation. IEEE Transactions on Neural Networks. Vol. 1, Nr. 4, pp. 303-305.

Weiss S and Kulikowski C, 1991. *Computer Systems that learn: classification and prediction methods from statistics, neural networks, machine learning and expert systems*. San Mateo, CA: Morgan Kaufman Publishers.

White H, 1989. Learning in Artificial Neural Networks: A Statistical Perspective. Neural computing. Vol. 1, pp. 425-464.

Curriculum Vitae of Gert Van der Linden

Dr Gert Van der Linden (Belgium) is an Associate Professor at Vesalius College (Belgium). He holds visiting positions at IFL (The Swedish Management Institute), at EAMS (The Euro-Arab Management School, Spain), and at CERAM-ESC (France). He was co-director of the Canon MBA Program that ran in conjunction with Nijenrode University. His research focuses on virtual organizations and the impact they have on managerial competencies, organizational processes, leadership and strategic change. He is currently researching managerial and organizational paradoxes.

A founding member of GP Group, Gert Van der Linden has acted as advisor and consultant for several international companies and senior managers. He is active in facilitating defining, developing and implementing strategic processes and corporate vision. He has experience as an interim/transition manager in several international companies. He has been involved in conceptualizing and designing several leadership/management development programmes and strategies as well as company-specific MBA and Leadership Programmes for several major European companies.

FURTHER READINGS

Acorn T, and Walden S, 1992. SMART: Support Management Automated Reasoning Technology for Compaq Customer Service. In Proceedings of the 4th Innovative Applications of Artificial Intelligence Conference.

Allen B P, 1994. Case-Based Reasoning: Business Applications. Communications of the ACM. Vol. 37, Nr. 3, pp. 40-42.

Argyris C, 1982. *Reasoning, Learning and Action: Individual and Organizational.* San Francisco: Jossey-Bass.

Argyris C, 1987. "Some Inner Contradictions in Management Information Systems." In *Information Analysis,* Galliers R (ed.). Addison-Wesley.

Backhouse J, Liebenau J and Land F, 1991. On the discipline of information systems. Journal of Information systems. Vol. 1, Nr. 1.

Baets W, 1987. Corporate Strategic Planning in an uncertain Environment. European Journal of Operational Research (EJOR). Vol. 32, Nr. 2, November.

Baets W, 1988. New generation decision support systems for optimal strategic management. Flanders Technology Seminars. Management 2000. Gent.

Baets W, 1990. Market choice for value added networks and services. Proceedings of European Telecom Conference. Blenheim Online. London/Brussels.

Baets W, Blandin J and Morel C, 1989. "Scoring system to evaluate company performance". Working Paper, Simuledge Benelux, Brussels; Second EURO Working Group on Financial Modeling, Padernborn.

Baets W and Venugopal V, 1994. No doubt, neural networks are alternative tools for statistical techniques: but yet... EURO XIII/OR 36 Conference. Glasgow.

Barley S, 1990. Images of Imaging: Notes on Doing Longitudinal Field Work. Organization Science. Vol. 1, Nr. 3, pp. 220-247.

Boland R, 1979. Control, causality and information system requirements. Accounting, Organizations and Society. Nr. 4, pp. 259-272.

Boland R, 1985. "Phenomenology: a preferred approach to research on information systems". In Research Methods in Information Systems, Mumford E, Hirschheim R, Fitzgerald G and Wood-Harper A, 1985. Proceedings of the IFIP WG 8.2 Colloquium, Manchester Business School.

Boynton A and Zmud R, 1987. Information Technology Planning in the 1990's: Directions for Practice and Research. MIS Quarterly. March.

Broadbent M, Hansell A, Lloyd P and Dampney C, 1992. Managing Information Systems in Australia and New Zealand: requirements for the 1990's. Australian Computer Journal. Vol. 34, Nr.1, pp. 1-11.

Broadbent M and Weill P, 1993. Developing Business and Information Strategy Alignment: A study in the banking industry. IBM Systems Journal. Vol. 32, Nr. 1.

Brown A, 1992. Grounding soft systems research. European Journal of Information Systems. Vol. 1, Nr. 6.

Caudill M and Butler C, 1990. *Naturally Intelligent Systems*. MIT Press.

Ciborra C, 1984. "Management Information Systems: a Contractual View." In *Beyond Productivity: Information Systems development for Organizational Effectiveness* (Ed. Bemelmans) North Holland.

Davis G, 1992. "An individual and Group Strategy for Research in Information Systems." In *Information Systems Research: Issues, methods and practical guidelines,* Galliers R (ed.). London: Blackwell Scientific Publications.

Desanctis G and Gallupe B, 1985. Group Decision Support Systems: a new frontier. Database. Winter, pp. 3-10.

Dyson R, 1990. *Strategic Planning: Models and Analytical Techniques*. West
Sussex: J Wiley and Sons.

Eden C, 1990. Strategic Thinking with Computers. Long Range Planning. Vol. 23,
Nr. 6, pp. 35-43.

Elias N, 1983. *The court society*. NY: Pantheon.

Everwijn S, Bomers G and Knubben J, 1993. Ability- or competence-based
education: bridging the gap between knowledge acquisition and ability to apply.
Higher Education. Nr. 25, pp. 425-438. Kluwer Academic Publishers.

Feeny D, Edwards B and Earl M, 1987. Complex organizations and the
information systems function. A research study. Oxford Institute of Information
Management research and discussion paper (RDP87/7). Templeton College,
Oxford.

Feigenbaum E, McCorduck P and Penny H, 1988. *The Rise of the Expert
Company*. MacMillan.

Fulk J, 1993. Social Construction of Communication Technology. Academy of
Management Journal. Vol. 36, Nr. 5, pp. 921-950.

Galliers R, 1993. Research Issues in Information Systems. Journal of Information
Technology. Nr. 8.

Hayes-Roth F and Jacobstein N, 1994. The State of Knowledge-based Systems.
Communications of the ACM. Vol. 37, Nr. 3, pp. 27-39.

Hedberg B and Jonsson S, 1978. Designing Semi-confusing Information Systems
for Organizations in Changing Environments. Accounting, Organizations and
Society. Vol. 3, Nr.1. Pergamon Journals Ltd.

Hennesy D and Hinkle D, 1992. Applying Case-based reasoning to autoclave
loading. IEEE Expert. Vol. 7, Nr. 5.

Hofstadter D, 1979. *Godel, Escher, Bach: an eternal golden braid.* NY: Basic Books.

Hofstadter D and Dennett D (eds.), 1981. *The Mind's I: Fantasies and reflections on self and soul.* NY: Basic Book.

Kamp Y and Hasler M, 1990. *Recursive Neural Networks for Associative Memory.* John Wiley.

Karger D, 1991. *Strategic planning and management: The Key to Corporate Success.* NY: Marcel Dekker Inc.

Kitano H, Shibata A, Shimazu H, Kajihara J, and Sato A, 1992. Building large-scale and corporate-wide case based systems : Integration of organizational and machine executable algorithms. In Proceedings of the 10th AAAI Conference. AAAI. San Jose, CA.

Kolf F and Oppeland H, 1979. A design-oriented approach to implementation research: the project PORGI. In *Design and implementation of computer-based information systems,* Szyperski N and Groschla E (eds.). Sijthoff & Noordhoff.

Kolodner J L, 1991. Improving Human Decision Making through Case-Based Decision Aiding. AI Magazine. Vol. 12, Nr. 2, pp. 52-68.

Leavitt H and Bahrami H, 1988. *Managerial Psychology: Managing Behavior in Organizations.* Chicago: The University of Chicago Press.

LehnerF, 1992. Expert systems for organizational and managerial tasks. Information & Management. Nr. 23, pp. 31-41.

Lorsch J and Allen S, 1973. Managing diversity and independence. PhD thesis. Division of Research, Graduate School of Business, Harvard University.

Lyytinen K, Klein H and Hirschheim R, 1991. The effectiveness of office information systems: a social action perspective. Journal of Information Systems. Vol. 1, Nr. 1.

Marton-Williams J, 1986. "Questionnaire design." In *Consumer Market Research Handbook*, third revised ed., Worcester R and Downham J (eds.). North Holland.

McConnell D and Hodgson V, 1990. Computer Mediated Communication Systems (CMCS) - Electronic Networking and Education. Management Education & Development. Vol. 21, Nr. 1, Spring.

Mingers J, 1992. Questions and suggestions in using soft systems methodology in practice. Systemist. Vol. 14, Nr. 2, pp. 54-61.

Mingers J and Taylor S, 1992. The use of soft systems methodology in practice. Journal of the Operational Research Society. Vol. 43, Nr. 4, pp. 321-332.

Minsky M and Papert S, 1969. *Perceptions*. Cambridge MA: MIT Press.

Mintzberg H, 1976. Planning on the left side and managing on the right side. Harvard Business Review. July-August.

Miyake S and Kanaya F, 1991. A Neural Network Approach to a Bayesian Statistical Decision Problem. IEEE Transactions on Neural Networks. Vol. 2, Nr. 5, September, pp. 538-540.

Mockler R J and Dologite D G, 1991. Using Computer Software to improve Group Decision Making. Long Range Planning. Vol. 24, Nr. 4, pp. 44-57.

Morecroft J, 1992. Executive knowledge, models and learning. European Journal of Operational Research. Vol. 59, Nr. 1.

Morecroft J and van der Heijden K, 1992. Modeling the oil industry knowledge in a behavioral simulation model. European Journal of Operational Research. Vol. 59, Nr. 1.

Morgan G, 1989. *Riding the waves of change: developing managerial competencies for a turbulent world*. San Francisco: Jossey-Bass.

Nelson M and Illingworth W, 1991. *A Practical Guide to Neural Nets*. New York: Addison-Wesley.

Neumann S, Ahituv N and Zviran M, 1992. A measure for determining the strategic relevance of IS to the organization. Information & Management. Nr. 22, 1992.

Nunamaker J F, 1989. GDSS: Present and Future. IEEE. November, pp. 6-16.

Nunamaker J F et al., 1989. Group Support Systems in Practice: experience at IBM. Proceedings of the Twenty-second Annual Hawaii International Conference on Systems Sciences Vol. III, Blanning R and King D (eds.). IEEE Computer Society Press.

Ornstein R, 1972. The psychology of consciousness. Harmondsworth: Penguin (1975) New York.

PA Technology, 1990. Banking on Survival. The situation in The Netherlands. July.

Pervan G and Klass D, 1992. The use and Misuse of Statistical Methods in Information Systems Research. In *Information Systems Research: Issues, Methods and Practical Guidelines,* Galliers R (ed.). London: Blackwell Scientific Publications.

Pettigrew A, 1983. Contextualist Research: A Natural Way to Link Theory and Practice. In Research Methods in Information Systems, Mumford E, Hirschheim R, Fitzgerald G and Wood-Harper A, 1985. Proceedings of the IFIP WG 8.2 Colloquium. Manchester Business School.

Ramprasad A and Poon E, 1985. A Computerized Interactive Technique for Mapping Influence Diagrams (MIND). Strategic Management Journal. Vol. 6, pp. 377-392.

Rangaswamy A, Burke R and Oliva T, 1993. Brand equity and the extendibility of brand names. International Journal of Research in Marketing. Vol.10, Nr.1, pp. 61-75.

Richmond B, Peterson S and Charyk C, 1990. ITHINK Documentation. High Performance Systems. Hanover. NH.

Rockart J and Short J, 1989. IT in the 1990's: Managing Organizational Interdependence. Sloan Management Review. Winter.

Russell S, 1989. *The Use of Knowledge in Analogy and Induction*, London: Pitman.

Scarbrough H and Corbett J M, 1992. *Technology and Organization*. London: Routledge.

Sejnowski T and Rosenberg C, 1986. NETtalk: A parallel network that learns to read aloud. John Hopkins University. January.

Singh S K, 1993. Using information technology effectively. Information & Management. Vol. 24, 1993.

Stefik M et al., 1987. Beyond the Chalkboard: Computer Support for Collaboration and Problem Solving in Meetings. Communications of the ACM. Vol. 30, Nr. 1, pp. 32-47.

Stowell F, West D and Stansfield M, 1991. The application of an expert system shell to an unstructured domain of expertise: using expert system technology to teach SSM. European Journal of Information Systems. Vol. 1, Nr. 4.

Sugerman, 1987. *Piaget's Construction of the Child's Reality*. Cambridge University Press.

Sunde L and Brodie R, 1993. Consumer evaluations of brand extensions: further empirical results. International Journal of Research in Marketing. Vol. 10, Nr. 1, pp. 47-53.

Van Den Broeck H, 1994. *Lerend Management*. Lannoo Scriptum.

Vennix J, Andersen D, Richardson G and Rohrbaugh J, 1992. Model building for group decision support: Issues and alternatives in knowledge elicitation. European Journal of Operational Research. Vol. 59, Nr. 1.

Vennix J and Gubbels J, 1992. Knowledge elicitation in conceptual model building: A case study in modeling a regional Dutch health care system. European Journal of Operational Research. Vol. 59, Nr. 1.

Walsham G, 1991. Organizational metaphors and information systems research. European Journal of Information Systems. Vol. 1, Nr. 2, March.

SUBJECT INDEX

AUTHOR INDEX